REA's Test Prep Books Are The Best!

(a sample of the <u>hundreds of letters</u> REA receives each year)

" The format of [REA's SAT II: French] publication is simple and understandable—the explanations and reasoning for each correct and incorrect answer extremely helpful—making it easy and delightful to learn. "

Student, Austin, TX

" I recently got the French SAT II Exam book from REA. I congratulate you on first-rate French practice tests. "

Instructor, Los Angeles, CA

" Five stars—terrific! [REA's book] helped me a lot, and actually let me pass my French SAT IIs! Thanks a lot! "

Student, New York, NY

" What I found in [REA's] book was a wealth of information sufficient to shore up my basic skills in math and verbal... The practice tests were challenging and the answer explanations most helpful. It certainly is the *Best Test Prep for the GRE*! "

Student, Pullman, WA

" Your book was such a better value and was so much more complete than anything your competition has produced—and I have them all! "

Teacher, Virginia Beach, VA

(more on next page)

(continued from front page)

" You don't really have to study your boring, cumbersome textbook. Just use this book instead and you have a guaranteed A+. "
Student, Singapore

" Your *Fundamentals of Engineering Exam* book was the absolute best preparation I could have had for the exam, and it is one of the major reasons I did so well and passed the FE on my first try. "
Student, Sweetwater, TN

" I used your book to prepare for the test and found that the advice and the sample tests were highly relevant... Without using any other material, I earned very high scores and will be going to the graduate school of my choice. "
Student, New Orleans, LA

" An excellent book for practicing review questions. The best thing about the book is that it's updated and the information is accurate. "
Student, Chicago, IL

" I really appreciate the help from your excellent book. Please keep up the great work. "
Student, Albuquerque, NM

" If you want more in-depth review for the exam, you should...look into the new study guide published by REA in C++. "
Student, Cerritos, CA

(more on back page)

THE BEST TEST PREPARATION FOR THE
SAT II: Subject Test

FRENCH

Linda Gregg
Language Coordinator
Brandeis University
Waltham, Mass.

Paulette Cuvillier
French Instructor
Broward Community College
Fort Lauderdale, Fla.

Miriam Ellis, Ph.D.
Chairperson, French Caucus
University of California at Santa Cruz
Santa Cruz, Calif.

Research & Education Association
61 Ethel Road West
Piscataway, New Jersey 08854
Dr. M. Fogiel, Director

The Best Test Preparation for the
SAT II: SUBJECT TEST IN FRENCH

Printed in the United States of America

Library of Congress Control Number 2002111911

International Standard Book Number 0-87891-451-X

Research & Education Association
61 Ethel Road West
Piscataway, New Jersey 08854

REA supports the effort to conserve and
protect environmental resources by
printing on recycled papers.

CONTENTS

Chapter 3

Chapter 4

Chapter 5

Chapter 6

About Research & Education Association

Research & Education Association (REA) is an organization of educators, scientists, and engineers specializing in various academic fields. Founded in 1959 with the purpose of disseminating the most recently developed scientific information to groups in industry, government, high schools, and universities, REA has since become a successful and highly respected publisher of study aids, test preps, handbooks, and reference works.

REA's Test Preparation series includes study guides for all academic levels in almost all disciplines. Research & Education Association publishes test preps for students who have not yet completed high school, as well as high school students preparing to enter college. Students from countries around the world seeking to attend college in the United States will find the assistance they need in REA's publications. For college students seeking advanced degrees, REA publishes test preps for many major graduate school admission examinations in a wide variety of disciplines, including engineering, law, and medicine. Students at every level, in every field, with every ambition can find what they are looking for among REA's publications.

Unlike most test preparation books—which present only a few practice tests that bear little resemblance to the actual exams—REA's series presents tests that accurately depict the official exams in both degree of difficulty and types of questions. REA's practice tests are always based upon the most recently administered exams, and include every type of question that can be expected on the actual exams.

REA's publications and educational materials are highly regarded and continually receive an unprecedented amount of praise from professionals, instructors, librarians, parents, and students. Our authors are as diverse as the subject matter represented in the books we publish. They are well-known in their respective fields and serve on the faculties of prestigious high schools, colleges, and universities throughout the United States and Canada.

Acknowledgments

We would like to thank Dr. Max Fogiel, President, for his overall guidance, which brought this publication to completion; Larry B. Kling, Quality Control Manager, for supervising revision of the book; David Bordeau, Editorial Assistant, for coordinating revision of this book; Nathan Lutz, Rutgers Preparatory School; Teresina Jonkoski, Associate Editor; and Omar J. Musni for their editorial contributions; Jeff LoBalbo, Senior Graphic Artist, for designing the cover; and Wende Solano for typesetting the manuscript.

INDEPENDENT STUDY SCHEDULE
SAT II: FRENCH SUBJECT TEST

This study schedule is set up to prepare you thoroughly for the SAT II: French Subject Test. Although it is designed to allow you to pace yourself comfortably over an eight-week preparation period, it can be condensed into a four-week course by collapsing each two-week period into a one-week interval. Be sure to set aside enough time—at least two hours each day—to study. No matter which study schedule works best for you, the more time you spend acquainting yourself with the subject matter and the test, the more prepared and relaxed you will feel on Test Day.

Week	*Activity*
1	Read the introduction to this book, which details critical aspects of the SAT II: French Subject Test for you. Then take Practice Test 1 to determine your strengths and weaknesses. Score each section by using the worksheet on page xviii. You'll now have a baseline for your study needs.
2	Carefully read and study the Course Review included in this book. Cover all the material, but highlight those areas that gave you trouble in Practice Test 1. Go through each of the items you answered incorrectly and make sure you understand how to arrive at the correct answer. Recognizing where you went wrong will boost your confidence and, as a practical matter, help you avoid making the same mistakes come Test Day.
3 and **4**	Take Practice Test 2 and Practice Test 3. After scoring each exam, flag your incorrect answers. For any types of questions or particular subjects that continue to pose difficulty for you, check our detailed explanations and consult our Course Review.
4 and **5**	Take Practice Test 4 and Practice Test 5. After scoring each exam, flag your incorrect answers. For any types of questions or particular subjects that continue to pose difficulty for you, check our detailed explanations and consult our Course Review. ➜

Week	Activity
7	Take Practice Test 6. After scoring your exam, carefully review the explanations for all your incorrect answers. By this point, you should be nearing mastery of the subject matter. Again, consult our Course Review as often as possible to ensure that you're sufficiently at ease with our model tests.
8	This is the week you'll consolidate your gains and eliminate any continuing subject-matter weaknesses. Retake one or more of the practice tests (as you deem necessary), paying special attention to the questions with which you had difficulty the first time around. Going through the practice tests once again will put you on completely familiar terms with the subject matter and the SAT II itself.

SAT II: SUBJECT TEST IN
FRENCH

INTRODUCTION

PASSING THE SAT II: FRENCH SUBJECT TEST

ABOUT THIS BOOK

This book provides you with an accurate and complete representation of the SAT II: French Subject Test. Inside you will find topical reviews packed with the information and strategies you'll need to do well on the exam, as well as six REA practice tests based on the actual College Board exam. Our practice tests contain every type of question that you can expect to encounter on the SAT II: French Test. Following each of our tests, you will find an answer key and step-by-step detailed explanations designed to help you master the test material.

ABOUT THE TEST

Who takes the test and what is it used for?

Planning to attend college? Then you should take the SAT II: French Subject Test if:

(1) Any of the colleges to which you're applying require the test for admission,

OR

(2) You wish to demonstrate proficiency in French.

The SAT II: French exam is designed for students who have at least two years of strong preparation in the language.

Who administers the test?

The SAT II: French Subject Test is developed by the College Board and administered by Educational Testing Service (ETS). The test development process involves the assistance of educators throughout the United States, and is designed and implemented to ensure that the content and difficulty level of the test are appropriate.

When should the SAT II: French Subject Test be taken?

Most students take the Subject Tests towards the end of their junior year or at the beginning of their senior year. You should take the SAT II: French Subject Test while you are taking a French class. You're likely to be rusty if you haven't been in a French class for several months. If you are applying to a college that requires SAT II: Subject Test scores as part of the admissions process, you should take the SAT II: French Subject Test in time for your colleges to see your score. If your scores are being used only for placement purposes, wait as long as you can to get the most preparation in your French courses as possible. Make sure to contact the colleges to which you are applying for more specific information.

When and where is the test given?

The SAT II: French Subject Test is administered six times a year—in October, November, December, January, May, and June—at test centers across the United States. The test given in November is the only one that includes a listening portion (which is not covered in this book).

To receive information on upcoming administrations of the exam, consult the publication *Taking the SAT II: Subject Tests,* which can be obtained from your guidance counselor or by contacting:

College Board SAT Program
P.O. Box 6720
Princeton, NJ 08541-6720
(609) 771-7070
Website: www.collegeboard.com

Is there a registration fee?

To take the SAT II: French Test, you must pay a registration fee. For a fee schedule, consult the publication *Taking the SAT II: Subject Tests.* Financial assistance may be granted in certain situations. To find out if you qualify and to register for assistance, contact your academic advisor.

HOW TO USE THIS BOOK

What do I study first?

The SAT II: French Subject Test is designed to test knowledge that you have acquired throughout your education. Therefore, the best way to prepare yourself for the actual exam is to refresh your knowledge by thoroughly studying our review material and test-taking tips and by taking the sample tests provided in this book. They will familiarize you with the types of questions, directions, and the format of the SAT II: French Subject Test.

To begin your studies, follow this simple plan: (1) Read over the reviews and the suggestions for test-taking. (2) Take one of our practice tests to determine your area(s) of weakness. (3) Study the review material, focusing on your specific problem areas. The reviews include the information you need to know when taking the exam. Make sure to take the remaining practice exams to further test yourself and become completely comfortable with the format and content of the actual SAT II: French Subject Test. Consult our study schedule for a detailed test-preparation timetable.

When should I start studying?

It is never too early to start studying for the SAT II: French Test. The earlier you begin, the more time you will have to sharpen your skills. Do not procrastinate! Cramming is *not* an effective way to study, since it does not allow you the time needed to learn the test material. The sooner you learn the format of the exam, the more comfortable you will be when you take it.

FORMAT OF THE SAT II: FRENCH SUBJECT TEST

The SAT II: French Test is a one-hour exam consisting of 85 to 90 multiple-choice questions—the number of items has been known to vary from one form of the test to another.

The questions you'll encounter on the SAT II: French Subject Test are designed to measure the gradual development of competence in the French language acquired over a period of years. The test measures your grasp of the language in three distinct areas:

• *Vocabulary-in-context: Approx. 30%.* Tests your knowledge of vocabulary and basic idioms within culturally authentic contexts.

- **Structure: 30–40%.** Tests your ability to choose words or expressions that are grammatically correct within a sentence or longer paragraphs.

- **Reading: 30–40%.** Tests your understanding of main and supporting ideas, themes, and settings of a text. Passages are drawn from texts like essays, historical works, newspapers, magazines, advertisements, and timetables.

ABOUT THE REVIEW SECTIONS

The reviews in this book will teach you the skills and concepts needed to approach SAT II: French Subject Test questions. We cover sentence structure, grammar, verb conjugation, spelling, and capitalization. Systematic review will help you identify the kinds of errors that often appear in vocabulary-in-context and structure questions. By using the reviews in conjunction with the practice tests, you will be able to sharpen your skills and put yourself in the best possible position to succeed on the SAT II: French Subject Test.

SCORING THE SAT II: FRENCH SUBJECT TEST

How do I score my practice tests?

The SAT II: French Test, like all other SAT subject tests, is scored on a 200-800 scale. Your exam is scored by crediting one point for each correct answer and deducting one-third of a point for each incorrect answer. There is no deduction for answers that are left blank. Use the formula below to calculate your raw score.

$$\underline{\hspace{3cm}} - (\underline{\hspace{3cm}} \times {}^1/_3) = \underline{\hspace{3cm}}$$

| Number Right | Number Wrong | Raw Score |

To convert your composite raw score to a scaled score, consult the Score Conversion Table at the end of this chapter.

STUDYING FOR THE SAT II: FRENCH SUBJECT TEST

It is vital that you choose the time and place for studying that works best for you. Some students may set aside a certain number of hours every morning, while others may study at night before going to sleep. Only you can determine when and where your study time will be most effective. Be consistent and use your time wisely. Work out a study routine and stick to it!

When you take the practice tests, try to make your testing conditions as much like the actual test as possible. Turn your television and radio off, and sit down at a quiet table free from distraction. Make sure to clock yourself with a timer.

As you complete each practice test, score your test and thoroughly review the explanations to the questions you answered incorrectly; however, do not review too much at any one time. Concentrate on one problem area at a time by reviewing the questions and explanations, and by studying the review until you are confident you completely understand the material.

Keep track of your scores. By doing so, you will be able to gauge your progress and discover general weaknesses in particular sections. You should carefully study the reviews that address your areas of difficulty; this will strengthen your skills and build your confidence.

TEST-TAKING TIPS

Although you may be unfamiliar with standardized tests such as the SAT II: French Subject Test, there are many ways to acquaint yourself with this type of examination and help alleviate your test-taking anxieties. Here are ways to help you become accustomed to the SAT II: French Subject Test, some of which may apply to other standardized tests as well.

Become comfortable with the format of the SAT II: French Subject Test. When you are practicing to take the test, simulate the conditions under which you will be taking the actual test. Stay calm and pace yourself. After simulating the test only a couple of times, you will boost your chances of doing well, and you will be able to sit down for the actual exam much more confidently.

Know the directions and format for each section of the test. Familiarizing yourself with the directions and format of the different test sections will not only save you time, but will also ensure that you are familiar enough with the SAT II: French Subject Test to avoid anxiety (and the mistakes caused by being anxious).

Work on the easier questions first. Within each group of questions, the easier ones are usually at the beginning. If you find yourself working too long on one question, make a mark next to it in your test booklet and continue to the next question. After you answer all the questions you can, go back to the ones you have skipped.

If you are unsure of an answer, guess. However—if you do guess, guess wisely. Use the process of elimination by going through each answer to a question and eliminating as many of the answer choices as possible. By eliminating two answer choices, you give yourself a fifty-fifty chance of answering correctly, since there will only be two choices left from which to make your guess.

Mark your answers in the appropriate spaces on the answer sheet. Each numbered row will contain four ovals corresponding to each answer choice for that question. Fill in the circle that corresponds to your answer darkly, completely, and neatly. You can change your answer, but remember to completely erase your old answer. Any stray lines or unnecessary marks may cause the machine to score your answer incorrectly. When you have finished working on a section, you may want to go back and check to make sure your answers correspond to the correct questions. Marking one answer in the wrong space will throw off the rest of your test, whether it is graded by machine or by hand.

You don't have to answer every question. You are not penalized if you do not answer a question. The only penalty you receive is if you answer a question incorrectly. Try to use the guessing strategy, but if you are truly stumped by a question, you do not have to answer it.

Work quickly and steadily. You have a limited amount of time to work on each section, so you need to work quickly and steadily. Avoid focusing on one problem for too long. Taking the practice tests in this book will help you to learn how to budget your time.

Before the Test

Make sure you know exactly where your test center is well in advance of your test day so you do not get lost on the day of the test. On the night before the test, gather together the materials you will need the next day:

- Your admission ticket

- Two forms of identification (e.g., driver's license, student identification card, or current alien registration card)

- Two No. 2 pencils with erasers

- Directions to the test center

- A watch, if you wish, but not one that makes noise, as it may disturb other test-takers

On the day of the test, you should wake up early (we hope after a decent night's rest) and have a good breakfast. Dress comfortably, so that you are not distracted by being too hot or too cold while taking the test.

Also, plan to arrive at the test center early. This will allow you to collect your thoughts and relax before the test, and will also spare you the stress of being late. If you arrive after the test begins, you will not be admitted or receive a refund.

During the Test

When you arrive at the test center, try to find a seat where you feel you will be comfortable. Follow all the rules and instructions given by the test supervisor. If you do not, you risk being dismissed from the test and having your scores canceled.

Once all the test materials are passed out, the test instructor will give you directions for filling out your answer sheet. Fill out this sheet carefully, since this information will appear on your score report.

Remember—since no scratch paper will be provided, you can write in your test booklet.

After the Test

When you have completed the SAT II: French Subject Test, you may hand in your test materials and leave. Then, go home and relax.

You should receive your score report about five weeks after you take the test. This report will include your scores, percentile ranks, and interpretive information.

SCORE CONVERSION CHART*

RAW SCORE	SCALED SCORE	RAW SCORE	SCALED SCORE
90	800	32	540
89	800	31	540
88	800	30	530
87	800	29	530
86	800	28	520
85	800	27	520
84	800	26	510
83	800	25	510
82	800	24	500
81	790	23	500
80	790	22	490
79	780	21	480
78	780	20	480
77	770	19	470
76	770	18	470
75	760	17	460
74	760	16	460
73	750	15	450
72	750	14	450
71	740	13	440
70	740	12	440
69	730	11	430
68	730	10	430
67	720	09	420
66	720	08	420
65	720	07	410
64	710	06	410
63	710	05	400
62	700	04	390
61	700	03	390
60	690	02	380
59	690	01	380
58	680	00	370
57	680	-01	370
56	670	-02	360
55	660	-03	360
54	660	-04	350
53	650	-05	350
52	650	-06	340
51	640	-07	340
50	640	-08	330
49	630	-09	320
48	630	-10	320
47	620	-11	310
46	620	-12	300
45	610	-13	290
44	610	-14	280
43	600	-15	270
42	600	-16	270
41	590	-17	260
40	590	-18	250
39	580	-19	250
38	570	-20	240
37	570	-21	230
36	560	-22	220
35	560	-23	210
34	550	-24	210
33	550	-25 through -30	200

*Your scaled scores on REA's practice tests may be slightly higher or lower than your score on the actual test. Bear in mind that scaled scores for different editions of the SAT II: French are adjusted to take into account small shifts in its level of difficulty and statistical weighting across the SAT II: French test-taker population.

SAT II:
SUBJECT TEST IN
FRENCH

REVIEW

CHAPTER 1

THE SOUNDS OF FRENCH

PRONUNCIATION HINTS

French is one of the Romance languages (the others are Spanish, Italian, Portuguese, Romanian, Catalan, and Provençal) and is "vocalic" in its sound, i.e., based on vowels. This structure gives the language its soft and flowing character. English speakers can attain good pronunciation if the following simple rules are kept in mind:

- There are **no diphthongs** in French, as there are in English: "boy" = "aw," "ee," "yuh." French vowels are clean and pure; e.g., *imiter* = "ee-mee-tay" (to imitate) and should be formed without any secondary movement of the jaw.
- Every syllable is of **equal importance** in volume and stress; e.g., English: de/VEL/op/ment and French: *dé/ve/lop/pe/ment*. There is a slight emphasis on the last syllable in words of two or more syllables and in a group of words: *dé/li/CIEUX; Je parle franÇAIS;* but it is not a strong stress.
- Consonants are **softened:** don't "explode" your d's, t's, b's, p's, g's, and k's and your accent will improve.
- There are **two sounds** that are generally difficult for English speakers: the "r," which can be achieved by "gargling," and the "u" (as in "*tu*"), which is made by puckering your lips as if to whistle, while you say "ee."

Further Pronunciation Details

French has the same alphabet as English; some letters are written but are not pronounced (e.g., most final consonants: *sans, chez, tard, livres*). Exceptions to this rule include the final "c," as in *bouc* (billy goat), "f," as in *chef* (head, chief), "l," as in *formel* (formal), and "r," as in *air*.

Also silent are "h," as in *homme, héros, théâtre*, and some combinations of letters, as in *parlent, monsieur, voudraient*.

In cognates (words that we recognize from English), spelling is often different from English, with letters added, deleted, or changed, giving the word a "French" look: *classe, indépendance, appartement, université*. The International Phonetic Alphabet (IPA), utilized in most good dictionaries, will help you understand the sounds of French vowels, which remain unchanged, even in different spelling groups.

THE INTERNATIONAL PHONETIC ALPHABET (IPA)

There are 17 consonants, 16 vowels (12 oral vowels pronounced in the mouth and 4 oral vowels articulated in the nasal passage), and 3 semi-vowels/semi-consonants halfway between vowels and consonants. These sounds are expressed by phonetic symbols which are always written between [ ].

Oral Vowels

Phonetic Symbol	French Example	English Approx.	Remarks
1. [a]	*avec*	Ah!	Open your mouth.
2. [ɑ]	*pâle*	Ahh!	Longer than [a].
3. [e]	*été*	say	Don't add "yuh."
4. [ɛ]	*elle*	elf	More open than [e].
5. [i]	*ici*	see	Smile; don't add "yuh."
6. [o]	*mot*	Moe	Don't add "wuh."
7. [ɔ]	*porte*	up	More open than [o].
8. [ø]	*peu*	put	Lips very rounded.
9. [œ]	*sœur*	purr	More open than [ø].
10. [u]	*nous*	noose	Don't add "wuh."
11. [y]	*tu*	No English equivalent	Round your lips as if to whistle while saying "ee."
12. [ə]	*je*	wood	Resembles [ø] but is much shorter: mute "e."

Nasal Vowels

Phonetic Symbol	French Example	English Approx.	Remarks
1. [ã]	*sans*	on	Say "on" with your mouth open.
2. [ɛ̃]	*pain*	can	Say "can" with your mouth open.
3. [ɔ̃]	*bon*	own	Say "own" with your mouth open.
4. [œ̃]	*un*	fun	Say "fun" with your mouth open.

Remember this little phrase, which includes all the nasal vowels: *Un bon vin blanc* [œ̃ bɔ̃ vɛ̃ blã]. (A good white wine.)

Denasalization, or **oral** pronunciation, of the nasal vowel occurs under **two** conditions:
1. When a nasal vowel **is followed by another "n" or "m"**: e.g., *intime* [ɛ̃tim]; *innocent* [inɔsã]; *important* [ɛ̃pɔrtã]; *immédiat* [imedja]; *enfant* [ãfã]; *ennemi* [ɛnmi]; *bon* [bɔ̃]; *bonne* [bɔn].
2. When a nasal vowel **is followed by another vowel**: e.g., *pain* [pɛ̃]; *peine* [pɛn]; *incident* [ɛ̃sidã]; *inutile* [inytil]; *profond* [prɔfɔ̃]; *chronique* [krɔnik].

Semi-Vowels/Semi-Consonants: Halfway Between Vowels and Consonants

1. [j]   *soulier* [sulje]; *bien* [bjɛ̃]; *hier* [jɛr]. ([j] is like biblical "yea.")
2. [w]   *mois* [mwa]; *Louis* [lwi]; *ouest* [wɛst]; *ouïr* [wir]; *soir* [swar].
3. [ɥ]   *huit* [ɥit]; *lui* [lɥi]; *cuisine* [kɥizin]. (Based on [y] + [i]; very closed.)

Consonants

Pronounce them softly!
Bi-labials: [p], [b], [m]. Both lips are used. *Papa, bébé, maman.*
Labio-dentals: [f], [v]. Teeth against lower lip. *Frère, vie.*
Dentals: [t], [d], [n], [l]. Put your tongue against the back of your upper teeth to soften the sound. Don't "explode" it! *Ton, de, non, la.*

Alveolars: [ʃ], [ʒ]. Air is forced between upper and lower teeth. [ʃ] *chanson, riche, acheter;* [ʒ] *Jean, Giverny, voyage.* In English: **sh**e, plea**s**ure.

Palatal: [ɲ]. "N" + yuh. *Champagne, Allemagne.* In English: He'll trai**n yuh.**

Velars: [k], [g]. Produced in the throat; make them soft. [k] *avec, qui, klaxon;* [g] *grand, fatigué.*

Uvular: [r]. Gargle it! *rue, Robert, tr*avail.

Spelling Groups

Phonetic symbols and examples of some common **spelling** combinations:

[e] é = *école;* ée = *fiancée;* ef = *clef* or *clé;* er = *chanter;* es = *ces;* et = *cadet;* ez = *nez;* ai = *j'ai;* e + il or ille = *pareil, merveille;* ay = *ayons.*

[ɛ] ai + consonant = *aide, aile, j'aime, palais, caisse, chaise, paix, faites;* è = *père, chèque, mène, achète, Thèbes, mèche, il lève;* ê = *tête, même, guêpe, gêne, chaîne;* e + tte = *dette;* e + l or lle = *sel, elle;* e + ige = *neige;* e + ine = *peine.*

[i] *ami, il y a.*

[o] *tôt, sauce, beau, ôter* [ote]*, haut.*

[ɔ] *porte, observer* (most words with initial "o" are pronounced [ɔ]).

[œ]*cœur, peur, jeune, beurre, seul, deuil* [dœj]*, bœuf.*

[u] *trou, toute, vous.*

[y] *vue, rhume* [rym]*, utile* [ytil].

[ə] *je, demain, menace* [mənas]*, fenêtre* [fənɛtrə].

THE FRENCH ALPHABET

Here is the phonetic pronunciation of the French alphabet:

Letter	Name	As in...
a	[a]	parc
b	[be]	belle
c	[se]	ici
d	[de]	dame
e	[ə]	école = [ekɔl]; père = [pɛr]; le = [lə]
f	[ɛf]	faire
g[1]	[ʒe]	gare; gomme; guerre; général; gilet

h²	*[aʃ]*	habiter = *[abite]*; *héros = *['ero]. The * and '* *indicate an aspirate "h," one which is not linked to a preceding consonant.*
i	*[i]*	idée; imiter = *[imite]*; inégal = *[inegal]*; ici; il y a; innocent = *[inɔsã]*; mystérieux
j¹	*[ʒi]*	jeune
k	*[ka]*	kilo. *Very few French words begin with "k"; most that do are borrowed foreign words.*
l	*[ɛl]*	laver; ville³ = *[vil]*; famille = *[famij]*
m	*[ɛm]*	mardi; ami
n	*[ɛn]*	noble; initial; animé
o	*[o]*	dormir; œuf = *[œf]*
p	*[pe]*	papa
q	*[ky]*	question = *[kɛstjɔ̃]*
r	*[ɛr]*	rire; pardon; irréel
s	*[ɛs]*	salle = *[sal]*; rester = *[rɛste]*; lisse = *[lis]: Initial "s," "s" before a consonant, and double "s" are pronounced "s." Plaisir = *[plezir]*: "s" between two vowels = *[z]*.*
t	*[te]*	tête; fait⁴
u	*[y]*	utile; tu
v	*[ve]*	voix = *[vwa]*; arriver
w	*[dubləve]*	walkman = *[wɔkman]*; wagon = *[vagɔ̃]*. *Many foreign words with an initial "w" are used in French. Some are pronounced "v" and some "w."*
x	*[ix]*	*Relatively few words have this initial letter.* – *xérès*
y	*[igrɛk]*	*Relatively few words have this initial letter.* – *yenx, yaourt*
z	*[zɛd]*	*Relatively few words have this initial letter.* – *zéro, zeste*

Note:
[1] "G" and "J": "g" is called [ʒe] (like "jay" in English) and "j" is called [ʒi] like "gee" in English. Remember that the names of these two letters are the opposite of what they are in the English alphabet.

[2] Aspirate "h" is not linked to a preceding consonant. Consider *"les héros"* [le ero]; if you link these words, the result is [lezero] *("les zéros")* and that is certainly not the usual intention when talking about heroes!

3   Three words and their derivatives that end in *"-ille"* are pronounced [il]: *mille, villes, tranquillité* [mil, vil, tra˜kil]. Similarly
pronounced are *million, milliard, village,* and *tranquilité. Lille*
(the city) is also [lil].

4   Sometimes the final "t" is pronounced: *C'est un fait.* [fet] or [fe].

ACCENTS

Accents are used in French to indicate pronunciation of vowels or to
differentiate between homonyms (two words that sound alike but have
different meanings, e.g., *où/ou; la/là*).

é = *accent aigu* (acute) is used only on closed "e" [∂] and sounds
approximately like "a" in the English word "say": *éléphant,
médecin* [medse], *j'ai chanté, je suis désolé.*

è = *accent grave* is used to give the sound of open "e" [ɛ] to a mute
"e" [∂] that stands before a consonant and is followed by another
mute "e." The open "e" of the *accent grave* sounds approximately
like the "e" in the English word "elf": *père, sèche, Hélène,
j'achète, deuxième.*

à, ù = *accent grave* is used to make a distinction between two words
that are spelled alike but have different meanings: There is no
difference in the pronunciation of these two words: *à Paris/Pierre
a une voiture; la femme/là-bas* (over there); *Où est Jean?/Marie
ou Simone* (or).

ç = *cédille* is used only on a "c" and is pronounced [s] before "a," "o,"
and "u." It sounds approximately like "s" in the English word
"sun": *ça, garçon, Je suis déçu.*

ä, ë, ï, ö, ü = *le tréma* is used on the second vowel when two vowels
occur together to indicate that they are to be pronounced separately: *haïr* [air]; *aïeux* [ajø]; *Noël.*

LIAISON

Liaison, or linking, occurs in speaking when a final consonant precedes an initial vowel or an "h": *cet homme; vous êtes; nos amies; un
anniversaire; un bel arbre; le bouc émissaire; un grand orchestre; un
patron ambitieux.*

Some Liaisons are to be Avoided

- Never link *"et"* to a following vowel: *Un chapeau et/un livre.*
- Never link a final "s" to an aspirate "h": *les/hors-d'œuvre* [le ɔrdœvrə].
- But do link the "h" in: *un hôpital, l'homme, des huîtres,* etc.
- In inversions, don't link the final "s" of the plural to a following vowel: *Avez-vous/une sœur? Vont-ils/en Europe? Sont-elles/ici?* In fact, the tendency among many young French speakers today is to avoid liaison, except where it is necessary for comprehension.

ELISION

When final and initial vowels come together, the final vowel is replaced by an apostrophe: *l'amie; c'est; l'examen; il n'est pas; l'heure; Est-ce qu'il faut parler?*

"Si" is elided before "i" but not before the other vowels: *s'il vous plaît; si elle accepte; si on arrive,* etc.

Exceptions: *le huit octobre; le onze février; tu as; tu es; Le Havre.*

SYLLABIFICATION

A French syllable is determined by the vowel within it: *é-té; a-mi; dé-ter-mi-ner; ré-pé-ti-tion; in-di-vi-du,* etc. When you wish to separate a word, either do so at the vowel itself, or if there is a double consonant, make the separation between the two letters: *fi-nis-sez; lit-té-ra-ture; syl-la-be,* etc.

CHAPTER 2

COGNATES — WORDS YOU RECOGNIZE

Many words are common to both French and English. Others have slight spelling differences, and still others have familiar characteristics which help to identify their meaning.

COGNATES COMMON TO BOTH LANGUAGES

restaurant	dessert	menu	service	table
art	culture	film	statue	tennis
football	sport	machine	science	client
magazine	concert	piano	cousin	parents
rouge	rose	violet	orange	automobile
route	train	promenade	taxi	suite
voyage	probable	possible	solitude	surprise
courage	brave	moment	content	secret

COGNATES WITH MINOR SPELLING CHANGES

la musique	la mémoire	le professeur	la leçon	la classe
magique	la saison	sophistiqué	l'artiste (m., f.)	
le poème	l'allée (f.)	répéter	le théâtre	
l'auteur (m.)	le poète	l'acteur (m.)	l'actrice (f.)	la comédie
la tragédie	première	l'opéra (m.)	la chambre	bleu
le/la touriste	élégant	la difficulté	l'hôtel (m.)	le président
le congrès	le sénateur	l'élection (f.)	la gouvernement	
voter	distingué	la démocratie	américain	
la nationalité	la loyauté	la télévision		

SPELLING PITFALLS

These common words are spelled differently from their English cognates and may cause confusion:

l'exemple (m.)	*indépendant*	*le mariage*	*l'appartement (m.)*
le rythme	*la rime*	*la littérature*	*la revue*
le peintre	*la personne*	*intéressant*	*fascinant*
l'automne (m.)	*l'erreur (f.)*	*l'exercice (m.)*	*la douzaine*
le dictionnaire	*la couleur*	*le danseur*	*le thé*
le riz	*le chrysanthème*	*le succès*	*le procès*
l'adresse (f.)	*le calendrier*	*le personnage*	*l'oignon (m.)*
la carotte	*l'omelette (f.)*	*les mathématiques*	

"FAUX AMIS" (FALSE FRIENDS)

Cognates are words that are common to two languages. Many times their spellings are the same, and other times there are slight spelling differences. The following are pairs of false cognates, or **faux amis (false friends)**, in which the words seem similar, but are not at all.

à l'heure actuelle – at the present time	*les actualités* – the news
actuellement – now	*en réalité* – actually
assister – to attend	*attendre* – to wait
la bague – a ring	*le sac* – bag
blesser – to wound	*le canapé* – sofa, couch
comment – how	*la déception* – disappointment
se douter de – to suspect	*sans doute* – probably
la figure – face	*ignorer* – not to be aware of
large – broad, wide	*la librairie* – book store
la bibliothèque – library	*l'occasion* – an opportunity, chance
la place – a square (Place Vendôme) or a seat at the theatre, on the bus, etc.	*regarder* – to look at, to watch
chargé – loaded, burdened	*crier* – to shout or yell
la prune – plum	*le raisin* – grape
rester – to stay or remain	*sensible* – sensitive, keen to senses
sensiblement – approximately	*le roman* – a novel
la romance – a story (fiction)	*la journée* – all day long
le voyage – a journey	*voyager* – to travel
quitter – to leave	*travailler* – to work
sale – dirty	*le sang* – blood
le stage – training course	*le store* – shade

SOME BORROWED WORDS

Some words that have been borrowed from French have been "Americanized," in that their pronunciation has changed somewhat. These words include:

la lingerie	*la chaise longue*	*le quai*	*le maître d'hôtel*
la femme	*à la mode*	*le salon*	*hors-d'œuvre*
le foyer	*le billet-doux*	*à la carte*	*le grand prix*
le chef-d' uvre	*tête-a-tête*	*le rendez-vous*	*le café*
la haute couture	*le chauffeur*	*le garage*	*la cuisine*
le croissant	*la vinaigrette*	*la détente*	*le coup d'état*
le chiffon	*le mot-clé*	*le tour de force*	*la liaison*
de luxe	*exposé*	*le gourmet*	*rouge*
au pair	*chic*	*le coup de grâce*	*le/la fiancé(e)*
beau	*le soufflé*	*voilà*	*le fait accompli*
la fête	*l'idiot savant (m.)*	*la suite*	*la raison d'être*
en garde	*le ballet*	*le pas de deux*	*l'entrepreneur (m.)*

French has borrowed many words from English, too. (This is derided as *"le franglais"* by purists.)

le week-end	*le parking*	*faire le shopping*
les fast-foods	*le steak*	*le jet-set*
un job	*"cool"*	*"super-cool"*
les spots télévisés	*faire du foot*	*les stars*
le rock and roll	*le marketing*	*le business*
le budget	*un manager*	*le "look"*
la "pub"[licité]	*le tunnel*	*un building de haut standing*
un superman	*un speaker*	*une speakerine*

CAPITALIZATION

Fewer words are capitalized in French than in English. Important examples are:

"*Je*" is capitalized only when it begins a sentence: *Je suis son ami.* But: *Ce matin, je vais rester ici. Elle sait que je veux partir. Que sais-je? Il faut que je te parle. Je vais au cinema et je vais acheter deux billets.*

Names of languages are not capitalized: *le français, le chinois, le russe, l'italien, l'anglais, le grec, l'allemand, le japonais.*

Days of the week and months of the year are not capitalized: *lundi, mardi, mercredi, dimanche; janvier, avril, décembre.*

Nationalities of people or national origins of things (adjectives) are not capitalized: *Vous êtes américain(e). Elle a une voiture danoise. J'aime la cuisine chinoise. Gildas est breton* (from Brittany). *Margot porte une robe parisienne.*

Nationalities (people) are capitalized: *Les Suisses font du chocolat magnifique. Connais-tu des Français? On croit que les Américains sont riches. Les Canadiens sont nos voisins. Nous avons rencontré beaucoup d'Européens.*

Names of cities, states, provinces, countries, rivers, oceans, mountains, and continents are capitalized: *Londres, la Californie, la Normandie, l'Italie, les États-Unis, l'Asie, l'Australie, la Seine, l'Atlantique, les Alpes.*

Capitalization varies for the titles of books, films, or plays: Generally the article is not capitalized but the first noun is: *l'Etranger; les Misérables; le Rouge et le noir; les Fleurs du mal.* But when the first word is not an article, only that word is capitalized: *Lettres de mon moulin; Tous les matins du monde; Autant en emporte le vent.* When the title is a clause and begins with a definite article, that is the capitalized word: *Les dieux ont soif; La guerre de Troie n'aura pas lieu; Le deuil sied à Electra.*

INTERROGATIVE SENTENCES

Questions are usually formed most simply by adding *"Est ce-que?"* to a declarative sentence:

Est-ce que Robert lit beaucoup? Does Robert read a lot?
Est-ce que tu veux aller avec nous? Do you want to go with us?
Est-ce que l'enfant sait lire? Does the child know how to read?

Questions are also formed by **inversion**, i.e., placing the verb **before** the **subject:**

Buvez-vous trop de café? Do you drink too much coffee?
Avons-nous les billets? Do we have the tickets?
Travailles-tu maintenant? Are you working now?

Note: When the subject is in the third person, **name the subject** and **then invert the verb-pronoun** for a question:

*Ces femmes **ont-elles** assez d'argent?* Do these women have enough money?

*La guerre **est-elle** nécessaire?* Is war necessary?

Note: Sometimes, when using inversion when the pronoun that is joined to the verb begins with a vowel and the verb itself has no strong ending consonants to pronounce, an extra "t" is added for the sake of pronunciation.

*Sylvie **prépare-t-elle** un grand dîner?* Is Sylvia making a big dinner?

***A-t-il** une grande famille?* Does he have a big family?

***A-t-on** des cahiers?* Does everyone have notebooks?

The "t" does not change the meaning of the sentence, but simply makes it easier to pronounce juxtaposed vowel sounds.

CHAPTER 3

BY THE NUMBERS

COUNTING FROM 1 TO 1,000,000,000

The French numerical system becomes somewhat complicated when you arrive at the 70's, 80's, and 90's. Otherwise the pattern of counting is regular:

un	[œ̃]	1	*onze*	[ɔ̃z]	11
deux	[dø]	2	*douze*	[duz]	12
trois	[trwa]	3	*treize*	[trɛz]	13
quatre	[katrə]	4	*quatorze*	[katɔrz]	14
cinq	[sɛ̃k]	5	*quinze*	[kɛ̃z]	15
six	[sis]	6	*seize*	[sɛz]	16
sept	[sɛt]	7	*dix-sept*	[disɛt]	17
huit	[ɥit]	8	*dix-huit*	[dizɥit]	18
neuf	[nœf]	9	*dix-neuf*	[diznœf]	19
dix	[dis]	10	*vingt*	[vɛ̃]	20

vingt et un	21	*vingt-sept*	27
vingt-deux	22	*vingt-huit*	28
vingt-trois	23	*vingt-neuf*	29
vingt-quatre	24	*trente* [trɑ̃t]	30
vingt-cinq	25		
vingt-six	26		

Continue the same pattern with:

trente et un, trente-deux, etc. 31, 32,...

quarante, quarante et un, quarante-deux, etc. 40, 41, 42,...
cinquante, cinquante et un, cinquante-deux, etc. 50, 51, 52,...

Note: Continue with *soixante, soixante et un* (60, 61) until you reach *soixante-neuf* (69). Now you will say 60 + 10, *soixante-dix,* for 70. After *dix,* continue with *onze,* so that you say:

soixante-dix	70	*soixante-quinze*	75
soixante et onze	71	*soixante-seize*	76
soixante-douze	72	*soixante-dix-sept*	77
soixante-treize	73	*soixante-dix-huit*	78
soixante-quatorze	74	*soixante-dix-neuf*	79

Now you are going to **multiply: 4 × 20 = *quatre* × *vingts* = *quatre-vingts*** (80). Note that there is an *"s"* in *quatre-vingts* and that there is **no** *"s"* and **no** *et* in *quatre-vingt-un* (81).

Now continue with *–deux:*

quatre-vingt-deux	82	*quatre-vingt-six*	86
quatre-vingt-trois	83	*quatre-vingt-sept*	87
quatre-vingt-quatre	84	*quatre-vingt-huit*	88
quatre-vingt-cinq	85	*quatre-vingt-neuf*	89

And now you say: **4 × 20 + 10 = *quatre-vingt-dix*** (90). Now continue with *onze* once again, this time eliminating *et*:

quatre-vingt-onze	91	*quatre-vingt-seize*	96
quatre-vingt-douze	92	*quatre-vingt-dix-sept*	97
quatre-vingt-treize	93	*quatre-vingt-dix-huit*	98
quatre-vingt-quatorze	94	*quatre-vingt-dix-neuf*	99
quatre-vingt-quinze	95		

cent	100	*deux cent un* (no *"s"*)	201
cent un (no *et*) [sɑ̃]	101	*trois cents*	300
deux cents	200		

quatre cents, cinq cents, six cents, sept cents, huit cents, neuf cents
mille [mil]   1.000

Note: **French** uses a **period** (.) where **English** uses a **comma** (,) to denote **thousands** or **millions**. Also, a **comma** (,) is used in **French** where **English** uses a **period** (.), as in **decimals**: *2,75* (Fr.) = 2.75 (Eng.); *,55* = .55; *,0426* = .0426, etc.

deux mille (no "s")	2.000
deux mille un	2.001
trois mille	3.000
etc.	
un million [miljɔ̃]	1.000.000
deux million (no "s")	2.000.000
etc.	
un milliard [miljar]	1.000.000.000

TELLING TIME

Quelle heure est-il? What time is it? ***Il est...*** It is...
une heure = 1h = 1:00
une heure cinq = 1h5 = 1:05
une heure dix = 1h10 = 1:10
une heure et quart = 1h15 = 1:15
une heure vingt = 1h20 = 1:20
une heure et demie = 1h30 =1:30

Note: *et* is used only for the **quarter-** and **half-hour.**

After the half-hour, you start to **subtract** from the following hour:

deux heures moins vingt-cinq = 1h35 = 1:35
deux heures moins vingt = 1h40 = 1:40 (or twenty-to-two)
deux heures moins le quart = 1h45 = 1:45 (the definite article *le* is
    used only for this measure of time.)
deux heures = 2h = 2:00
midi (cf. midday) = 12 noon   *minuit* = 12 a.m.

The French often denote the hours between noon and midnight in
military time; this is especially true when referring to the time of appoint-
ments, films, concerts, programs, etc. For example, *quatorze heures* (14h)
= 2 p.m.; *vingt heures* (20h) = 8 p.m.; etc. Midnight is *vingt-quatre
heures.*

Hint: Subtract 12 from the military time to get p.m. time.

DESCRIBING TIME

Ways of talking about time:

Quelle est la date aujourd'hui? What's today's date?
Quel jour sommes-nous? What day is it?
C'est le 15 avril. It's April 15.
C'est mardi, le 15 avril. It's Tuesday, April 15.
C'est le 15 aujourd'hui. It's the 15th today.
On est le quinze. It's the 15th.
C'est le quinze avril, mille neuf cent quatre-vingt-quatorze. It's April
   15, 1994.

DAYS OF THE WEEK

*Les jours de la semaine: lundi, mardi, mercredi, jeudi, vendredi,
samedi, dimanche.* The days of the week are not capitalized in French.

Note: The French week begins on **Monday,** rather than Sunday.

Hint: Never say *"à" lundi, "en" lundi,* or *"sur" lundi* for **on** Monday;
the day of the week alone is sufficient:

*Je verrai Pierre **lundi**.* I'll see Peter **on Monday.**
*Margot est arrivée **mardi**.* Margot arrived **on Tuesday.**
*Nous allons partir **jeudi**.* We're leaving **on Thursday.**

For the **day in general** use the definite article:

*Elle travaille **le lundi** jusqu'à minuit.* **Mondays** she works until mid-
   night.
*Le **mercredi**, ils se rencontrent en ville.* They meet in town **on
   Wednesday(s).**
*Les enfants n'aiment pas **le dimanche**.* Children don't like **Sundays.**

MONTHS

The months are very similar to their English cognates but are **not
capitalized:** *janvier, février, mars, avril, mai, juin, juillet, août,
septembre, octobre, novembre, décembre.*

Quel est votre anniversaire? When is your birthday?
C'est le 25 mai. It's May 25.
Je suis né(e) le 13 octobre. I was born on October 13.
Mon anniversaire c'est le premier août. My birthday is August 1st.
Quelle est la date de la fête nationale américaine? When is America's
   national holiday?
C'est le 4 juillet. It's July 4th.

THE FOUR SEASONS: *LES QUATRE SAISONS*

Le printemps, l'été, l'automne, l'hiver. Spring, summer, autumn (note
French spelling change), winter.

In autumn = *en automne; en hiver, en été,* but **au printemps** because
the preposition now precedes a **consonant.**

EXPRESSING THE YEAR

You may use either form:
1492   *mille quatre cent quatre-vingt-douze* or
       quatorze cent quatre-vingt-douze
1776   *mille sept cent soixante-seize* or
       dix-sept cent soixante-seize
1812   *mille huit cent douze* or
       dix-huit cent douze
1994   *mille neuf cent quatre-vingt-quatorze* or
       dix-neuf cent quatre-vingt-quatorze
2001   *deux mille un*

PHONE NUMBERS

Quel est votre numéro de téléphone? What's your phone number?

US: (219) 468-9876. *Indicatif régional: deux cent dix-neuf. Quatre
   cent soixante-huit, quatre-vingt dix-huit, soixante-seize.* Area code:
   two hundred nineteen. Four hundred sixty-eight, ninety-eight, sev-
   enty-six.

French numbers are quoted in four pairs; a typical number in the Paris
area is (1) 60.42.27.99. *Composer le un* (Dial 1), *soixante, quarante-deux,
vingt-sept, quatre-vingt-dix-neuf.*

EXPRESSING AGE

To talk about **age,** use *"avoir"*:

Quel âge avez-vous? How old are you?
J'ai 23 ans. I'm 23.
Ma sœur a 25 ans et mes parents ont 47 ans. My sister's 25 and my
parents are 47.
La France a plus de mille ans. France is more than 1,000 years old.

CALCULATIONS

For **addition, subtraction, multiplication,** and **division:**
$2 + 2 = 4$ *Deux **plus** deux **font** quatre*
$10 - 3 = 7$ *Dix **moins** trois **égalent** sept*
$20 \times 2 = 40$ *Vingt **fois** deux **font** quarante*
$10 \div 5 = 2$ *Dix **divisé** par cinq **égale** deux*

COMPARISONS

Comparisons of **equality, inferiority,** and **superiority** are made by
using the following structures:

Equality

*Jean a deux sœurs. Pierre a deux sœurs. Jean a **autant de sœurs que**
Pierre.* John has two sisters. Pierre has two sisters. John has **as
many** sisters as Peter.
*Marie-France gagne 3.000 francs par mois; Simone touche le même
salaire. Simone gagne **autant d'argent que** Marie-France.* Marie-
France earns 3,000 francs a month; Simone earns the same salary.
Simone earns **as much** money as Marie-France.

autant de + noun + *que* = comparison of equality: as much as, as
many as...

Inferiority

*Nous visitons trente villes; vous visitez trente-deux villes. Nous visitons
moins de villes que vous.* We visit thirty cities; you visit thirty-two
cities. We visit **fewer cities than** you.

*Les Duval boivent trois bouteilles de vin mais leurs cousins n'en boivent que deux. Leurs cousins boivent **moins de vin que** les Duval.* The Duvals drink three bottles of wine but their cousins only drink two. Their cousins drink **less wine than** the Duvals.

moins de + noun + *que* = less than (singular or plural quantity)

Superiority

*Robert a dix-huit livres; tu as quinze livres. Il a **plus de livres que** toi.* Robert has eighteen books; you have fifteen books. He has more books than you.

*Margot passe trois jours à Paris; sa mère y passe cinq jours. Sa mère passe **plus de temps** à Paris **que** Margot.* Margot spends three days in Paris; her mother spends five days. Her mother spends more time in Paris than Margot.

plus de + noun + *que* = more than (singular or plural quantity)

Generalized Comparisons

For comparisons that do not entail numbers but are more **generalized**, use *autant que, moins que, plus que:*

*Tu lis **autant que** moi.* You read as much as I do.
*Paul parle **moins que** son père.* Paul talks less than his father (does).
*Elise voyage **plus que** sa sœur.* Elise travels more than her sister.

ORDINAL NUMBERS

To express numbers that represent **consecutive order** (first, tenth, twenty-first, thirtieth, etc.) use:

premier, première	first (m. & f.)
deuxième	second
troisième	third
quatrième	fourth
cinquième	fifth
vingt et unième	twenty-first
etc.	

Note: While the English form of these numbers varies, aside from *premier,* French uses the suffix *"—ième"* for **all numbers.**

Dates are expressed by **cardinal** numbers: *le cinq mai, le vingt-deux septembre, le trente juillet,* even though English uses **ordinal** numbers: the 5th of May, the 22nd of September, July 30th, etc.

Exception: The first day of the month is expressed by the **ordinal** form: *le **premier** juin, le **premier** décembre,* etc.

CHAPTER 4

NOUNS AND ARTICLES

GENDER

The gender of French nouns is something that needs to be memorized. There is a trick for guessing the gender of a noun, **although it is not a rule and is subject to having exceptions**. The rule refers to the *ending sounds* of words, not the *ending letters*.

Many masculine nouns end in a vowel sound:
e.g., le camion [õ]
       le chocolat [â]

Many femine nouns end in a consonant sound:
e.g., la salle [l]
       la bombe [b]

Masculine Nouns

Nouns which refer to **masculine beings,** both humans and animals:

l'homme, le garçon, le prince, l'empereur, le roi, le duc, le mâle, le cheval, le coq, etc.

Guide to Identifying Masculine Nouns

Ending of Noun	Examples	Exceptions
"—age"	*l'âge*	*une image*
	le fromage	*une cage*
	le nuage	*la plage*
	un étage	*une page*
	Quel dommage!	
"—eur"	*un professeur*	*la faveur*
	le docteur	*une rumeur*
	un auteur	*la chaleur*
	un ordinateur	
	le bonheur	
	l'extérieur	
"—isme"	*le capitalisme*	
	le patriotisme	
	le socialisme	
	le féminisme	
	l'impressionnisme	
"—ment"	*l'appartement*	
	le département	
	les renseignements	
	un compliment	
	le médicament	
	les vêtements	
Vowels other than [ə]	*le cinéma*	*la radio*
	le trou	*l'eau*
	le piano	*la vertu*
	le bureau	
	le café	
	le hibou	
Consonant	*le raisin*	*la saison*
	le jour	*l'amour*
	le nez	*la clef*
	le doigt	*la nuit*
	le champ	*la mort*
	le ciel	

Ending of Noun	Examples	Exceptions
Foreign words	*le pique-nique*	*une interview*
	le bifteck	
	le weekend	
	le marketing	
	le base-ball	
	le parking	

The names of languages are masculine: *le français, le russe, le japonais, l'anglais, l'espagnol, l'italien, . . .*

Feminine Nouns

Nouns that are used to describe **female beings,** both humans and animals:

la femme, une fille, une mère, une tante, la nièce, la reine, la princesse, la poule, la vache, la chatte, la chienne

Guide to Identifying Feminine Nouns

Ending of Noun	Examples	Exceptions
"—ade"	*une promenade*	
	une tirade	
	la limonade	
"—ance" or "—ence"	*la naissance*	*le silence*
	la distance	
	l'indépendance	
	la différence	
	la patience	
	la science	
"—oire"	*la gloire*	*le mémoire* – (student paper)
	l'histore	
	une poire	
	la victoire	
	la mémoire	
"—sion" or "—tion"	*une impression*	
	une décision	
	la télévision	
	la libération	
	une condition	
	une répétition	
	la constitution	

Ending of Noun	Examples	Exceptions
"—son"	la saison une maison la raison la liaison une chanson	le son
"—é" or "—ée"	la pensée l'idée la liberté l'égalité la bonté	le comité

Feminine Nouns/Masculine Beings

Some **feminine** nouns can refer to **masculine** beings:

*Philippe est **la sentinelle** ce soir.* Philip is the sentry tonight.
*Georges était **une victime** de l'épidémie.* George was a victim of the epidemic.
*Henri est **une personne** importante.* Henry is an important person.

Masculine Nouns/Feminine Beings

Some **masculine** nouns can refer to **feminine** beings:

*Elle est **écrivain**.* She's a writer. (or) *C'est une femme **écrivain**.*
***Le soprano** était magnifique.* The soprano was wonderful.
***Mon professeur** est une femme intelligente.* My professor is an intelligent woman.

Identical Forms/Different Meanings

Some nouns have identical masculine and feminine forms but different meanings:

Masculine		Feminine	
un livre	a book	une livre	a pound
un page	a page-boy	une page	a page
un tour	a turn	une tour	a tower
un vase	a vase	la vase	mud or sludge
le critique	the critic	la critique	criticism

FORMATION OF FEMININE NOUNS

Many feminine nouns are formed by adding "e" to the masculine: *l'ami/l'amie, le cousin/la cousine, un voisin/une voisine, le berger/la bergère, l'étudiant/l'étudiante*

Irregular Feminine Noun Forms

Some feminine nouns can be formed by substituting the masculine ending *-eur* with *-euse* or *-rice*.

-eur to -euse	*-eur to -rice*
le vendeur/la vendeuse	*l'acteur/l'actrice*
le danseur/la danseuse	*le directeur/la directrice*
le menteur/la menteuse	*le lecteur/la lectrice*
le coiffeur/la coiffeuse	*le tuteur/la tutrice*

Variant Forms

Some feminine nouns are quite different from their masculine counterparts:

Masculine	Feminine
le père	*la mère*
le frère	*la sœur*
l'homme	*la femme* (woman)
le mari	*la femme* (wife)
un dieu	*une déesse*
le roi	*la reine*
un neveu	*une nièce*
un oncle	*une tante*
un héros	*une héroïne*
le beau-fils	*la belle-fille*
un coq	*une poule*
un cerf	*une biche*

Same Form for Masculine and Feminine

Some nouns use the same form for describing both male and female:

un/une enfant; un/une artiste; un/une camarade; un/une esclave; un/une philosophe; un/une secrétaire, etc.

PLURAL NOUNS

Normally, as in English, the plural of nouns is formed by adding an "s" to the singular:

> *le stylo/les stylos; la table/les tables; l'arbre/les arbres; l'ami/les amis* and *l'amie/les amies,* etc.

Nouns Ending in "s," "x," or "z"

Nouns that end in "s," "x," or "z" do not add "s" for the plural:
> *le repas/les repas; la croix/les croix; le nez/les nez*

Some Irregular Plural Nouns

Singular Ending	Plural	Exceptions
—al, —ail:		
journal	*journaux*	*bals*
animal	*animaux*	*récitals*
cheval	*chevaux*	*carnavals*
canal	*canaux*	*festivals*
métal	*métaux*	*chacals*
mal	*maux*	
vitrail	*vitraux*	*chandails*
travail	*travaux*	*détails*
—au, —eu, —eau:		
noyau	*noyaux*	*pneus*
eau	*eaux*	
neveu	*neveux*	
niveau	*niveaux*	
—ou: Most take "s" in the plural.		**7 exceptions:**
fou	*fous*	*bijoux*
cou	*cous*	*cailloux*
sou	*sous*	*choux*
trou	*trous*	*genoux*
		hiboux
		joujoux
		poux

Three Plural Nouns That Are Very Irregular

un œil/les yeux – an eye/eyes
le ciel/les cieux – sky, as in weather/Heaven
le jeune homme/les jeunes gens – young man/young folks

Note: *"Ciels"* is also used in poetry and in discussing paintings,
e.g., *"les ciels de Gaugin."*

Three Feminine Nouns That Are Always Plural

les mathématiques (often shortened to *"les maths"*)
les vacances
les fiançailles

Family Names

Family names do not change in the plural form except for those of royal dynasties:

les Duval – the Duvals; *les Mitterrand* – the Mitterrands
la famille Duval, la famille Mitterrand
but:
les Bourbons, les Plantagenêts

Plural of Compound Nouns

Some compound nouns contain verbs and adverbs which are invariable. Nouns and adjectives are sometimes pluralized.

Singular	Plural
un gratte-ciel	*des gratte-ciel* ("sky" is singular)
une pomme de terre	*des pommes de terre* ("earth" is singular)
un coffre-fort	*des coffres-forts*
un arc-en-ciel	*des arcs-en-ciel*
un chef-d'œuvre	*des chefs-d'œuvre*

Check the dictionary to be sure of the correct plural form of compound nouns.

THE ARTICLE

The article introduces the noun and may be definite or indefinite. **It is usually repeated before each noun.** Although in English we often omit articles, in French the noun **must** always be preceded by an article.

Definite Articles: "The"

	Masculine	**Feminine**
Singular	*le garçon*	*la femme*
	le billet	*la maison*
	le soir	*la plage*
Plural	*les garçons*	*les femmes*
	les billets	*les maisons*
	les soirs	*les plages*

Note: When a singular noun begins with a vowel, the article becomes *l'*:

	Masculine	**Feminine**
	l'ami	*l'amie*
	l'aéroport	*l'école*
	l'œil	*l'usine*

Repetition of the Article

Articles are generally repeated before each noun in a series:

J'ai invité tout le monde: la mère, le fils, la fille, l'oncle, et les cousins.
I invited everyone: the mother, son, daughter, uncle, and cousins.

Contractions with an Article

After the prepositions *à* and *de* (at the, to the, in the, of the, from the), some forms of the definite article contract:

$$à + la \quad = \quad à\ la$$
$$à + le \quad = \quad \underline{au}$$
$$à + l' \quad = \quad à\ l'$$
$$à + les \quad = \quad \underline{aux}$$

Nous sommes allés à l'école. We went to the school.
Nous avons parlé à la secrétaire. We spoke to the secretary.
Au début de la semaine, il écrira aux clients. At the beginning of the
    week, he'll write to the customers.
Il fera beau au printemps. It will be nice weather in the spring.

de + la	=	*de la*
de + le	=	<u>*du*</u>
de + l'	=	*de l'*
de + les	=	<u>*des*</u>

Jean est le père de l'enfant. John is the father of the child.
As-tu appris les paroles de la chanson? Did you learn the words to the
    song?
C'est le plus beau pays du monde, le pays des merveilles. It's the most
    beautiful country in the world, the land of marvels.
Ils reviennent du sud. They're returning from the south.

SPECIAL USES OF THE DEFINITE ARTICLE

The definite article is used to make generalized observations:

Les voitures de sport sont chères. Sports cars are expensive.
Les oiseaux mangent tout le temps. Birds eat constantly.

Note: In English we often omit the article in these kinds of statements.

The Definite Article with *aimer, préférer, adorer, détester*

An easy acronym is "A PAD."

Since these four verbs express one's **general** feelings about a person,
place, or thing, they **always** take the definite article.

Nous aimons les films français. We like French films.
Laure adore la vanille mais elle déteste le chocolat. Laura loves va-
    nilla but hates chocolate.
Préfères-tu le bleu ou le rouge? Do you prefer blue or red?

With Titles, Professions, and Countries

The definite article is used when addressing or describing titled or important individuals:

Titles:
le président, la comtesse, le sénateur, etc.
Oui, monsieur le Président. Le Président Mitterrand a parlé. Yes, Mr. President. President Mitterrand spoke.

Professions:
Le docteur Duval est arrivé. Doctor Duval has arrived.

Countries: "Feminine" countries (i.e., those whose final letter is *"e"*) are preceded by the definite article when they are the **subject** or **direct object** of the verb:

La France est belle. France is beautiful.
J'ai visité l'Italie et la Belgique. I visited Italy and Belgium.

Use *le* for **"masculine" countries** (those which end in a consonant):

Le Japon exporte beaucoup de produits électroniques. Japan exports a lot of electronic products.
Elles vont visiter le Danemark et le Brésil. They will visit Denmark and Brazil.

Exceptions:

1. *Le Mexique.* Mexico.
2. No article is used when discussing islands: *Tahiti est très beau.* Tahiti is very beautiful.
3. No article is used before Israel: *Ils connaissent bien Israël.* They know Israel well.

Les is used for plural countries:

Les États-Unis. The United States.
Les Pays-Bas. The Netherlands.

THE INDEFINITE ARTICLE

The indefinite articles "a," "an," "some," "any" are used to refer to a non-specific noun.

Masculine	Feminine	Plural
un *livre*	**une** *lettre*	**des** *cousins*
un *stylo*	**une** *jupe*	**des** *lunettes*
un *jardin*	**une** *chanson*	**des** *bonbons*

*Ils ont acheté **des** légumes.* They bought some vegetables.
*Jacques a reçu **une** lettre.* Jack received a letter.
*C'est **un** bon livre.* It's a good book.

Special Uses of the Indefinite Article

Use the indefinite article to answer a question:

Qu'est-ce que c'est? What is it? (or "this")?
*C'est **une** discussion importante.* It's an important discussion.
Qui est-ce? Who is it? (or "this")?
*C'est **une** bonne amie.* She's a good friend.

Also use the indefinite article to describe a profession, or a religious or political persuasion:

*Voilà Pierre. C'est **un** médecin célèbre.* There's Peter. He's a famous doctor.
*Mme. Aumont, c'est **une** catholique orthodoxe.* Mrs. Aumont is a devout Catholic.

Remember the rule: *C'est un, une, des, le, la, les* + noun **for identification.** *Ce sont* + *les* or *des* may be used for plural nouns.

CHAPTER 5

THE PARTITIVE ARTICLE (*LE PARTITIF*)

GENERAL USE

The partitive is based on describing **"a part** of all the ... that exists in the world." While in English, "some" or "any" may be omitted, the partitive article must be expressed in French, except in certain structures.

FORMATION

		Partitive	Example
Masculine	*de + le*	*du*	*Voulez-vous **du** vin?* Do you want some/any wine?
	de + l'	*de l'*	*As-tu **de l'**argent?* Do you have any money?
Feminine	*de + la*	*de la*	*Elle a acheté **de la** crème.* She bought some cream.
	de + l'	*de l'*	*Va-t-il dépenser **de l'**argent?* Is he going to spend any money?

		Partitive	Example
Plural	*de + les*	*des*	*Nous cherchons **des** livres intéressants.* We're looking for some interesting books. *Margot a acheté **des** robes chic.* Margot bought some chic dresses.

OMISSION OF THE DEFINITE ARTICLE AFTER *"de"*

With Negative Expressions

pas de   *Simon n'a **pas d'**amis.* Simon doesn't have any friends.

plus de   *Nous ne voulons **plus de** problèmes.* We don't want any more problems.

jamais de   *Il ne porte **jamais de** cravate.* He never wears a tie.

Before a Plural Noun Preceded by an Adjective

In cases when the noun that the partitive article reflects has an adjective before it, the partitive article is omitted and only *de* is used.

*Nous avons vu **de belles maisons**.* We saw some beautiful homes.
*Nous avons vu **des maisons** blanches.* We saw some white houses.
*Ce chien a **de grands yeux**.* This dog has big eyes.
*Ce chien a **des** yeux intéressants.* This dog has interesting eyes.

With Adverbs of Quantity

Adverbs that describe quantity use only *de* before a noun.

beaucoup de   *Elle a eu **beaucoup de** chance.* She had lots of luck.

trop de   *Manges-tu **trop de** pain?* Do you eat too much bread?

assez de   *Il n'avait pas **assez d'**argent pour le billet.* He didn't have enough money for the ticket.

un peu de/   *Nous voulons **un peu de** soupe et **peu de** viande.*
peu de   We want a little soup and not much meat.

After Certain Expressions

There are certain expressions that call for the omission of the definite article before a noun.

avoir besoin de   *J'**ai besoin de** vacances.* I need a vacation.

avoir envie de   *As-tu **envie de** gâteau?* Do you feel like having some cake?

DEFINITE, INDEFINITE, OR PARTITIVE ARTICLE

The Definite Article

The definite article **describes a specific noun:**

Nous avons visité le musée, la tour, et les vieux bâtiments. We visited the museum, the tower, and the old buildings.

The definite article **makes a general observation:**

Les vitamines sont bonnes pour la santé. Vitamins are good for your health.

Indefinite Article

The indefinite article refers to a class of persons or things that are **not specifically identified:**

Un homme lui a parlé. A man spoke to her.
Nous avons lu une histoire triste. We read a sad story.
Y a-t-il des chats chez toi? Are there (any) cats at your house?

The Partitive Article

The partitive article describes quantities that are **a part of an entire class of people or objects:**

Nous avons rencontré des gens intéressants. We met (some) interesting people.
Il n'a pas lu beaucoup d'articles. He didn't read many articles.
Nos invités prennent du thé le matin. Our guests drink tea in the morning.

Résumé

"Voulez-vous **de l'eau?**"

"Non, merci, je ne veux **pas d'eau** parce que **je n'aime pas l'eau.** Je préfère **le coca.**"

"Mais **l'eau** ici est spéciale. Prenez seulement **un peu d'eau** et vous verrez."

"D'accord. Mais ne me donnez qu'**un petit verre d'eau** et nous resterons **de bons amis.**"

"Do you want some water?"

"No, thanks, I don't want any water because I don't like water. I prefer Coke."

"But the water here is special. Have just a bit of water and you'll see."

"All right. But give me only a small glassful and we'll remain good friends."

CHAPTER 6

ADJECTIVES

FUNCTION

Adjectives **qualify** or **describe** nouns and pronouns and may be either concrete or abstract in meaning.

> *C'est une **grande** maison.* It's a large house.
> *C'est un examen **important**.* It's an important exam.

Agreement in Gender and Number

Adjectives vary in **number** and **gender** to **agree** with the nouns they modify.

> ***Philippe** est **blond** et ses **sœurs** sont **blondes** aussi.* Phillip is blonde and his sisters are blonde too.
> *La **vieille église** se trouve à côté d'un **vieux château**.* The old church is situated near an old castle.
> *Elle porte **des bas blancs** et **des souliers noirs**.* She's wearing white stockings and black shoes.

FORMATION OF FEMININE

Regular adjectives add an "e" to the masculine to make the feminine form:

petit/petite; rond/ronde; fort/forte

Adjectives that end in "e" are invariable:

une rue large; un stylo rouge; un/une autre enfant

Chic is also invariable; as is *génial, super, extra*

un hôtel chic; une robe chic

Common Irregular Forms

There are several irregular forms:

Masculine	Feminine
un mur épais	*une tête épaisse*
un faux ami	*une fausse amie*
un esprit vif	*une couleur vive*
un air doux	*une chanson douce*
un garçon malin	*une fille maligne*
un stylo favori	*une robe favorite*
un vin sec	*une peau sèche*
un homme sérieux	*une femme sérieuse*
de l'air frais	*une idée fraîche*

The plural form of these irregular adjectives agrees in gender with the subject it modifies.

des esprits vifs	uses the regular masculine form of the adjective because *esprit* is masculine.
des choses favorites	uses the irregular feminine form of the adjective because *chose* is feminine.

POSITION OF ADJECTIVES

The majority of adjectives **follow** the noun:

> *un vin blanc*
> *une maison blanche*

However, there are about a dozen adjectives that precede the nouns they modify. They include:

Masculine	Feminine
un **autre** cheval	une **autre** personne
un **beau*** garçon	une **belle** fille
un **bon** livre	une **bonne** histoire
un **certain** homme	une **certaine** femme
un **grand** problème	une **grande** montagne
un **gros** nez	une **grosse** poule
un **jeune** enfant	une **jeune** enfant
un **joli** chapeau	une **jolie** robe
un **long** chemin	une **longue** leçon
un **mauvais** jour	une **mauvaise** vie
un **nouveau*** complet	une **nouvelle** situation
un **vieux*** soldat	une **vieille** dame

* Each of these three adjectives has another form used before **masculine nouns with initial vowels or "h":**

	beau	*nouveau*	*vieux*
Singular	*bel*	*nouvel*	*vieil*
Plural	*beaux*	*nouveaux*	*vieux*

un bel arbre – a beautiful tree
de beaux arbres – beautiful trees
un nouvel endroit – a new place
de nouveaux endroits – new places
un vieil état – an old state
de vieux états – old states
un vieil homme – an old man

Remember that the correct form of the plural is *de grandes montagnes* and *de jolis chapeaux* because when a plural adjective precedes a noun the partitive article is omitted.

Before or After a Noun with the Same Meaning

Many adjectives may be placed before or after the noun for stylistic effect, **without a change in meaning:**

Joyeux Noël/un Noël joyeux; une merveilleuse surprise/une surprise merveilleuse

Change in Position, Change in Meaning

Some adjectives may change meaning with a change in position:

un pauvre enfant – a poor child
un enfant pauvre – a child without money

un professeur ancien – an aged teacher
un ancien professeur – a former teacher

une brave personne – a good person (in character)
une personne brave – a courageous person
mon cher oncle – my dear uncle
ma voiture chère – my expensive car

un grand homme – a great man (famous, important)
un homme grand – a tall man

le même jour – the same day
le jour même – the very day

> *Nous arrivons **le même jour** que toi.* We're arriving the same day as you are.
> *Il est parti **le jour même** de son mariage.* He left on the very day of his wedding.

le mois dernier – last month (compared to this month)
le dernier mois – the last month (in a series)

> *Décembre est **le dernier mois** de l'année.* December is the last month of the year.

propre – showing possession
propre – clean

> *Elle utilise **sa propre voiture.*** She uses her own car.
> *Cette **maison propre** est admirable.* This clean house is admirable.

certain – a vague number
certain – sure

> ***Certaines** gens* sont impolies.* Some people are impolite.
> *Son voyage est **certain.*** His trip is a sure thing.

41

* Note: *"Gens"* is **feminine** when it has an adjective **preceding** it and **masculine** when it has an adjective **following** it: *de bonnes gens; des gens heureux.*

Adjectives of Color

Most adjectives of color are placed after the noun and form the feminine by adding "e":

vert/verte; gris/grise; noir/noire

Note these exceptions:

*un ciel **bleu***	*une cravate **bleue***	*des livres **bleus***
*un chien **blanc***	*une chemise **blanche***	
*un ruban **violet***	*une veste **violette***	
*un crayon **marron***	*une table **marron*** *	*des yeux **marron***

* Note: *Marron* (brown) is an invariable adjective.

*un chapeau **bleu marine***	*une robe **bleu marine*** (navy blue)
*un papier **rose foncé*** (deep pink)	*une **robe rose clair*** (light pink)

* Note: *Clair, foncé,* and compound colors are invariable.

COMPARING WITH ADJECTIVES

For comparisons of **equality,** use *aussi* + **adjective** + *que:*

*Françoise est **aussi intelligente que** son frère.* Françoise is as smart as her brother.
*Jeannette est **aussi jolie que** sa sœur.* Jeannette is as pretty as her sister.
*Un chien est **aussi amusant qu'**un chat.* A dog is as much fun as a cat.

Superiority and Inferiority

For comparisons of **superiority** and **inferiority,** regular adjectives add *plus* or *moins:*

*Ce livre est **plus cher** que l'autre.* This book is more expensive than the other.

*Sa veste est **plus longue** que la mienne.* His jacket is longer than mine.

*As-tu un **plus petit morceau** de gâteau?* Do you have a smaller piece of cake?

*Elle cherche une **plus jolie maison** qui est **moins chère**.* She is looking for a nicer house that's cheaper.

Bon/Meilleur

The comparative of *bon* is *meilleur* and of *bonne* is *meilleure*.
Just as you don't say "gooder" in English, you don't say it in French!

*Ce vin est **meilleur** que le vin suédois.* This wine is better than Swedish wine.

*Je voudrais acheter **une meilleure télévision**.* I'd like to buy a better television.

The **negative** comparative of *bon* is *pire*, which means "worse."
(You can also use *plus mauvais* which means "more bad" or *moins bon* which means "less good" to make a negative comparison.)

*Celui-ci est un mauvais restaurant mais Chez Jean est **pire**.* This is a bad restaurant but Chez Jean is worse.

Petit/Moindre

Petit has an irregular form when used in an abstract sense:

*Cette **loi** est de **moindre importance**.* This law is of lesser importance.

When used in a concrete sense:

*Leur bateau est **plus petit** que le nôtre.* Their boat is smaller than ours.

Superlatives

Just as in English, the superlative is formed by **adding the definite article to the comparative.**

For adjectives that precede the noun: *le plus, le moins* + adjective + *de* + noun (the most, the least…in the…)

*Il a acheté **la plus belle voiture du village.*** He bought the most beautiful car in the village.

La plus petite fille de l'école va chanter. The smallest girl in the school is going to sing.

*Voilà **le moins bon vin de la saison.*** There's the worst wine of the season.

*Il choisit **les meilleurs desserts** pour la fête.* He's choosing the best desserts for the party.

Adjectives that follow the noun: The superlative is formed by **naming the noun** and **adding the article and the adjective.** Note that there are **two definite articles** in this structure.

*Nous avons vu **le film le plus populaire** de l'année.* We saw the most popular film of the year.

*Quel est **l'étudiant le moins intelligent** du lycée?* Who is the least intelligent student in the high school?

*J'ai rencontré **la femme la plus célèbre** de Washington.* I met the most famous woman in Washington.

POSSESSIVE ADJECTIVES

Since all adjectives **agree with the nouns they modify,** possessive adjectives also follow this rule. Unlike English, where the **possessor** determines the number and gender (his car, her uncles), in French the **object possessed** determines the adjective's gender and number.

Masculine

Masculine singular: one owner, one object

mon livre	my book
ton ami	your friend (**You** can be male or female; the **friend** is male.)
son oncle	his or her uncle (Gender of the **possessor** is determined by the **context.**)

Masculine plural: one owner, two or more objects

mes livres	my books
tes amis	your friends
ses oncles	his or her uncles

Feminine

Feminine singular: one owner, one object

ma robe	my dress
ta cousine	your cousin (**You** can be male or female; the **cousin** is female.)
sa maison	his or her house

Feminine plural: one owner, two or more objects

mes robes	my dresses
tes cousines	your female cousins
ses maisons	his or her houses

Plural Owners

Plural owners: one masculine or feminine object

notre père – our father
votre mère – your mother
leur jardin – their garden

Plural owners: two or more masculine or feminine objects

nos voitures – our cars
vos parents – your parents
leurs bateaux – their boats

Mon, Ton, and *Son* Before a Feminine Noun

Always use *mon, ton,* and *son* before a feminine noun that begins with a vowel. However, if there is an adjective that precedes the feminine noun beginning with a vowel, use the regular feminine forms *ma, ta,* and *sa*.

Feminine Nouns Beginning with a Vowel	*Feminine Nouns Beginning with a Vowel that have Preceding Adjectives*
*Voilà **mon amie** Lara.* There's my friend Lara.	*Voilà **ma bonne amie** Lara.* There is my good friend Lara.
*Elle a oublié **ton adresse.*** She forgot your address.	*Elle ne sait pas **ta nouvelle adresse.*** She doesn't know your new address.
***Son enfant** est malade.* Her child is sick.	***Sa petite enfant** est malade.* Her small child is sick.

DEMONSTRATIVE ADJECTIVES ("THIS," "THESE")

As the name indicates, these adjectives indicate which of several objects or people are being singled out.

Masculine singular: *Ce livre est bon.*
Feminine singular: *Cette jupe me plaît.*
Masculine and **feminine plural:** *Ces hommes, ces femmes sont jeunes.*

Note: Before a **masculine singular** noun with an initial vowel, use *cet:*

cet arbre; cet homme; cet état; cet article

The **plural** of *cet* is *ces:*

ces arbres; ces articles; etc.

Before a **feminine singular** noun with an initial vowel, use *cette:*

cette industrie; cette école; cette amie

The **plural** of *cette* is *ces:*

ces écoles; ces amies; etc.

Note: You may add *"–ci"* or *"–là"* to the noun to indicate if the object is closer or farther away:

Ce village-ci est plus grand que ce village-là. This town (here) is larger than that one (there).

INTERROGATIVE ADJECTIVES

To ask "which" or "which one" of a group of things, use *quel, quelle, quels,* or *quelles*.

Quel jour sommes-nous? What day is it?
Quelle plage préfères-tu? Which beach do you prefer?
Quels amis t'ont téléphoné? Which friends phoned you?
Quelles chansons vont-ils présenter? Which songs will they perform?

Note: *Quel* may also be an exclamation:

Quelle belle femme! What a beautiful woman!
Quels problèmes! What problems!

ADJECTIVES OF NUMBER

Cardinal numbers are invariable, except for *un, vingt,* and *cent,* which under certain conditions **agree with the noun** they modify:

*Il a écrit **quatre-vingts** articles.* He wrote 80 articles. **But:**
*Il a écrit **quatre-vingt-trois** articles.* He wrote 83 articles.
*Il y a seulement **une** femme dans la chambre.* There is only one woman in the room. **But:**
*Il y a **deux** femmes dans la chambre.* There are two women in the room.
*Son manteau coûte **deux cents** dollars.* Her coat costs $200. **But:**
*Cela coûte **deux cent cinq** dollars.* This coat costs $205.

Remember that if the number is more than 200, there is no agreement. "S" is put onto *cent* only when there is not another number following it:

trois cents / trois cent trois
300   303

DEMI(E): HALF

When *demi* is used in expressions of time, it should agree with the gender of the noun it reflects.

*Le train arrivera à **une heure et demie.*** The train will arrive at 1:30. "Demie" agrees with "heure," which is feminine.
*Nous déjeunons à **midi et demi.*** We have lunch at 12:30. "Midi" is masculine.

However, when *demi* **precedes** the noun it reflects, it is **masculine:**

*Je voudrais bien prendre une **demi-tasse** de café.* I would like a half cup of coffee.

INDEFINITE ADJECTIVES

As the name indicates, they describe a generalized and non-specific noun:

Indefinite Adjectives

Masculine	Feminine	Definition, Example
Singular:		
tout	*toute*	All of **one** class of things: *tout le monde; toute la famille; tout le livre* (the entire, or whole book). The verb is **singular.**

Masculine	Feminine	Definition, Example
Plural:		
tous	*toutes*	*Tous mes amis; toutes les chansons.* The verb is **plural.**
plusieurs	*plusieurs*	Several: *plusieurs amis/amies*
quelque(s)	*quelque(s)*	Some, a few: *quelque temps; quelque part; quelques cartes*
aucun (sing. only)	*aucune*	Not one, no: *aucun cadeau; aucune femme*
certain(s)	*certaine(s)*	Certain, some: *certaines personnes; certains jours*
chaque	*chaque*	Each, every: *chaque jour; chaque fois*
différent(s)	*différente(s)*	Different: *Il y a de différents livres; de différentes femmes.*
n'importe quel(s)	*n'importe quelle(s)*	Any...whatsoever: *Vous trouverez de bons vins dans n'importe quelle région de France.*

CHAPTER 7

PRONOUNS

Pronouns take the place of nouns and have many functions in French. **Personal pronouns** may replace persons or things and act as **subjects** and **direct** or **indirect objects.**

SUBJECT PRONOUNS

Subject pronouns perform the action of the verb.

First Person

Je	I
nous	we (masc. or fem.)

Je *fais le travail.*	I do the work.
Nous *l'aimons.*	We like it.

Second Person

tu	you (masc. or fem., familiar)
vous	you (singular, formal)
vous	you (plural)

Tu *danses bien.*	You dance well.
Vous *partez tôt.*	You're leaving early.

Third Person

il	he, it (masc.)
elle	she, it (fem.)
on	one, everyone, we, you, they (indef.)

ils	they (masc. plural or masc. and fem. plural: *Jean et Marie = ils*)
elles	they (fem. plural)

Elle est malade. She's sick.
Ils comprennent tout. They understand everything.

DIRECT OBJECT PRONOUNS

Direct object pronouns **receive** the action of the verb **directly** without any interference from another person or object.

First Person

me	me (masc. or fem.)
nous	us (masc. or fem.)

Edgar me déteste. Edgar hates me.
Mon ami nous invite. My friend's inviting us.

Second Person

te	you (masc. or fem., familiar)
vous	you (masc. or fem., singular or plural)

Sam t'aime. Sam loves you.
Irma vous regarde.* Irma's looking at you.

Third Person

le	him, it (masc.)
la	her, it (fem.)
les	them (masc. or fem. plural)

Je cherche le chat. Je le cherche.* I'm looking for the cat. I'm looking for him.
Il voit la table. Il la voit. He sees the table. He sees it.
Tu fais les exercices. Tu les fais. You're doing the exercises. You're doing them.
J'écoute la radio. Je l'écoute.* I listen to the radio. I listen to it.
J'attends l'autobus. Je l'attends.* I'm waiting for the bus. I'm waiting for it.

* Note: *"Regarder"* (to look at) and *"chercher"* (to look or search for) take a **direct object** in French. Similarly, *"écouter"* (to listen to) and *"attendre"* (to wait for) take **direct objects.**

Position in Sentence

Object pronouns **precede** the verb. Whereas in English, the word order is **subject–verb–object** (I see you), in French, it is **subject–object–verb** (*Je te vois*).

INDIRECT OBJECT PRONOUNS

Indirect object pronouns include the preposition *à* (to) in their meaning. Only the third person pronouns change for indirect objects; *me, te, nous, vous* appear in the same forms for **direct and indirect** objects.

*Gaston **m'**a parlé.* Gaston spoke to me.
*Il va **t'**écrire.* He'll write to you.
*Marie **nous** a envoyé des fleurs.* Marie sent us flowers.
*Paul veut **lui** téléphoner.* Paul wants to phone her.

Note: *"Téléphoner à quelqu'un"* takes an **indirect object** in French.
Hint: Just as the word "indirect" is longer than the word "direct," third person indirect object pronouns are **longer** than direct object pronouns:

Direct Object Pronouns
Third person: *le, la, les*

Indirect Object Pronouns
Third person: *lui* – to him, to her; *leur** – to them (masc. or fem.)

* Note: ***Leur*** (to him, to her) is invariable. Do not confuse it with the possessive adjective ***leur*** *mère* (their mother) or ***leurs*** *amis* (their friends).

Position of Indirect Object Pronouns

As with direct object pronouns, indirect object pronouns **precede** the verb:

*Nous **lui** envoyons une lettre.* We're sending him (or her) a letter.
*Nancy répond à ses cousins. Elle **leur** répond.* Nancy answers her cousins. She answers them.

Note: ***"Répondre à"*** takes an **indirect object.**

WITH TWO VERBS TOGETHER

With two verbs together, place the object pronoun **before the infinitive:**

*Il veut faire ce dîner. Il veut **le** faire.* He wants to make dinner. He wants to make it.

*Margot va **lui** écrire.* Margot will write to him.

WITH TWO OBJECT PRONOUNS TOGETHER

When two object pronouns are in the same sentence, they appear in this order before the verb:

Me, te, se, nous, vous are always first.
Le, la, les follow next.
Lui, leur are always last.

*Il donne son livre à moi. Il **me le** donne.*
*Paul envoie vos cadeaux à vous. Paul **vous les** envoie.*
*Bill vend sa voiture à Mireille. Il **la lui** vend.*
*Elle offre ces photos à ses parents. Elle **les leur** offre.*

Y AND *EN; PENSER À; PARLER DE*

Y and ***en*** replace things, places, ideas, or expressions, but do not replace people.

Y replaces prepositional phrases of location.

Y can also replace expressions in which the object of the preposition *à* is a thing.

Y can never refer to a person.

*Il va **à l'aéroport**. Il **y** va.* He's going to the airport. He's going there. (Prepositional phrase of location)

*Les fleurs sont **sur la table**. Elles **y** sont.* The flowers are on the table. They're on it. (Prepositional phrase of location)

*Nous avons mis son argent **dans le tiroir**. Nous **y** avons mis son argent.* We put his money in the drawer. We put his money there. (Prepositional phrase of location)

*Elle a répondu **à ta question**. Elle **y** a répondu.* She answered your question. She answered it. (Object of the preposition *à* is a thing)

*Les bons citoyens obéissent **aux lois.** Ils **y** obéissent.* Good citizens obey the laws. They obey them. (Object of preposition *à* is a thing)

Note for ***penser:***

Penser à + a thing = to think about something:

*Il pense à son voyage. Il **y** pense.* He thinks about his trip. He's thinking about it.

Note:

Penser à + a person = disjunctive pronoun (see 55 for further information about disjunctive pronouns):

*Je pense à mon père. Je pense à **lui.*** I think about my father. I'm thinking about him.

En replaces expressions with *de.* ***En*** also replaces nouns that are preceded by a number or description of quantity:

*Ma sœur revient **de Paris.** Elle **en** revient.* My sister's returning from Paris. She's returning from there.

*A-t-il parlé **de ses aventures?** Oui, il **en** a parlé.* Did he speak about his adventures? Yes, he spoke about them.

*Il parle souvent **de ses problèmes.** Il **en** parle souvent.* He often talks about his problems. He often talks about them.

When *en* replaces nouns preceded by numbers or quantities, the noun is replaced but the number or quantity remains in the sentence:

*Il a pris cinq verres. Il **en** a pris cinq.* He had five drinks. He had five of them.

*As-tu beaucoup **de temps libre?** Non, je **n'en** ai pas beaucoup.* Do you have much free time? No, I don't have much.

*Jean-François a onze cousins. Il **en** a onze.*
Jean-François has eleven cousins. He has eleven of them.

Note: The verb ***"parler"*** + *de* + an idea, place, or thing = ***en:***
*Sam parle de son travail. Il **en** parle.* Sam talks about his work. He talks about it.

But: *parler de* + a person = a disjunctive pronoun:

Sam parle de ses parents. Il parle d'eux. Sam is talking about his parents. He's talking about them.

Note: *parler à* + a person = indirect object pronoun:

Sam parle à sa petite amie. Il lui parle. Sam is talking to his girlfriend. He's talking **to** her.

1. Use *y* to replace expressions with *à* and other prepositions (besides *de*).
2. Use *en* to replace expressions with *de.*
3. The verbs *penser* and *parler* make a distinction between pronouns which replace things or people.
    a. *Penser à* + a thing = *y*
    b. *Penser à* + a person = disjunctive pronoun (*à moi, à lui,* etc.)
    c. *Penser de:* This form is used only **in a question** seeking an **opinion.** *Que penses-tu de mon chapeau? Qu'en penses-tu?* Answer: *Je pense qu'il est chic.*
    d. *Penser de* + a person = disjunctive pronoun. *Que penses-tu de Jean? Que penses-tu de lui?* Answer: *Je pense qu'il est gentil.*

Word order with *y* and *en*: These two pronouns come after direct and indirect object pronouns; *y* precedes *en.*

Je mets les stylos dans la boîte. Je les y mets. I put them there.
Tu as donné de l'argent à Pierre. Tu lui en as donné. You gave him some.

Note: There is never any agreement with *en.*

Nous leur avons envoyé des fleurs. Nous leur en avons envoyé. We've sent them some (flowers).

Hint: Remember, the expression *"Il y en a"* answers the question *"Y a-t-il (des roses sur la table)?"* — *Oui, il y en a.*

INTERROGATIVE SENTENCES WITH PRONOUNS

As with declarative sentences, pronouns **precede the verb** in **interrogative** sentences:

*Avons-nous assez **d'argent? En** avons-nous assez?* Do we have
  enough money?
*Est-ce que tu connais **Marcie?** Est-ce que tu **la** connais?* Do you know
  her?
*Ont-ils pris **mon stylo? L'**ont-ils pris?* Did they take it?
*Pierre est-il **à New York** maintenant? **Y** est-il?* Is he there?

  * Note: The **adverb** *"assez"* is repeated.

DISJUNCTIVE PRONOUNS

  Disjunctive pronouns are **not joined** to the verb, as are those discussed
so far. Their forms are: *moi, toi, lui, elle, nous, vous, eux, elles.* Their
principal uses are:
  a. After a preposition: *Je vais **chez toi.** Le livre est **devant lui.***
  b. After *c'est: Qui parle? C'est **elle.** C'est **lui.***
  c. With a double subject: *Simon et **moi,** nous allons à Paris.*
  d. With *parler de* + a person. *Je parle de **mes amis.** Je parle **d'eux.***
  e. With *penser à* + a person and *penser de* + a person.
  f. To emphasize a strong statement: *Moi, j'ai dit cela?* I said that?
  g. To compare and contrast two elements: *Paul, **lui** est riche mais
      Marie, **elle** est pauvre.*

RELATIVE PRONOUNS

  Relative pronouns link or relate two ideas or two clauses. They must
have an **antecedent** (a noun or pronoun which comes before the pronoun
to which it refers).

Simple Relative Pronouns

  Simple relative pronoun forms: *qui* (subject), *que* (object), and *où* (for
places and time).

  *Nous regardons l'homme **qui danse** si bien.* We're watching the man
      who dances so well. *Qui* links the two ideas and is the **subject** of
      the verb *danse.* Antecedent: *l'homme.*
  *Le livre **que tu cherchais** a disparu.* The book for which you were
      looking has disappeared. *Que* is the **object** of the verb *chercher.*
      Antecedent: *le livre.*

*Voilà le café **où** Bill travaille.* There's the café where Bill works. ***Où*** designates **"the place where."** Antecedent: ***le café.***

*Minuit est l'heure **où** nous nous couchons.* Midnight is the time (when) we go to bed. Antecedent: ***l'heure.***

Hint: To differentiate **subject** from **object,** remember that *qui* always **precedes the verb directly;** *que* always has **another subject before the verb.**

Ce qui, ce que

Ce qui, ce que are used in sentences where there is **no antecedent.** *Ce* = "the thing that" or "what":

*Tu ne sais pas **ce qui** est bon.* You don't know what's good.

*Je comprends **ce que** Sam dit.* I understand what Sam is saying.

Lequel, laquelle, lesquels, lesquelles

Unlike the simple relative pronouns, *lequel* is a relative pronoun used only after a preposition. It replaces a thing.* *Lequel* must agree in gender and number with its antecedent (*lequel, laquelle, lesquels, lesquelles*).

*C'est le stylo **avec lequel** le Président a signé la loi.* That's the pen with which the President signed the law.

*Où est la maison **dans laquelle** tu habitais?* Where's the house in which you used to live?

*Voici les gens **sans lesquels** nous ne pouvons pas partir.* Here are the people without whom we can't leave.

When it is preceded by the preposition *à* or *de*, contractions are made: *auquel, auxquels, auxquelles, duquel, desquels, desquelles.*

*Le grand banquet **auquel** elle a assisté était marveilleux.* The big banquet she attended was astonishing.

*Je n'ai rien à dire au sujet **duquel** vous parlez.* I don't have anything to say about the subject of which you are speaking.

*There are two cases in which *lequel* can be used to replace people:

After the adverb ***parmi**: Voilà des étudiants **parmi lesquels** se trouve ta cousine.* There are some students, among whom is your cousin.

When there is a need to emphasize or clarify the gender or number of the antecedent: *Connaissez-vous les enfants **pour lesquelles** il a* *écrit ses poèmes?* Do you know the children for whom he wrote his poems?

Because *enfants* is invariable, we only know the gender of the children from the feminine for *lesquelles*.

Dont

Dont is the relative pronoun used to replace *de*. *Dont* is used to replace people in phrases with *de*.* It is also regularly used instead of *duquel*, *de laquelle*, etc., to replace things:

La personne dont vous parlez n'est plus en ville. The person of whom you're speaking is not in town.

J'ai dîné au restaurant dont mes parents parlent de temps en temps. I dined at the restaurant of which my parents speak from time to time.

Remember that in French, you cannot end a sentence with a preposition. Use *dont* to avoid ending a sentence with *de*:

C'est le livre dont j'ai besoin.
It's the book that I need.

*To replace a person after a preposition other than *de* use *qui*.
Voilà la fille avec qui j'ai parlé.
There's the girl with whom I spoke.

Dont also acts as a relative pronoun meaning "whose":

Yves, dont le frère est Paul, comprend la situation. Yves, whose brother is Paul, understands the situation.

C'est l'étudiant dont l'examen n'était pas lisible. It's the student whose exam wasn't legible.

Ce dont is used when there is **no antecedent** (the thing about which, the thing of which) and when *de* is being replaced in the sentence:

Je ne comprends pas ce dont vous avez besoin. [*avoir besoin + de*]. I don't understand what you need.

Ce dont ils parlent me fait peur. [*parler + de*]. What they are talking about frightens me.

POSSESSIVE PRONOUNS

Possessive pronouns take the place of nouns and agree with them in number and gender.

Forms of Possessive Pronouns

Remember that the pronoun agrees with the object possessed, **not with the gender of the possessor.**

First Person	Second Person	Third Person
le mien – mine, m. s.	*le tien* – yours, m. s.	*le sien* – his, hers, m. s.
les miens – mine, m. pl.	*les tiens* – yours, m. pl.	*les siens* – his, hers, m. pl.
le nôtre – ours, m.s.	*le vôtre* – yours, m. s.	*le leur* – theirs, m. s.
la mienne – mine, f. s.	*la tienne* – yours, f. s.	*la sienne* – his, hers, f. s.
les miennes – mine, f. pl.	*les tiennes* – yours, f. pl.	*les siennes* – his, hers, f. pl.
les nôtres – ours, m. or f. pl.	*les vôtres* – yours, m. or f. pl.	*les leurs* – theirs, m. or f. pl.
la nôtre – ours, f. s.	*la vôtre* – yours, f. s.	*la leur* – theirs, f. s.

Où sont tes amis? **Les miens** *sont ici.* Where are your friends? Mine are here.

Ta robe est jolie. **La sienne** *est laide.* Your dress is pretty. Hers is ugly.

Nos oncles sont là. **Les leurs** *sont partis.* Our uncles are here. Theirs left.

CHAPTER 8

VERBS

Verbs are the heart of the sentence and **express an action or a state of being, mental or physical.** There are several **moods** of verbs (means of communication) and each mood contains **tenses** (time of the action). *L'indicatif, l'impératif, le conditionnel,* and *le subjontif* are the principal moods we will discuss.

L'INDICATIF

L'indicatif (the indicative) indicates or relates information in either declarative or interrogative sentences. It has three main conjugations: *–er, –ir,* or *–re* verbs. The *infinitif* (the "to" form) is made up of **a stem + an ending.**

Regular *–er* verbs

Regular *–er* verbs: *chanter, danser, manger, donner, parler,* etc.
Note: The great majority of French verbs are of this conjugation.
Present tense of *chanter* (to sing). *Chant* = stem (or radical) + *er* = ending.

Chanter (to sing)	**present participle:** *chantant*
je chante	*nous chantons*
tu chantes	*vous chantez*
il (elle, on) chante	*ils (elles) chantent*

–ir verbs

There are two classes of *–ir* verbs, those that add *-iss-* to the plural forms *(maigrir, finir, choisir, réussir, fleurir, brunir)* and those that do not *(dormir, sortir, partir)*. The **present participles** of *finir = finissant* (finishing) and *dormir = dormant* (sleeping) also reflect these differences.

Finir (to finish)
  je finis
  tu finis
  il (elle, on) finit
  to il, (elle, on)

present participle: *finissant*
  nous finissons
  vous finissez
  ils (elles) finissent

Dormir (to sleep)
  je dors
  tu dors
  il (elle, on) dort

present participle: *dormant*
  nous dormons
  vous dormez
  ils (elles) dorment

Regular *–re* verbs

Regular verbs ending in *–re (vendre, rendre, attendre, descendre, entendre):*

Attendre (to wait for)
  j'attends
  tu attends
  il (elle, on) attend

present participle: *attendant*
  nous attendons
  vous attendez
  ils (elles) attendent

Verbs ending in *–oir*

Verbs ending in *–oir (voir, recevoir, pouvoir, vouloir, devoir,* etc.) are irregular but commonly follow a pattern: 1st, 2nd, 3rd persons singular and 3rd person plural are **similar**:

Voir (to see)
  je vois
  tu vois
  il (elle, on) voit

present participle: *voyant*
  nous voyons
  vous voyez
  ils (elles) voient

Vouloir (to want, to wish) **present participle:** *voulant*
    je veux   nous voulons
    tu veux   vous voulez
    il (elle, on) veut   ils (elles) veulent

Recevoir (to receive) **present participle:** *recevant*
    je reçois   nous recevons
    tu reçois   vous recevez
    il (elle, on) reçoit   ils (elles) reçoivent

Note: No cedilla is used under the "c" when it is before "e."

Spelling Changes in *–er* Verbs

Some otherwise regular *–er* verbs have **spelling changes** in the *nous* and *vous* forms:

appeler:	j'appe**lle**	nous appelons	vous appelez
jeter:	je je**tte**	nous jetons	vous jetez
acheter:	j'ach**è**te	nous achetons	vous achetez
espérer:	j'esp**è**re	nous espérons	vous espérez
préférer:	je préf**è**re	nous préférons	vous préférez
manger:	je mange	nous mangeons*	

Manger (ranger, changer) takes an extra *"e"* in the *nous* form in order to maintain consistency with pronunciation.

Common Irregular Verbs

Common irregular verbs (with present participle)

Être (étant) *Avoir (ayant)*
  je suis   nous sommes   j'ai   nous avons
  tu es   vous êtes   tu as   vous avez
  il (elle) est   ils (elles) sont   il (elle) a   ils (elles) ont

Faire (faisant) *Aller (allant)*
  je fais   nous faisons   je vais   nous allons
  tu fais   vous faites   tu vas   vous allez
  il (elle) fait   ils (elles) font   il (elle) va   ils (elles) vont

Note: *ils **ont** (avoir); ils **sont** (être); ils **font** (faire); ils **vont** (aller)*

Venir (venant)

je viens	nous venons
tu viens	vous venez
il (elle) vient	ils (elles) viennent

Pouvoir (pouvant)

je peux	nous pouvons
tu peux	vous pouvez
il (elle) peut	ils (elles) peuvent

Dire (disant)

je dis	nous disons
tu dis	vous dites
il (elle) dit	ils (elles) disent

Envoyer (envoyant)

j'envoie	nous envoyons
tu envoies	vous envoyez
il (elle) envoie	ils (elles) envoient

Prendre (prenant)

je prends	nous prenons
tu prends	vous prenez
il (elle) prend	ils (elles) prennent

Écrire (écrivant)

j'écris	nous écrivons
tu écris	vous écrivez
il (elle) écrit	ils (elles) écrivent

Craindre (craignant)

je crains	nous craignons
tu crains	vous craignez
il (elle) craint	ils (elles) craignent

Savoir (sachant)

je sais	nous savons
tu sais	vous savez
il (elle) sait	ils (elles) savent

Boire (buvant)

je bois	nous buvons
tu bois	vous buvez
il (elle) boit	ils (elles) boivent

Lire (lisant)

je lis	nous lisons
tu lis	vous lisez
il (elle) lit	ils (elles) lisent

L'IMPÉRATIF

L'impératif, another **mood,** expresses **commands** or **orders.** The impératif is formed by using a verb in the present tense of the *tu, nous,* and *vous* forms.

For the informal commands, use the *tu* form.
For the formal commands, use the *vous* form.
For collective commands, use the *nous* form.

Affirmative Commands

Réponds, Jim!	Answer, Jim!
Choisis une pomme!	Take an apple!
Rends mon argent!	Give back my money!
Marie, regarde la lune!	Mary, look at the moon!
Donne le stylo à ton papa!	Give your dad the pen!
Va avec Sam!	Go with Sam!

Note: There is no "s" in the *tu* form of *-er* verbs.

Marchons vite!   Let's walk fast!
Écrivons la lettre!   Let's write the letter!
Fermez la porte!   Close the door!
Finissez le vin!   Finish the wine!
Prenez votre manteau!   Take your coat!

Negative Commands

To form **negative commands** use the same verb forms, but place *ne* in front of the verb and *pas* after it:

Ne réponds pas!   Don't answer!
Ne rends pas mon argent!   Don't give back my money!
Ne fermez pas la porte!   Don't close the door!
Ne prenez pas votre manteau!   Don't take your coat!

Irregular Imperatives

There are only **three irregular imperative forms:**

Avoir: aie, ayons, ayez
Être: sois, soyons, soyez
Savoir: sache, sachons, sachez

N'aie pas peur! Don't be afraid!
Soyez calme! Be calm!
Sachons la vérité! Let's learn the truth!

Imperative + Pronoun

Imperative + pronoun: With **affirmative** commands, use *le, la, les, nous* for **direct objects** and *moi, nous, lui, leur* for **indirect objects**. Place pronouns **after the verb:**

Regarde-le! Look at it!
Mange-les! Eat them!
Fais-le! Do it!
Écrivez-moi! Write to me!
Parlons-lui! Let's speak to him (her)!

With Negative Commands

With negative commands, place the pronoun **before the verb:**

*Ne **le** regarde pas!* Don't look at it!
*Ne **les** mange pas!* Don't eat them!
*Ne **le** fais pas!* Don't do it!
*Ne **m'**écrivez pas!* Don't write to me!
*Ne **lui** parlons pas!* Don't talk to him.

With Two Pronouns

With two pronouns place **people** at the end of the sentence for emphasis in **affirmative commands.** Use regular pronoun order in **negative commands:**

*Donne-le-**moi**!* Give it to me! **But:** *Ne **me** le donne pas!*
*Envoyez-les-**nous**!* Send them to us! **But:** *Ne **nous** les envoyez pas!*
*Ecrivez-la-**leur**!* Write it to them! **But:** *Ne **la** leur écrivez pas!*

Y and *en*

Y and *en* follow personal pronouns in both affirmative and negative commands.

*Mettez-**les-y**!*	Put them there!
*Ne **les** y mettez pas!*	Don't put them there!
*Parlez-**lui-en**!*	Speak to him about it!
*Ne **lui** en parlez pas!*	Don't speak to him about it!
*Donne-**m'en**!*	Give me some!
*Ne **m'en** donne pas!*	Don't give me any!

Note: When using *y* and *en* in affirmative commands in the *tu* form, the "s" of the *tu* form of *-er* verbs is retained.

Vas-y!	Go to it!
But: *N'y va pas!*	Don't go to it!
Manges-en!	Eat some of it!
But: *N'en mange pas!*	Don't eat any of it!

LE PASSÉ COMPOSÉ

Le passé composé is a past tense of a verb in the indicative mood. It is used to express a completed action in the past. The name of this tense (compound past) illustrates the fact that it is made up of **more than one part.** (A "simple" verb has only one component.) There are **two parts** to the *passé composé*: an **auxiliary verb** *(avoir* or *être)* and a **past participle,** which is a verb form that **can never stand alone as a verb.** The auxiliary verb is conjugated, but the past participle is invariable.

Formation of the *Passé Composé*

–er **verbs:** To form the past participle, drop the *–er* of the infinitive and add *"é."*

donner: to give
*j'ai donné (*I gave, I did give, I have given)
tu as donné (you gave)
il (elle) a donné (he/she gave)
nous avons donné (we gave)
vous avez donné (you gave)
ils (elles) ont donné (they gave)

Note: *Avoir* is conjugated; the participle is invariable.

–ir **verbs:** To form the past participle, drop the "r" of the infinitive.

choisir: to choose
j'ai choisi   *nous avons choisi*
tu as choisi   *vous avez choisi*
il (elle) a choisi   *ils (elles) ont choisi*

–re **verbs:** To form the past participle, drop the *–re* and add "u" to the stem.

vendre: to sell
j'ai vendu   *nous avons vendu*
tu as vendu   *vous avez vendu*
il (elle) a vendu   *ils (elles) ont vendu*

Past Participles of Irregular Verbs

The above patterns apply to all **regular** verbs; for **irregular** verbs, participles must be learned separately. Here is a list of some of the irregular past participles:

avoir: j'ai eu	*être: j'ai été*	*écrire: j'ai écrit*
courir: j'ai couru	*boire: j'ai bu*	*croire: j'ai cru*
dire: j'ai dit	*prendre: j'ai pris*	*ouvrir: j'ai ouvert*
tenir: j'ai tenu	*faire: j'ai fait*	*lire: j'ai lu*
voir: j'ai vu	*savoir: j'ai su*	*vouloir: j'ai voulu*
pouvoir: j'ai pu	*mettre: j'ai mis*	*vivre: j'ai vécu*
recevoir: j'ai reçu	*plaire: j'ai plu*	

L'Accord (Agreement)

In the *passé composé* with the auxiliary *avoir,* if there is a **direct object** (noun or pronoun) that **precedes** the **verb,** the participle must "agree" with the direct object in gender and number (for feminine and plural). Masculine singular objects that precede the verb do not affect the participle.

> *Pierre a pris **ces chemises**. ("Chemises"* is the direct object of *"a pris.") **Il les a prises**. ("Les"* is the feminine plural direct object that precedes the verb; therefore, you add "es" to the participle *"pris.")*
> *Nous avons vendu **la voiture**. Nous l'avons **vendue**. ("Voiture"* is feminine singular; *"l"* replaces *"voiture"; "vendu"* must agree; therefore, you add an "e.")*

Note: When the **direct object follows the verb** *("ces chemises," "la voiture"),* the participle is **invariable.**

> *As-tu **rencontré** Marie? L'as-tu **rencontrée**?* Did you meet Marie? Did you meet her?

Attention:
*Nous avons téléphoné à nos amis. Nous **leur** avons **téléphoné**.*

(Agreement is made **only** with the preceding **direct object,** not the **indirect object.**)

Passé Composé with *être*

There are about 20 verbs that form the *passé composé* with *être,* rather than with *avoir* (cf., "Joy to the World/the Lord **is** come" in old English). These verbs deal with movement, such as comings and goings.

aller – to go
arriver – to arrive
descendre – to come down
devenir – to become
entrer – to enter
monter – to go up, climb
mourir – to die
naître – to be born
partir – to leave, depart

parvenir – to reach or achieve
passer – to pass, drop by, spend time
rentrer – to come or go home
rester – to stay, remain
retourner – to return
revenir – to come back, return
sortir – to go out
tomber – to fall
venir – to come

Agreement with *être*

The past participle used with *être* must agree in number and gender with the subject.

*Elles **sont nées** à Paris.* They (fem. pl.) were born in Paris.
*Son amie **est morte** hier.* His friend (fem.) died yesterday.
*Nous **sommes arrivés** en retard.* We arrived late.
*Mathilde **est tombée** de son lit.* Mathilde fell from her bed.

Transitive and Intransitive Verbs

Rentrer, sortir, monter, descendre, passer may be used **transitively** (with a direct object) or **intransitively** (with no object). When they are **transitive verbs,** they take *avoir:*

*J'ai **rentré** la voiture.* I brought the car inside.
*Marie **a monté** la rue Diderot.* Marie went up Diderot Street.
*Bill **a descendu** les valises.* Bill brought the suitcases down.
*Yvette **m'a passé** le pain.* Yvette passed me the bread.

Note: Rules of agreement for *avoir* apply to these five verbs when they are **transitive**. The participle agrees with the preceding **direct object.**

*Je l'ai **rentrée**.* I brought it (the car) in.
*Marie l'a **montée**.* Marie went up it (the street).
*Bill les a **descendues**.* Bill brought them (the suitcases) down.

Interrogative in the *Passé Composé*

With *est-ce que:*
*Est-ce que Jacques **a téléphoné**? **Est-il passé** ce matin?* Did Jack call? Did he come by this morning?

With **inversion:**

Jacques a-t-il téléphoné? (Note: In conversation, the structure
   "Jacques a téléphoné?" is more common.)
Où êtes-vous allés, mes amis? Where did you go, my friends?
Tes parents sont-ils partis? Did your folks leave?

Negative

Since all negatives have two parts *(ne...pas, ne...jamais, ne...pas encore,* etc.), place *ne* before the **verb** *(avoir* or *être)* and *pas, plus,* etc. after
the verb, which is conjugated.

Il n'a pas vu ton chien. He didn't see your dog.
Nous n'avons plus parlé de lui. We didn't speak of him any longer.
Jeanne n'est jamais allée à Nîmes. Jeanne never went to Nîmes.
Pourquoi n'ont-ils pas encore écrit? Why haven't they written yet?

Negative interrogative + object pronoun with *avoir:* (With *être,* the
object pronoun is used only in pronominal verb constructions — see below.)
A-t-elle mis la robe? Ne l'a-t-elle pas mise? Did she wear the dress?
   Didn't she wear it?
*Les Duval n'ont-ils pas acheté cette maison? Ne l'ont-ils pas
achetée?* Didn't the Duvals buy that house? Didn't they buy it?

L'IMPARFAIT

The term **"imperfect"** signifies **"not perfected** or **finished,"** and this
attribute distinguishes it from the *passé composé.* Unlike the *passé
composé,* it is a simple form (with no auxiliary).

Formation

Take the *nous* form of the present tense; remove the ending *-ons.* To the
remaining stem add: *–ais, –ais, –ait, –ions, –iez, –aient.*
Exception: *être: j'étais, tu étais, il était, nous étions, vous étiez, ils
étaient.*

Je dansais. I danced, I used to dance, I was dancing.

   ***Donner:** je donnais*   ***Finir:** je finissais*

Écrire: j'écrivais   *Étudier:* j'étudiais, nous étudions
Manger: je mangeais   *Commencer:* je commençais
Préférer: je préférais   *Appeler:* j'appelais

Usage

Unlike the *passé composé,* which denotes **an action completed within a specified or implied time frame,** the imperfect is a tense of **description, condition, repetition,** or **habitual action.** This time frame can also be prolonged when using the *imparfait* for a repeated, habitual, or routine action in the past. For example: *Tous les matins, je me promenais au bord de la mer.* Every morning, I used to (I would) go for a walk by the ocean.

Quand j'étais jeune, je faisais beaucoup de sport. [General description of habitual, repeated action.] When I was young, I played a lot of sports.

Puisque Marc avait mal au dos, il ne pouvait pas marcher vite. [Description of physical/mental condition.] Since Marc had a backache, he couldn't walk fast.

Le ciel était bleu, le vent touchait légèrement le bout des fleurs, qui semblaient heureuses. Il faisait très beau et nous avions envie de rester au jardin mais il fallait rentrer dans la maison. The sky was blue, the wind lightly touched the edges of the flowers, which seemed to be happy. It was a beautiful day, and we felt like staying in the garden, but we had to go inside the house. [As you can see, an entire passage may be expressed in the imperfect, if it involves description of the weather, the décor, mental and/or physical conditions, i.e., "how things were."]

Quand

Two **simultaneous actions** that took place in the past may be expressed by the imperfect using *quand.*

Quand nous parlions, elle regardait la télé. When we were speaking, she was watching TV.

Claudette avait cinq ans quand son père travaillait à Nice. Claudette was five years old when her father was working in Nice.

Quand tu entrais, nous sortions. When you were coming in, we were going out.

Attention:

*Robert ne **savait** pas quand son cousin **allait** revenir.* Robert didn't know when his cousin was going to return.

Note: *Aller* is **always** used in the **imperfect** as an auxiliary to express the future in the past ("was going to do something").

L'imparfait versus *le passé composé*

Although theoretically any verb may be used in any tense, some verbs are used **almost exclusively** in the **imperfect** because of their meaning, e.g., *être, avoir, pouvoir, vouloir, savoir, aimer, détester, préférer,* etc., which describe conditions, states of mind, or emotions.

Under certain circumstances, these verbs may be used in the *passé composé* in order to isolate a particular moment or an extraordinary situation or event.

*Ce matin elle **a eu** mal à la tête à cause de son accident hier.* This morning she had a headache because of her accident yesterday. [The headache is gone now.]

*Le garçon regardait attentivement le film et tout à coup il **a pu** comprendre l'histoire.* The boy watched the movie carefully and all at once he could understand the story. [He succeeded in grasping it.]

*Le chat a vu le chien et soudain il **a voulu** courir.* The cat saw the dog and suddenly he tried to run. [The sense of *vouloir* is "to try" in this case.]

Hint: Key words like ***tout à coup, soudain, immédiatement*** often indicate the extraordinary circumstances that call for the use of the *passé composé* for these verbs.

Remember:

*Use the *imparfait* for description, condition, repetition, and habitual action.

*Certain verbs are used almost exclusively in the *imparfait* (*être, avoir, pouvoir, vouloir, savoir, aimer, détester, préférer,* etc.).

*The *passé composé* stands for an action completed in a specified or implied time. The *imparfait* is ongoing and has no indicated beginning or end.

Compare:

*Nous **écrivions** une carte postale quand le train **est arrivé**.* We were
   writing a post card when the train arrived. [*Passé composé* inter-
   rupts the ongoing action of the imperfect.]

*Sophie **a ouvert** la boîte et elle **a ri** de plaisir.* Sophie opened the box
   and laughed with pleasure. [Two actions in the *passé composé*; one
   inspires the other. Both actions are completed within a specific
   time.]

*Sam **était** fatigué et il **ne voulait pas** manger.* Sam was tired and didn't
   want to eat. [Two descriptive actions, both imperfect because both
   have no indicated beginning or end.]

LE PLUS-QUE-PARFAIT

Le plus-que-parfait (a.k.a., *pluperfect*) denotes something further
away in the past. It is a compound tense that is used **to compare two past
actions.** It may be used with the *passé composé* or the imperfect.

Formation

The imperfect form of *avoir* or *être* is used as an **auxiliary** with the
past participle. The same rules of **agreement** that apply to the *passé
composé* govern the *plus-que-parfait*.

*Hier **j'ai reçu** la lettre que Jean **avait envoyée** il y a trois semaines.*
   Yesterday I received the letter that John (had) sent three weeks
   ago. [The action of sending the letter precedes its receipt. Both
   actions are in the past.]

*Gigi **était déjà arrivée** quand **nous avons téléphoné**.* Gigi had already
   arrived when we phoned.

*Philippe **oubliait** toujours le nom des gens qu'il **avait rencontrés**.*
   Philip always used to forget the names of people he (had) met.

LE FUTUR PROCHE

Le futur proche (the near future) is a way of expressing actions that
are going to be done in the future. In fact, in English, the *futur proche*
means "to be going to do something." It is formed by using *aller* in the
present tense (as an auxiliary) and the infinitive.

*Nous **allons voir** le nouvel ami de Laure ce soir.* We're going to see
   Laure's new friend this evening.

Vas-tu payer cette facture? Are you going to pay this bill?
L'année prochaine ils ne vont pas visiter *le Midi.* Next year they're
   not going to visit the South of France.

LE FUTUR

This tense expresses an action that is going to happen in the future. It
is a simple tense (unlike the *futur proche,* which is a compound tense). In
English the future is indicated by the words "will" or "shall."

Formation of Future Tense for Regular Verbs

The *futur* is based on the infinitive. To form a future verb, simply add the
appropriate ending -*ai, -as, -a, -ons, -ez, -ont* to the infinitive of the verb.

–*ar* verb	–*ir* verb	–*re* verb
je parler**ai**	je finir**ai**	je vendr**ai**
tu parler**as**	tu finir**as**	tu vendr**as**
il parler**a**	il finir**a**	il vendr**a**
elle parler**a**	elle finir**a**	elle vendr**a**
nous parler**ons**	nous finir**ons**	nous vendr**ons**
vous parler**ez**	vous finir**ez**	vous vendr**ez**
ils parler**ont**	ils finir**ont**	ils vendr**ont**
elles parler**ont**	elles finir**ont**	elles vendr**ont**

Common Irregular Verbs

Stems change; endings do not.

avoir: j'**aur**ai	être: je **ser**ai	faire: je **fer**ai
aller: j'**ir**ai	dire: je **dir**ai	venir: je **viendr**ai
courir: je **courr**ai	pouvoir: je **pourr**ai	vouloir: je **voudr**ai
savoir: je **saur**ai	essayer: j'**essaier**ai	voir: je **verr**ai

Quand je serai *à Paris,* j'irai *le voir.* When I'm in Paris, I'll go see
   him.
Je ne sais pas quand elle partira. I don't know when she's leaving.

Note: When *"quand"* is followed by a **future action,** the verb must be
in the **future,** even though in English we often translate it in the present.

Expressing Probability

The future can be used to express **probability:**

*Il est minuit, Paul **sera** déjà endormi.* It's midnight; Paul is probably asleep already.

*Christine **aura** reçu mon cadeau.* Christine has probably received my present.

LE CONDITIONNEL

The conditional is a **mood** (with a present and past tense) that is always based on a **hypothetical situation** ("if" certain circumstances occur, "then"...). The "if" may be expressed or implied.

Formation

Like the future, the conditional uses the **infinitive** as its stem. To form the conditional, add the appropriate ending: *-ais, -ais, -ait, -ions, -iez, -aient* to the infinitive. Irregular conditional verbs use the same stems as irregular future verbs.

*je parler**ais***	*je finir**ais***	*je vendr**ais***
*nous parler**ions***	*nous finir**ions***	*nous vendr**ions***
*ils parler**aient***	*ils finir**aient***	*ils vendr**aient***

Hint: There is always an "r" in the conditional to differentiate it from the imperfect, which has the same endings.

Imperfect	Conditional	Imperfect	Conditional
je dansais	*je danser**ais***	*je voulais*	*je voudr**ais***
je venais	*je viendr**ais***	*j'étais*	*je ser**ais***
j'avais	*j'aur**ais***	*je faisais*	*je fer**ais***
je voyais	*je verr**ais***	*je finissais*	*je finir**ais***
je pouvais	*je pourr**ais***	*j'allais*	*j'ir**ais***

*Sans son aide, nous ne **saurions** pas utiliser cette machine.* Without his help, we wouldn't know how to use this machine.

*Pauline **serait** ravie de recevoir ce livre.* Pauline would be delighted to receive this book.

*Je **viendrais** te parler ce soir.* I'd come to talk to you tonight.

*Daniel **voudrait** du poisson et de la salade.* Daniel would like some fish and salad. [The conditional of **vouloir** is used for politeness instead of the present of the indicative *je veux*.]

The Past Conditional

The past conditional is further away in possibility and time, and often expresses regret.

Formation: The conditional of *avoir* or *être* + **past participle.**

*J'**aurais voulu** le voir.* I would have liked to see him.
*Elle **serait allée** avec toi.* She would have gone with you.
*Nous **ne** leur **aurions pas raconté** cette histoire.* We wouldn't have told them that story.

The Future and Conditional with "If" Clauses

If...	Result...
Present: *Si j'ai le temps*	Future: *j'irai chez lui.*
Imperfect: *Si j'avais le temps*	Conditional: *j'irais chez lui.*
Pluperfect: *Si j'avais eu le temps*	Past Conditional: *je **serais allé** chez lui.*

These structures correspond to English: If I **have** the time, **I'll go** to his house. If I **had** the time, I **would go** to his house. If I **had had** the time, I **would have gone** to his house.

L'INFINITIF

When two present tense verbs are used together, the **second verb** is always in the **infinitive.** The following verbs are followed **directly** by the infinitive with **no preposition:**

*Nous **aimons** danser.* We like to dance.
*Ils ne **savent** pas lire.* They don't know how to read.
*Margot **déteste** travailler.* Margot hates to work.
*Cet homme **adore** manger.* This man loves to eat.

As a Noun

The infinitive may also be used as a noun, as the subject or object of the sentence, or as the object of a preposition:

*Bien **dormir** est très important.* Sleeping well is very important.
*Je n'aime pas **dire** "adieu."* I don't like to say "goodbye."

L'infinitif passé

L'infinitif passé uses ***avoir*** or ***être*** as the **auxiliary + the past participle** *(après avoir vu; après être venu)* to express "after having done something." ***Avant de* + the infinitive** *(avant de voir; avant de venir)* is used for "before doing something."

> ***Avant de faire** son lit, Marie a cherché des draps.* Before making her bed, Mary looked for some sheets.
> *Jacques prépare son dîner **après avoir étudié.*** Jacques made his dinner after having studied.
> *Elle nous a vus **après être rentrée.*** After coming home, she saw us.
> ***Après être tombée,** Suzy a ri.* After falling down, Susie laughed.
> *Il nous écrira **avant de partir.*** He'll write to us before he leaves.

Note: **One subject** performs **both actions**. The participle agrees with the **subject** with ***être*** and with the **preceding direct object** with ***avoir***. The verb in the second action may be in the present, past, or future tense.

LE PARTICIPE PRÉSENT

The present participle is formed by adding *–ant* to the stem of the *nous* form of the present:

parlant, finissant, rompant. **Exceptions:** *étant, ayant, sachant.*

As an Adjective

The present participle may act as an **adjective:**

*"L'homme est un roseau **pensant."** (Pascal)* "Man is a thinking reed."

With *"en"*

The **only** preposition used with the present participle is *en* ("by," "while," or "upon" doing something):

> *En fermant la porte, il a laissé son chat dehors.* By closing the door, he left his cat outside.
> *Le vieillard est mort heureux en sachant la vérité.* The old man died happy, upon learning the truth.
> *Elle peut chanter en dansant.* She can sing while dancing.

Note: The **same subject** performs both actions.

LES VERBES PRONOMINAUX

As the name implies, pronominal verbs are always accompanied by a **pronoun** *(me, te, se, nous, vous, se)*. They are used in **reciprocal, reflexive,** and **idiomatic** constructions.

Reciprocal

Reciprocal verbs indicate a reciprocal action between two parties. They are usually translated with the English expression "each other."

> *Roméo et Juiliette s'aiment.* Romeo and Juliet **love each other**.
> *Nous nous écrivons chaque mois.* We **write to each other** every month. [The first *nous* is the subject; the second is the indirect object pronoun.]
> *Vous vous regardez longtemps.* You **look at each other** for a long time.
> *Ils se voient tous les jours.* They **see each other** every day.

Reflexive

Reflexive verbs indicate that the action of the verbs falls on the subject. It corresponds to the English expressions "to do something to oneself" or "to do something for oneself." The auxiliary verb for every pronomial verb in a compound tense, such as the *passé composé,* is *être.*

> *Bette se lave.* Bette washes herself.
> *Bette se lave les mains.* Bette washes her hands (for herself).
> *Bette s'est lavé les mains.* Bette washed her hands.

With reflexive verbs, follow the rule of agreement for *être* (participle agrees with the subject) unless there is a direct object preceding the verb. In that case, follow the rule of *avoir* (participle agrees with object).

Bette s'est lavée. Bette washed herself.
Bette se les est lavées. Bette washed them (for herself).

Note that the direct object *les* now precedes the verb. Therefore, agreement is made with *les*, which refers to *mains*, a feminine plural noun.

Common Idiomatic Use of Pronominal Verbs

To express the **passive voice** (i.e., the action falls on the subject instead of an object), the **reflexive form** is often used:
Le français se parle au Canada. French is spoken in Canada.
Monsieur, cela ne se fait pas ici! Sir, that isn't done here!
Les journaux se vendent au kiosque. Papers are sold at the kiosk.

Note: The verb agrees in number with the subject.

TWO OTHER PAST TENSES OF THE INDICATIVE

Two other past tenses of the indicative are *le passé simple* and *le passé antérieur.* Both of these tenses are used in writing, rather than in conversation. (Many modern writers use the *passé composé, imparfait*, and *plus-que-parfait* instead of these tenses.)

Le passé simple (historic or literary past) describes an action finished at a well-defined moment in the past.

Formation of regular verbs: Add to the stem the following endings:

–er verbs	*–ir* verbs	*–re* verbs
je parlai	*je finis*	*je vendis*
tu parlas	*tu finis*	*tu vendis*
il parla	*il finit*	*il vendit*
nous parlâmes	*nous finîmes*	*nous vendîmes*
vous parlâtes	*vous finîtes*	*vous vendîtes*
ils parlèrent	*ils finirent*	*ils vendirent*

*Napoléon **entra** dans la salle et **prit** son épée.* Napoleon entered the room and took his sword.

*Les princes **rendirent** le terrain aux paysans.* The princes gave back the land to the peasants.

Some Irregular Forms of the *Passé Simple*

avoir: j'eus	*être: je fus*	*savoir: je sus*
faire: je fis	*pouvoir: je pus*	*connaître: je connus*
écrire: j'écrivis	*vouloir: je voulus*	*falloir: il fallut*
lire: je lus	*voir: je vis*	*craindre: je craignis*

Le passé antérieur

Le passé antérieur, another literary tense, is used to show action that **immediately precedes** the *passé simple.* (Their relationship is similar to that of the *plus-que-perfect* and the *passé composé.*)

Formation: Use the *passé simple* of *avoir* or *être* with the *past participle:*

*Quand ils **eurent trouvé** la maison, ils **frappèrent à la porte.*** When they (had) found the house, they knocked at the door.

*Marcel **arriva** aussitôt que son père **fut parti.*** Marcel arrived right after his father left.

CHAPTER 9

THE SUBJUNCTIVE

The subjunctive is a **mood** that communicates emotions, wishes, desires, opinions, doubts — the subjective state of mind — of one agent acting upon another. Certain factors must be present for its use:

1. There must be **two different** subjects in **two clauses: one main, one subordinate;**
2. the subordinate clause must be introduced by *que*;
3. an expression of emotion, doubt, necessity, etc., must be present in the main clause.

FORMATION: REGULAR VERBS

To form the subjunctive drop the *-er, -ir,* or *-re* ending of the regular verb and add the following subjunctive endings: *e, es, e, ions, iez, ent.*

–er verbs	*–ir* verbs	*–re* verbs
que je mange	*que je dorme*	*que je rende*
que tu manges	*que tu dormes*	*que tu rendes*
qu'il mange	*qu'il dorme*	*qu'il rende*
que nous mangions	*que nous dormions*	*que nous rendions*
que vous mangiez	*que vous dormiez*	*que vous rendiez*
qu'ils mangent	*qu'ils dorment*	*qu'ils rendent*

Formation: Irregular Verbs

Irregular verbs have the same endings as regular verbs, except their stems are irregular.

Some common irregular forms:

faire: que je fasse
dire: que je dise
pouvoir: que je puisse
mettre: que je mette
craindre: que je craigne
vivre: que je vive
savoir: que je sache
rire: que je rie, que nous riions
lire: que je lise
écrire: que j'écrive, que nous écrivions
prendre: que je prenne, que nous prenions, qu'ils prennent
vouloir: que je veuille, que nous voulions, qu'ils veuillent
aller: que j'aille, que nous allions, qu'ils aillent
venir: que je vienne, que nous venions, qu'ils viennent
voir: que je voie, que nous voyions, qu'ils voient
boire: que je boive, que nous buvions, qu'ils boivent
mourir: que je meure, que nous mourions, qu'ils meurent
devoir: que je doive, que nous devions, qu'ils doivent
recevoir: que je reçoive, que nous recevions, qu'ils reçoivent

Note:

être	*avoir*
que je sois	*que j'aie*
que tu sois	*que tu aies*
qu'il soit	*qu'il ait*
que nous soyons	*que nous ayons*
que vous soyez	*que vous ayez*
qu'ils soient	*qu'ils aient*

USES OF THE SUBJUNCTIVE IN SUBORDINATE CLAUSES

When using the subjunctive in subordinate clauses:

With **expressions of <u>necessity</u>**:

> *Il faut que Pierre me **rende** cet argent.* Pierre must give that money
> back to me. (Or) It's necessary that Pierre give....
> *Est-ce qu'il est **nécessaire que** tu **ailles** chez tes parents?* Do you
> have to go to your parents' house?

*Ses amis **exigent que** Diane leur **écrive** des lettres.* Her friends insist that Diane write them letters.

With **expressions of <u>desire</u> or <u>will</u>**:

***Voulez**-vous **que** nous **venions** à midi?* Do you want us to come at noon?

*L'enfant **préfère que** sa mère lui **tienne** la main.* The child prefers that his mother hold his hand.

*Nous **désirons que** la paix **soit** faite au monde.* We want peace to be made in the world.

*Je **souhaite que** Marcel te **dise** la vérité.* I wish that Marcel would tell you the truth.

With **expressions of <u>emotion</u>**:

*Laurent **n'aime pas que** tu **partes** si tôt.* Laurent doesn't like you to be leaving so soon.

*Ils **ont peur que** cette voiture **ne puisse pas** faire le voyage.* They're afraid that this car can't make the trip.

*Votre père **est heureux que** vous **compreniez** le problème.* Your father is glad that you understand the problem.

With **expressions of <u>doubt</u>**:

*Il **est douteux que** nous **fassions** ce dîner.* It's doubtful that we'll make that dinner.

*Je **ne suis pas certaine que** Jean **vienne** avec nous.* I'm not sure Jean is coming with us.

*Elle **n'est pas convaincue que** cette situation **soit** bonne.* She's not convinced that this situation is a good one.

With **impersonal <u>expressions</u> (that convey a <u>subjective</u> idea)**:

*Il **est important que** tu **étudies** cette leçon.* It's important that you study this lesson.

*Il **est temps que** nous **nous en allions**.* It's time for us to leave.

*C'est **dommage que** tu **ne saches pas** son adresse.* It's too bad you don't know her address.

*Il **est inutile que** vous **vous dépêchiez**.* It's useless for you to hurry.

*Il **est possible que** cet homme **veuille** travailler ici.* It's possible that this man wants to work here.

Note: When there is more **certainty** than doubt, the **indicative** is used:

> *Il est probable que nous allons à Marseille.* We will probably go to Marseilles.
>
> *Elle est certaine que son mari peut réparer la télé.* She's sure her husband can repair the TV.
>
> *On est sûr que les voisins ont acheté une nouvelle maison.* We're sure the neighbors bought a new house.
>
> *Sans doute que Richard gagnera plus que toi.* Doubtless Richard will earn more than you.

With *espérer, penser,* and *croire:* When these verbs are in the **affirmative** ("I hope," "I think," "I believe"), the verb is in the **indicative:**

> *Vous espérez que leur avion partira à l'heure.* You hope their plane will leave on time.
>
> *Je pense que Sylvie est très intelligente.* I think Sylvie is very smart.
>
> *Le petit croit que son père va jouer avec lui.* The child thinks his father will play with him.

However, when these verbs are either **negative** or **interrogative,** since there may be doubt involved, the **subjunctive** is used:

> *Je n'espère pas qu'elle m'écrive.* I don't hope she'll write me.
>
> *Pense-t-il que sa cousine revienne bientôt?* Does he think his cousin will be back soon?
>
> *Je ne crois pas que Sara puisse nous accompagner.* I don't think Sara can go with us.

USES OF THE SUBJUNCTIVE AFTER CERTAIN CONJUNCTIONS

After certain conjunctions which convey a sense of doubt or fear, the subjunctive is required:

> *Avant que tu le saches, l'hiver arrivera.* Before you know it, winter will be here.
>
> *Pourvu que mes amis voient Robert, ils nous téléphoneront.* Provided that my friends see Robert, they'll call us.

Conjunctions and Prepositions

Many of these conjunctions have corresponding **prepositions** which are used when there is only **one subject:**

Conjunction (+ Subjunctive) (Two subjects)	Preposition (+ Infinitive) (One subject for both actions)
à condition que – provided that	*à condition de*
afin que – in order that	*afin de*
à moins que – unless	*à moins de*
avant que – before	*avant de*
de crainte que – for fear that	*de crainte de*
de peur que – for fear that	*de peur de*
pour que – so that	*pour*

> **De crainte d'oublier le rendez-vous, j'ai écrit** la date. For fear of forgetting the appointment, I wrote down the date. (one subject)
>
> **Avant de** partir, **viens nous voir.** Before you leave, come see us. (one subject)
>
> *Elle* **achètera** *cette voiture,* **à condition d'***avoir assez d'argent.* She'll buy the car, provided that she has enough money. (one subject)

But:

Elle recevra cette voiture, à condition que son père ait assez d'argent. She will receive the car, provided that her father has enough money. (two subjects)

Conjunctions with the Subjunctive

Some conjunctions do not have a prepositional equivalent and require the **subjunctive, even with one subject:**

bien que *quoique* *encore que* *malgré que*	although
avant que	before
malgré que	despite the fact that

de peur que *de crainte que*	for fear that
afin que *pour que*	in order that
non que *ce n'est pas que*	not that
pourvu que *à condition que*	provided that, on condition that
tel que	such as
de façon que *de manière que* *de sorte que* *si bien que*	such that, so that, in such a way
à supposer que *supposé que* *en supposant que* *en admettant que*	supposing that
à moins que	unless
jusqu'à ce que	until
soit que	whether
en attendant que	while waiting for
sans que	without

Bien qu'il dorme *beaucoup, il est toujours fatigué.* Although he sleeps
    a lot, he's always tired.

*Elle attendra ici **jusqu'à ce qu'elle apprenne** le résultat.* She'll wait
    here until she finds out the results.

Quoique *Sam **fasse** de son mieux, il ne réussit pas.* Although Sam is
    doing his best, he isn't succeeding.

Note: The form **quoi que** (two words meaning "whatever" or "no
matter what") also takes the subjunctive:

Quoi que tu dises, on ne va pas te croire. No matter what you say, they won't believe you.

LE PASSÉ DU SUBJONCTIF

The **past subjunctive** is a comparative tense used to contrast **an action in one tense** (in the principal clause) with **an action that preceded it** (in the subordinate clause). The auxiliary *avoir* or *être*, in the **subjunctive form,** is used with the **past participle.**

*Nous **sommes contents** que nos amis **soient** enfin **arrivés**.* We're happy (now) that our friends finally arrived (before now).

*Est-ce que tu **étais surprise** que Jeanne **t'ait envoyé** l'argent?* Were you surprised (yesterday) that Jeanne had sent you the money?

*Maurice **n'a pas cru** que sa fille **soit née**.* Maurice didn't believe his daughter had already been born.

Agreement of Tenses *(La concordance du temps)*

When two actions (one of which calls for the subjunctive) take place at the same time or in rapid chronological order, the present subjunctive is used. This applies to two simultaneous actions in past contexts as well. (Remember that the past subjunctive is only used to contrast an action in the principal clause with an action in the subordinate clause that happened before it.)

*Monique **était heureuse que** Virginie **ne parte pas**.* Monique was happy that Virginie wasn't leaving.

*Il **a parlé** lentement **afin que** nous **puissions** le comprendre.* He spoke slowly so that we were able to understand him.

*Il **fallait que** les employés **fassent** attention au patron.* The employees had to pay attention to the boss.

*Je **voulais que** mes amis **suivent** l'autre route.* I wanted my friends to take the other route.

*Tout le monde **doute que** Jacques **revienne** demain.* Everyone doubts that Jack's coming back tomorrow.

CHAPTER 10

ADVERBS

As in English, French adverbs modify verbs, adjectives, or other adverbs. There are adverbs of time, place, manner, quantity, negation, opinion, and adverbs that link ideas.

FORMATION OF ADVERBS

Many adverbs are formed by adding the suffix *–ment* (equivalent to the English suffix "–ly") to the **feminine** form of the adjective:

heureux	*heureuse*	*heureusement* (happily, luckily)
lent	*lente*	*lentement* (slowly)
doux	*douce*	*doucement* (softly, slowly, gently)
égal	*égale*	*également* (equally)
certain	*certaine*	*certainement* (certainly, surely)

Adjectives that End with Vowels

Adjectives that end in "e" or in **another vowel**, simply add *–ment*:

rapide	*rapidement*	*vrai*	*vraiment* (really, truly)
sincère	*sincèrement*	*absolu*	*absolument*
infini	*infiniment*		

IRREGULAR FORMS

(a) *Bien — mieux.*

(b) Adjectives that end in *–ant* and *–ent* form their adverbs by adding *–amment* or *–emment* as suffixes:

constant	*constamment*	*Elle chante **constamment**.* She sings constantly.
prudent	*prudemment*	*Nous avons agi **prudemment**.* We acted prudently (cautiously).
courant	*couramment*	*Parlent-ils **couramment**?* Do they speak fluently?

(c) Some adjectives form adverbs with the suffix *–ément:*

profond	*profondément*	*Nous avons été **profondément** émus.* We were deeply (profoundly) moved.
précis	*précisément*	*Vous avez reçu **précisément** ce que vous vouliez.* You received just what you wanted.
décidé	*décidément*	*C'était **décidément** sérieux.* It was decidedly (definitely) serious.
assuré	*assurément*	*Vous serez **assurément** à l'heure.* You'll surely be on time.

(d) ***bref – brièvement.*** *Il a parlé brièvement.* He spoke briefly.

(e) ***gentil – gentiment.*** *Elle m'a répondu **gentiment**.* She answered me politely.

PLACEMENT OF THE ADVERB

The adverb **precedes** an **adjective** or another **adverb:**

*Sam était **complètement** surpris.* Sam was completely surprised.
*Il m'a parlé **bien** sérieusement.* He spoke to me quite seriously.

With Simple Verbs

The adverb **follows** a simple verb:

*Nous le lui dirons **doucement**.* We'll tell him gently.
*Yves allait **souvent** chez eux.* Yves used to go to their house often.

With Compound Verbs

With a **compound** verb, the adverb **follows the auxiliary** (especially with short forms) or may **follow the participle** (with forms in *–ment*):

Simone est presque partie sans nous. Simone nearly left without us.
Il a toujours aimé jouer. He has always loved to play.
Elle a déjà fini. She finished already.
Nous lui avons parlé calmement. We spoke to her calmly.
Ils sont entrés bruyamment. They came in noisily.

Adverbs of Time and Space

Place adverbs of time and space **after** the participle or at the **beginning** of the sentence:

Hier nous avons vu Charles. We saw Charles yesterday.
Le cheval est tombé là-bas. The horse fell down over there.
Vous m'avez souvent* écrit autrefois. You often wrote me in the past.

*Note: *Souvent* (often), *déjà* (already), and *toujours* (always) are placed **before** the participle.

COMPARATIVE OF ADVERBS

As with adjectives, add *aussi*, *plus*, or *moins* for equal, superior, or inferior comparisons:

Nous avons voyagé aussi longtemps qu'eux. We traveled as long as they did.
Jean écrit plus correctement que toi. John writes more correctly than you.
Sara nous parlait moins librement que Bette. Sara spoke to us less freely than Bette did.

Hint: Remember that the comparative of *bien* is *mieux* (better) without *plus*. For **"less well,"** use *moins bien:*

Angélique parle allemand moins bien que sa sœur. Angelique speaks German worse than her sister.
Sophie chante mieux que moi. Sophie sings better than I do.

THE SUPERLATIVE

The superlative is formed by adding *le* to the comparative form and is **invariable:**

*Nancy danse **le plus gracieusement** de toute la famille.* Nancy dances the most gracefully of everyone in the family.
*C'est Philippe qui téléphone **le moins souvent.*** Phillip's the one who phones the least often.

SOME COMMON ADVERBS

Of assent, dissent, and reasoning:

ainsi – thus	*cependant* – however
néanmoins – nevertheless	*non* – no
oui – yes	*peut-être* – perhaps
pourquoi – why, because	*pourtant* – however

Of consequence:

alors – then	*comme* – as

Of manner:

bas – low, quietly	*ensemble* – together
haut – high, loud	*vite* – quickly

Of place:

dehors – outside	*ici* – here
là, là-bas – there, over there	*loin* – far
près – near	

Of quantity, intensity:

assez – enough	*aussi* – also
beaucoup – much	*même* – even
peu – little	*plus* – more
presque – almost	*si* – so
tant – so much	*tout* – quite, entirely
tout à fait – entirely	*très* – very
trop – too, too much	

Of time, frequency:

après – afterward	*aujourd'hui* – today
autrefois – in the past	*bientôt* – soon

dèjà – already
d'habitude – usually, generally
enfin – finally, last
hier – yesterday
longtemps – a long time
parfois – sometimes
quelquefois – sometimes
tard – late
toujours – always, still
tout de suite – immediately

demain – tomorrow
encore – still, yet, again
ensuite – then, afterwards
jamais – never
maintenant – now
puis – then
souvent – often
tôt – soon, early
tout à coup – suddenly

INTERROGATIVE ADVERBS

où – where
comment – how
combien – how much, how many

quand – when
pourquoi – why

ADVERBS THAT CONNECT NOUNS, PHRASES, AND CLAUSES

d'abord – first, at first
enfin – finally, at last
mais – but

ensuite – next, then
car, parce que – because

D'abord *il ouvre la porte et* **ensuite** *il appelle son chien.* First he opens the door and then he calls his dog.

CHAPTER 11

PREPOSITIONS AND CONJUNCTIONS

PREPOSITIONS

A preposition introduces a phrase and has a noun, pronoun, or infinitive as its **object.** Prepositions are invariable.

Simple Prepositions:

avec – with	*sans* – without	*dans* – in
sur – on	*pour* – for	*par* – by
sous – under	*de* – of, from	*devant* – in front of
dans – in	*à* – at, to	*derrière* – behind
en – in	*contre* – against	*entre* – between

avant – before (in time)

parmi – among (more than two things). *C'est **parmi** mes papiers.* It's among my papers.

après – after (in time and space). *Viens **après** cinq heures.* Come after 5 o'clock. *Il est arrivé après moi.* He arrived after me.

COMPOUND PREPOSITIONS

Compound prepositions are composed of more than one word:

à côté de – next to	*autour de* – around (in space)
près de – near	*loin de* – far from
au-dessous de – underneath	*le long de* – along

en haut de – at the top of
en face de – opposite
à gauche de – to the left of
au milieu de – in the middle of

en bas de – below
à droite de – to the right of
au-dessus de – above
jusqu'à – until (in time and space)

PREPOSITIONS WITH GEOGRAPHIC NAMES

For **cities,** always use *à:*

Je vais à Nice. I'm going to Nice.
Ils habitent à Chicago. They live in Chicago.
Allez-vous à Rome? Are you going to Rome?
Nous arriverons à Québec. We'll arrive in Québec.

Note: A few cities have an **article** in their name:

On s'arrête au Havre et à la Nouvelle Orléans. We're stopping at Le Havre and New Orleans.

For **large islands,** use *à:*

Ils sont à Hawaii. Elles sont à Cuba. They are in Hawaii. They are in Cuba.

For **"feminine" states, provinces, countries,** or **continents** (those that end in an *"e"*) use *en:*

Ils ont habité en Californie, en Floride, en France, en Allemagne, en Espagne, en Angleterre, en Afrique, en Europe, en Asie, en Italie, en Bretagne, et en Provence.

For **"masculine" countries** (those not ending in *"e"*) use *au:*

Je vais au Japon, au Portugal, au Canada, au Pérou.
Je reviens du Danemark, du Congo, du Brésil, du Maroc, des États-Unis.

Exceptions: *au Mexique; en Israël*

For the **names of states in the U.S.,** the same rule applies:

*Nous voyageons **en** Californie, **en** Pennsylvanie, **en** Floride, et **en** Virginie.*

*Nous voyageons **au** Texas, **au** Missouri, **au** New Jersey, **au** Washington, et **au** Kansas.*

Note: A good "rule of thumb" is to use ***dans l'état de...** + **the name of the state** when you're not sure of its gender:

*Il pleut beaucoup **dans l'état de** Nebraska, de Michigan, d'Indiana, de North Dakota, etc.*

COMMON VERBS + PREPOSITION + INFINITIVE

Verb + *à*

When an infinitive follows certain verbs, the preposition *à* is used. These verbs include *aider à, commencer à, hesiter à, inviter à, se mettre à, reussir à,* etc.

*J'**aide** ma mère **à faire** le dîner.* I help my mother make dinner.
*Elle **a commencé à danser**.* She started to dance.
*Nous **hésitons à le dire**.* We hesitate to say it.
*On **invite** le professeur **à parler**.* We invite the professor to speak.
*Il s'**est mis à pleurer**.* He started to cry.
*Ont-elles **réussi à finir** le travail?* Did they succeed in completing the work?

Verb + *de*

Likewise, there are other verbs that take the preposition *de* when followed by an infinitive. They include *accepter de, choisir de, conseiller de, décider de, demander de, empêcher de,* etc.

*Margot **accepte de** lui téléphoner.* Margot agrees to call him.
*Simon **a choisi d'acheter** cette maison.* Simon chose to buy this house.
*Je te **conseille d'aller**.* I advise you to go.
*Continues-tu **de souffrir**?* Are you still suffering?

Note: The verb *continuer* can be used with either *à* or *de.*

*Ils ont **décidé de partir**.* They decided to leave.

*J'ai **demandé à** Anne **de** m'écrire.* I asked Anne to write to me.
*Il m'**empêche de parler.*** He prevents me from speaking.

Note: See Chapter 12 for discussion of the verb ***manquer.***

CONJUNCTIONS

Conjunctions join words, phrases, or clauses. **Compound conjunctions** are followed by a clause.

Commonly used **simple conjunctions** include:

et – and	*mais* – but	*ou* – or
car – because	*donc* – thus, so	*comme* – as, since
quand – when	*lorsque* – when	*or* – well, so

Commonly used **compound conjunctions** include:

parce que – because	*dès que* – as soon as
alors que – while	*puisque* – since

CHAPTER 12

BASIC IDIOMATIC EXPRESSIONS

An "idiom" cannot be translated literally.

EXPRESSIONS WITH *AVOIR*

Expression	Example
avoir besoin de	*J'ai besoin d'argent.* I need money.
avoir crainte de	*Il a crainte de toi.* He's afraid of you.
avoir peur de	*Elle a peur de Jean.* She's afraid of John.
avoir honte de	*Ils ont honte de cela.* They're ashamed of it.
avoir envie de	*Tu as envie de rire.* You feel like laughing.
avoir l'air + adj.	*Elle a l'air riche.* She seems to be rich.
avoir l'air de + nom.	*Jim a l'air d'un idiot.* Jim looks like a fool.
avoir l'air de + inf.	*Il a l'air de souffrir.* He seems to be suffering.
avoir lieu	*Le concert a eu lieu hier soir.* The concert took place last night.
avoir mal	*Elle a mal à la tête.* She has a headache.
avoir chaud	*Avez-vous chaud?* Are you warm?
avoir faim	*C'est midi; j'ai faim.* It's noon; I'm hungry.
avoir soif	*Bill a toujours soif.* Bill's always thirsty.
avoir froid	*Nous avons très froid.* We're very cold.
avoir raison	*Sa mère a raison.* Her mother is right.
avoir sommeil	*As-tu sommeil?* Are you sleepy?
avoir tort	*Ils ont eu tort.* They were wrong.
avoir + *ans* = age	*Claire a 22 ans.* Claire is 22.
avoir + âge	*Quel âge avez-vous?* How old are you?

Expression	Example
avoir beau	*Tu **as beau** insister.* It's no use insisting.
avoir à + inf.	*Nous **avons à** le faire.* We have to do it.
avoir du mal à + inf.	*Il **a du mal à** lire.* He has trouble reading.
en avoir à quelqu'un	*J'**en ai à** Thomas.* I've got it in for Thomas.
en avoir assez	*Sa femme **en a assez**.* His wife is fed up.
en avoir pour + time	*J'**en ai pour** une heure.* It will take me an hour.
il y a	***Il y a** six livres ici.* There are six books here.
il y a + time	*Je l'ai vu **il y a** un mois.* I saw him a month ago.
	***Il y a** un an que je l'ai vu.* It's a year since I saw him.
il n'y a pas de quoi	*Merci, madame. **Il n'y a pas de quoi**.* Thanks, madam. Don't mention it. [Often: ***Pas de quoi**.*]

EXPRESSIONS WITH *FAIRE*

ça, cela fait + **time:**

***Cela fait un an** que tu étudies.* You've been studying for a year.

Expression	Example
ça fait	*Arrête! **Ça fait** mal!* Stop! That hurts!
	***Ça** te **fera** du bien.* It will do you good.
faire semblant de	*Il **fait semblant de** l'aimer.* He pretends to like it.
s'en faire	*Ne **vous en faites** pas!* Don't worry!
faire la connaissance	*Enchanté de **faire votre connaissance**.* I'm pleased to meet you.
faire un voyage	*Ils **font** beaucoup de **voyages**.* They travel a lot.
faire une promenade	***Faites une promenade**.* Go for a walk.
faire le plein	*Je **fais** toujours **le plein**.* I always fill the gas tank.
faire de la fièvre	*Le bébé **a fait de la fièvre**.* The baby had a fever.
faire Paris-Nîmes	*Le TGV **fait Paris-Nîmes** en trois heures.* The TGV goes from Paris to Nimes in three hours.
faire les magasins	*Anne **faisait tous les magasins**.* Anne went to all the stores.
faire un rôle	*Il va **faire** Roméo.* He's going to play Romeo.
n'avoir que faire de	*Je **n'ai que faire de** tes promesses!* I don't need your promises!
faire attention	***Fais attention!*** Watch out! [Pay attention!]
faire face à quelque chose	*Irène **fait face à** tous ses **problèmes**.* Irene is dealing with all her problems.

Expression	Example
faire partie de	*Ils **font partie du** club.* They belong to the club.
faire de son mieux	*As-tu **fait de ton mieux** à l'examen?* Did you do your best on the exam?
faire sa médecine	*Simone **fait sa médecine** à Nice.* Simone is studying medicine in Nice.
faire ses valises	***Faites vos valises!*** Pack your bags!
se faire à quelque chose	*Nous nous **faisons à la situation**.* We're getting used to the situation.

Faire causatif

The **subject causes someone else to do the action:**

*Il **se fait** construire une maison.* He's having a house built for himself.
*Elle **se fait** toujours remarquer.* She always makes people notice her.
*Nous **ferons** jouer cette musique.* We'll have that music played.
*Il **s'est fait faire** un complet.* He had a suit made for himself.
*Ils **ont fait lire** l'histoire par l'enfant.* They had the child read the story.

IMPERSONAL EXPRESSIONS WITH *IL*

Time:
Il est deux heures; il est minuit; il est trois heures moins le quart. [See Chapter 3 for a discussion of time.]

Il fait jour. It's daybreak.
Il fait nuit. Night is falling.
Il se fait tard. It's getting late.

Weather:
Il fait beau; mauvais; froid; chaud; lourd; frais. It's a beautiful day; nasty; cold; hot; humid; cool.
Il fait du soleil; des nuages; de la pluie; du brouillard. It's sunny; cloudy; rainy; foggy.

Other Idiomatic Expressions with *il*

Il s'agit de: it's a question of; it's a matter of; it deals with

*Dans ce film, **il s'agit de** justice.* This film is about (concerns itself with) justice.

Note: The verb *s'agir* is **only** conjugated in the third person masculine singular (like ***falloir** = il faut*).

Il s'agit de is usually prefaced by *"Dans ce livre/roman/film..."* or *"Dans cette situation..."* The past tense is expressed by the imperfect form of ***il s'agissait de...*** (It was a question of...; a matter of...)

il arrive	***Il arrive** que Georges est malade.* It happens that George is sick.
il reste	***Il** nous **reste** dix francs.* We have 10 francs left.
il vaut [mieux]	***Il vaut mieux** lui écrire.* It's better to write him.
il convient	***Il convient** de téléphoner.* It's proper to phone.
il suffit de	***Il suffit de** m'envoyer une carte postale.* It's enough if you send me a post card.
il importe de	***Il importe d'arriver** à temps.* It's important to arrive on time.

To Make General Observations

Use the formula *il est* + **adjective** + *de* + **infinitive:**

Il est important de bien manger. It's important to eat well.
Est-il nécessaire de le lui dire? Is it necessary to tell it to him?
Il est triste de ne pas la voir. It's sad not to see her.
Il est possible d'être content. It's possible to be happy.

Il faut que + subjunctive

***Il faut que** je **parte** maintenant.* I must leave now.
***Il** ne **faut** pas **que** vos amis **sachent** la vérité.* Your friends must not know the truth.
***Faut-il que** nous **venions** à midi?* Do we have to come at noon?

To **avoid the subjunctive** with *il faut,* use an **indirect object pronoun + the infinitive:**

Il** ne lui **fallait** pas **rester. She didn't have to stay.
*Est-ce qu'**il leur faut déménager?*** Must they move?

Il nous faudra passer chez eux. We'll have to go by their house.
Vous a-t-il fallu travailler? Did you have to work?

IDIOMATIC EXPRESSIONS WITH *ÊTRE*

être sur le point de	*Elle est sur le point de se marier.* She's about to get married.
	faire quelque chose
être d'accord	*Es-tu d'accord avec moi?* Do you agree with me?
être en train de	*Nous sommes en train de dîner.* We're in the midst of having dinner.
être plus fort	*C'est plus fort que moi!* It's too much for me.
être d'avis de	*Papa est toujours de ton avis.* Dad always agrees with you.
être de retour	*Le chef sera de retour demain.* The boss will be back tomorrow.
être dans son assiette	*Il n'est pas dans son assiette.* He doesn't feel very well.
être bien	*Êtes-vous bien dans ce lit?* Are you comfortable in that bed?
en être	*Nous en sommes à la page 29.* We're up to page 29.
y être	*J'y suis.* I've got it! (to understand, to "get it")

THE VERB *MANQUER*

Manquer: to miss, to fail, to be short of, "nearly"

J'ai manqué le train. I missed the train.
Ne manquez pas de nous avertir. Don't fail to let us know.
As-tu tout l'argent necessaire? --Non, il me manque cinq francs. Do you have all the money you need? --No, I'm five francs short.
Elise a manqué de tomber. Elise nearly fell.

Note: "Missing someone" is expressed by "He/she **is missing to me**" rather than by "I miss him/her":

Pierre est parti; il nous manque. Pierre left; we miss him.
Où est Agnès? Elle me manque. Where's Agnes? I miss her.
Puisque leur mère habitait très loin, elle leur manquait. Since their mother lived very far away, they missed her.

*Quand tu seras en vacances sans Anne, **tu lui manqueras**.* When you're on vacation without Anne, she'll miss you.

MEASURING TIME WITH *DEPUIS/DEPUIS QUE*

To express the passage of time from one point in the past to another point, either in the past alone or including the present, use *depuis* + **measure of time:**

*Marc **étudie** le piano **depuis deux ans**.* Marc has been studying the piano for two years. [The verb is in the **present** because he's still studying.]

*François **travaillait** à Boston **depuis six mois quand** il a rencontré Monique.* François had been working in Boston for six months when he met Monique. [The verbs are in the imperfect and *passé composé* because both actions are in the past and do not extend to the present.]

Using *depuis que* with a Subject and Verb

***Depuis que tu as rencontré** Cécile, tu sors plus souvent.* Since you met Cécile, you go out more often.
*Nous sommes moins nerveux **depuis que nous avons** un chien.* We've been less nervous since we have had a dog.
*Il ne nous voit plus jamais **depuis qu'il s'est blessé**.* He never sees us anymore since he was hurt.

Note: Don't confuse *depuis* (since) with *pendant* (during or while):

*Il a plu **pendant** la nuit.* It rained during the night.
*Nous travaillons **pendant** l'été.* We work during the summer.

Use *pendant que* with a **subject and verb:**

***Pendant que** Maurice parlait, tout le monde s'endormait.* Everyone fell asleep while Maurice was talking.
***Pendant que** j'y pense, prenez la clé.* While I'm thinking of it, take the key.

CONNAÎTRE AND *SAVOIR*

While both verbs may be translated as "to know," French differentiates between knowing people, places, works of art (including wine!), i.e., what one learns primarily through the senses, and things that one learns intellectually, by studying, practicing, or learning.

> *Mon frère* **connaît** *bien* **Rome et Paris** *mais je* **connais** *mieux* **New York et Los Angeles.** My brother knows Rome and Paris well, but I know New York and Los Angeles better.
>
> **Connaissez-vous les Duval? Savez-vous leur adresse?** Do you know the Duvals? Do you know their address?
>
> *Jeanne* **connaît** *un bon restaurant où l'on* **sait** *préparer une bouillabaisse formidable.* Jeanne knows a good restaurant where they know how to make a great fish stew.
>
> **Savent-ils** *que ta voiture est en panne?* **Connaissent-ils** *un garagiste honnête?* Do they know that your car broke down? Are they acquainted with an honest mechanic?
>
> *Elle* **connaît la musique** *de Chopin et elle* **sait la jouer** *aussi.* She knows Chopin's music and how to play it, too.

MISCELLANEOUS EXPRESSIONS

vouloir dire:
Que **veut dire** *"ordinateur?"* What does *"ordinateur"* **mean**?

se rendre compte de:
Il **se rend compte de** *sa faute.* He **realizes** his mistake.

tout de suite:
Venez **tout de suite!** Come **at once**!

rendre visite à quelqu'un:
Je **rendrai visite** *à ma tante ce weekend.* I'll **visit** my aunt this weekend.

Note: *Voir* or *rendre visite* are used for visiting **a person**. *Visiter* is used for **a place:** *Vas-tu visiter Chicago?*

n'en pouvoir plus:
Le pauvre chaton **n'en peut plus.** The poor kitten is **exhausted**.

passer un examen:
A-t-elle passé l'examen? Did she **take** the test?

réussir à un examen:
Oui, et elle (y) a réussi. Yes, and she **passed** it.

passer une nuit blanche:
Je suis très fatiguée; j'ai passé une nuit blanche. I'm very tired; I **spent a sleepless night**.

à la fois:
Ils sont à la fois gentils et bêtes. They're both nice and foolish at the **same time**.

en même temps:
Nous sommes arrivés en même temps que Julie. We arrived **at the same time** as Julie.

à son gré:
Le dîner était à notre gré. The dinner was **to our liking**.

CHAPTER 13

NEGATION

There are always **two** parts to a negative expression: *ne* precedes the verb and another expression follows it *(pas, jamais, aucun,* etc.).

POSITIVE AND NEGATIVE ADVERBIAL EXPRESSIONS

encore: still	*Fabian chante-t-il **encore?*** Does Fabian still sing?
ne...plus	*Non, il **ne** chante **plus.*** He no longer sings.
toujours: always	*Irène sort-elle **toujours** avec ces jeunes gens?* Does Irène always go out with those young people?
ne...jamais	*Elle **ne** sort **jamais** avec eux.* She never goes out with them.
partout: everywhere	*Va-t-elle **partout** ce soir?* Is she going everywhere tonight?
ne...nulle part	*Elle **ne** va **nulle part.*** She's not going anywhere.
déjà: already	*Ont-ils **déjà** déjeuné?* Have they already had lunch?
ne...pas encore	*Non, ils **ne** sont **pas encore** descendus.* No, they haven't come down yet.
et: both, and	*Nous avons rencontré **et** Claude **et** David. Ont-ils téléphoné?* We met Claude and David. Did they call?
ni...ni...ne	***Ni** Claude **ni** David **n'**ont téléphoné.* Neither Claude nor David has phoned.

Note: The verb is **plural** in French for **"neither, nor."**

Other Negations

ne...pas	*Tu n'as pas d'amis ici.* You have no friends here.
ne...guère	*Elle n'a guère répondu.* She hardly answered.
ne...que	*Elise n'a que deux chapeaux.* Elise has only two hats.
ne...aucun	*Il n'a lu aucun livre cet été.* He hasn't read a single book this summer.

Note: *Aucun* can be used as a **pronoun** as well as an **adjective.** It can be masculine or feminine, but it is always **singular:**

> *A-t-elle reçu mes lettres? --Non, aucune n'est arrivée.* Did she receive my letters? No, not one has arrived.

ne...personne	*Personne ne nous a téléphoné.* No one called us.
ne...rien	*Rien n'est important quand on est malade.* Nothing is important when you're sick.
ne...ni...ni	*Charles ne veut ni écouter ni discuter l'histoire.* Charles neither wants to listen to the story nor to discuss it.

QUELQUE CHOSE DE/RIEN DE + ADJECTIVE

To express the general idea of "something" or "nothing" + an adjective, use *quelque chose de* or *rien de*:

> *Patrice, as-tu quelque chose d'intéressant à nous raconter? Non, je n'ai rien d'important à vous dire.* Patrice, do you have something interesting to tell us? No, I've nothing of importance to say to you.
>
> *Est-ce que quelque chose d'amusant est arrivé? Rien d'amusant n'est arrivé.* Did something amusing happen? Nothing amusing took place.
>
> *Avez-vous acheté quelque chose de délicieux au marché? Non, il n'y avait rien de délicieux à acheter.* Did you buy something delicious in the market? No, there was nothing delicious to buy.

Note: The adjective is always masculine singular in these structures.

For "someone," "anyone," or "nobody" use *quelqu'un de* or *personne de*:

> *Connaissent-ils quelqu'un de riche et de célèbre? Non, ils ne connaissent personne de riche ni de célèbre.* Do they know anyone

rich and famous? No, they don't know anybody who's rich and famous.

*Est-ce que **quelqu'un** d'intelligent ferait cela? Non, **personne** d'intelligent ne le ferait.* Would someone intelligent do that? No, nobody intelligent would do it.

CHAPTER 14

USEFUL VOCABULARY

SCHOOL (*L'ÉCOLE*)

l'assistance (f.) – attendance
assister au cours – to attend class
la manifestation – demonstration
obtenir son diplôme – to graduate
l'horaire (m.) – class schedule
la biblio(thèque) – the library
l'ordinateur (m.) – computer
sa spécialisation – one's major
s'inscrire aux cours – to register for classes
l'école élémentaire (f.) – grammar school
des livres d'occasion (m.) – used books
des cours obligatoires (m.) – required classes

le collège – middle school
un mémoire – a paper
échouer, rater – to fail
la lecture – reading
réussir – to pass
la librairie – the bookstore
la conférence – lecture
le lycée – high school

ANIMALS (*UN ANIMAL; LES ANIMAUX*)

le bœuf – bull
le cerf – deer
le coq – rooster
le mouton – sheep
le chien – dog
un mulet / une mule – mule (both masculine and feminine)
un âne – donkey

la vache – cow
la biche – doe
la poule – hen
le chat – tomcat
un cheval – horse
un lapin – rabbit

un poisson – a fish
un ours – bear

un renard – fox
un oiseau – bird

THE BODY *(LE CORPS)*

la tête – head
la joue – cheek
les oreilles (f.) – ears
la chevelure – head of hair
les lèvres (f.) – lips
la langue – tongue
la poitrine – chest
la jambe – leg
le pied – foot
le bras – arm
le poignet – wrist
le dos – the back
le cœur – heart

un œil; les yeux – one eye, the eyes
les cheveux (m.) – hair
la bouche – mouth
les dents (f.) – teeth
le cou – neck
le ventre – stomach
le genou – knee
la cheville – ankle
le coude – elbow
la main – hand
l'épaule (f.) – shoulder
le foie – liver

THE CITY *(LA VILLE)*

le centre-ville – downtown
visiter la ville – sightseeing in town
une visite – a tour
Où se trouve…? – Where is…?
à gauche – to the left
à la droite – to the right
tout droit – straight ahead
la place – the square
la rue – the street
le boulevard – the boulevard
le musée – the museum
le parc – the park
la préfecture – police station
le bureau de poste – post office
Renseignements (m.) – Information (booth)
le jardin zoologique – the zoo

la cité – the old part of town
une excursion – a guided sightseeing tour
l'hôtel de ville (m.) – town hall
la fontaine – fountain
le trottoir – the sidewalk
le cinéma – the movies
le tarif, droit d'entrée – admission fee
un banc – a bench
les chèques de voyage (m.) – travelers checks
l'immeuble (m.) – building
la banque – the bank
l'agent de police (m.) – policeman
des timbres (m.) – stamps
l'agence de voyage (f.) – travel agency

CLOTHING *(LES VÊTEMENTS)*

un chemisier – a blouse
un pantalon – pants
un sac – a purse
les chaussures (f.) – shoes
un maillot – a bathing suit
la veste – a jacket (suit)
un manteau – a coat
des bas (m.) – stockings
un peignoir – a bathrobe
l'imperméable (l'imper) (m.) –
    a raincoat
les chaussettes (f.) – socks
un complet – a man's suit
une cravate – a tie
le linge – linen

une jupe – a skirt
un chapeau – a hat
une robe – a dress
un tailleur – a lady's suit
les gants (m.) – gloves
un blouson – outside jacket
une écharpe – scarf
le short – shorts
le bleu-jean – jeans
le tricot, le pull, le chandail –
    sweater, pullover
une ceinture – belt
une chemise – a shirt
un gilet – a vest
la manche – sleeve

COLORS *(LES COULEURS)*

le bleu – blue
le gris – gray
le noir – black
le rose – pink
le violet – purple
le beige – beige

le jaune – yellow
le blanc – white
le rouge – red
le vert – green
le brun – brown
le marron – chestnut brown

DRINKS *(LES BOISSONS)*

le vin – wine
la bière – beer
l'eau minérale (f.) – mineral water
la citronnade – lemonade
le coca – Coke
une boisson gazeuse – a soft drink
le café crème – coffee with cream
le café noir – black coffee
le café express – espresso coffee
le café décaféiné – decaffeinated
    coffee
le thé – tea

un demi – glass of beer
le jus de fruits – fruit juice
la limonade – soda (7-Up)
le soda – club soda
le sucre – sugar
le café – coffee
le café au lait – coffee with milk
le café turc – Turkish coffee
le lait – milk
un café serré – small cup of
    coffee, black, very strong
le thé anglais – tea with milk

le thé glacé – iced tea
le chocolat chaud – hot chocolate

un apéritif (l'apéro) – cocktail
un digestif – a liqueur; after-
    dinner drink

THE FAMILY *(LA FAMILLE)*

le père – the father
un bébé – a baby
un garçon – a boy
le fils – the son
la tante – the aunt
la grand-mère – the grandmother
le cousin, la cousine – the cousin
la nièce – the niece

la mère – the mother
un(e) enfant – a child (boy or girl)
une fille – a girl, a daughter
papa, maman – dad, mom
l'oncle – the uncle
le grand-père – the grandfather
le neveu – the nephew

FOODS *(LES ALIMENTS)*

Fruits *(Les fruits):*
une banane – banana
une poire – pear
une prune – plum
une cerise – cherry
une fraise – strawberry
un ananas – pineapple
un pamplemousse – grapefruit

une pomme – apple
une pêche – peach
une orange – orange
un abricot – apricot
une framboise – raspberry
un citron – lemon
des raisins secs (m.) – raisins

Vegetables *(Les légumes):*
une carotte – carrot
une pomme de terre – potato
un oignon – onion
le maïs – corn
les brocolis (m.) – broccoli
le poivron – pepper
    (red or green)

une tomate – tomato
la laitue – lettuce
des haricots (m.) – beans
les petits pois (m.) – peas
les épinards (m.) – spinach
le concombre – cucumber

Meat and Poultry *(La viande et la volaille):*
le bœuf – beef
le veau – veal
le porc – pork
le mouton – lamb
le canard – duck

le bifteck – steak
le jambon – ham
les saucisses (f.) – sausage
le poulet – chicken
la dinde – turkey

Desserts *(Les desserts)*:

la tarte aux pommes – apple pie

la glace – ice cream

la crème brûlée – custard

un beignet – a doughnut

une crêpe – a thin pancake

la pâtisserie – pastry

le gâteau au chocolat – chocolate cake

la tarte aux fruits – fruit pie

les parfums (m.) – the flavors

un petit gâteau – cookie

le gaufre – waffle

le yaourt – yogurt

le chou à la crème – a cream puff

ILLNESSES *(LES MALADIES)*

avoir mal... – to have pain in...

aller chez le médecin – to go to the doctor's office

avoir les frissons – to have chills

la tension – blood pressure

avoir des nausées – to be nauseous

l'antibiotique (m.) – antibiotic

une piqûre – an injection

démangeaison – an itching

un rhume – a cold

l'hôpital (m.) – hospital

l'ordonnance (f.) – prescription

être allergique à – to be allergic (to)

la douleur – pain

le pouls – pulse

vomir – to throw up

le médicament – medicine

une pilule – a pill

une éruption – a rash

la grippe – the flu

l'infirmière (f.) – the nurse

les honoraires (m.) – doctor's fee

PROFESSIONS, OCCUPATIONS *(LES PROFESSIONS, LES MÉTIERS)*

Note: For many professions, there is no female form. The word *femme* or *une* precedes the profession or the masculine form is used.

un(e) avocat(e) – lawyer

un ingénieur – engineer

un, une secrétaire – secretary

une actrice – actress

un chauffeur de taxi – taxi driver

un serveur, une serveuse – waiter, waitress

un commis – clerk

un juge – judge

un chef – cook

un acteur – actor

un, une artiste – artist

un professeur – secondary or college teacher

un vendeur, une vendeuse – salesperson

le coiffeur, la coiffeuse – hairdresser

la ménagère – housewife

le fermier, la fermière – farmer
un pilote – pilot
un musicien, une musicienne – musician
le pharmacien, la pharmacienne – pharmacist

le policier, la policière –
    policeman, policewoman
le banquier – banker
un chimiste – chemist

SPORTS/LEISURE (LES SPORTS ET LES PASSE-TEMPS)

faire du vélo – to ride a bicycle
faire de la pêche – to fish
faire de la plongée – to scuba dive
faire de la voile or *faire de la
    planche à voile* – to windsurf
faire de l'aérobic (m.) – to do
    aerobics
faire de l'équitation (f.) – to
    horseback ride
faire du ski nautique – to waterski
faire du canöe – to canoe
faire du cyclisme – to cycle
faire du jogging – to jog
faire du patin à roulettes –
    roller skating
faire du roller en ligne – to do
    in-line skating
faire du surf – to surf
jouer au baseball – to play baseball
jouer à des jeux vidéo – to play
    video games
jouer au golf – to play golf
jouer au hockey – to play hockey
jouer au rugby – to play rugby
jouer au volley – to play volleyball
jouer aux dames – to play checkers

faire de la chasse – to hunt
faire de la natation – to swim
faire de la pêche sous-marin –
    to deep-sea fish
faire de l'alpinisme (m.) – to
    mountain climb
faire de l'escalade (f.) – to
    mountain climb
faire du bateau à voile – to sail
faire du canotage – to go boating/
    rowing
faire du patin – to skate
faire du patin à glace – ice skating
faire du plongeon – to deep sea
    dive
faire du ski – to ski
    faire du vélo – to ride a bicycle
jouer au basket – to play basketball
jouer au football – to play soccer
jouer au football américain –
    to play football
jouer au ping-pong – to play
    ping-pong
jouer aux cartes – to play cards
jouer aux échecs – to play chess

COUNTRIES (LES PAYS)

l'Algérie (f) – Algeria
l'Australie (f) – Australia

l'Argentine (f) – Argentina
l'Autriche (f) – Austria

la Belgique – Belgium
le Canada – Canada
l'Egypte (f) – Egypt
la France – France
la Grèce – Greece
l'Inde (f) – India
Israël – Israel
la Cote de'Ivoire – Ivory Coast
le Japon – Japan
le Liban – Lebanon
le Luxembourg – Luxembourg
Monaco (f) – Monaco
les Pays-Bas (m) – Netherlands
le Pérou – Peru
la Pologne – Poland
la Russie – Russia
la Corée du Sud – South Korea
la Suisse – Switzerland
la Tunisie – Tunisia
les États-Unis (m) – United States

le Brésil – Brazil
la Chine – China
l'Angleterre (f) – England
l'Allemagne (f) – Germany
la Hollande – Holland
l'Irlande (f) – Ireland
l'Italie (f) – Italy
la Jamaïque – Jamaica
la Jordanie – Jordan
la Libye – Libya
le Mexique – Mexico
le Maroc – Morocco
la Corée du Nord – North Korea
les Philippines (f) – Phillippines
le Portugal – Portugal
le Sénégal – Senegal
l'Espagne – Spain
la Syrie – Syria
la Turquie – Turkey
le Viêt-nam – Vietnam

PROFESSIONS (LES PROFESSIONS)

un(e) dentiste – dentist
un(e) mécanicien(ne) – mechanic
un(e) sécretaire – secretary
un(e) téchnicien(ne) – technician
un(e) vétérinaire – veterinarian
un archéologue – archaeologist
un(e) assistant(e) social – social worker
un banquier – banker
un caissier/une cassière – cashier
un chauffeur de taxi – taxi driver
un(e) commerçant(e) – merchant
un danseur/une danseuse – dancer
un écrivain – writer
un facteur/une factrice – postal worker
un homme de foyer/ une femme de foyer – homemaker

un(e) gérant(e) – store manager
un(e) scientifique – scientist
un(e) styliste de mode – fashion designer
un agent de police – police officer
un(e) architecte – architect
un(e) athlète – athlete
un(e) avocat(e) – lawyer
un bijoutier/une bijoutière – jeweller
un coiffeur/une coiffeuse – hairdresser
un directeur/une directrice – company manager/director
un homme d'affaires/une femme d'affaires – businessman/businesswoman
un infirmier/une infirmière – nurse
un ingénieur – engineer

un mannequin – fashion model
un ouvrier (une ouvrière) – worker
un peintre en bâtiment – painter
    (of buildings)
un pompier – firefighter
un routier – truck driver

un médecin – doctor
un peintre – painter (of art)
un pilote – pilot
un plombier – plumber
un rédacteur/une rédactrice – editor

SAT II:
SUBJECT TEST IN
FRENCH

PRACTICE
TEST I

FRENCH TEST I

PART A

Time: 1 Hour
        90 Questions

DIRECTIONS: This part consists of a number of incomplete statements, each followed by four suggested completions. Select the most appropriate completion and blacken the corresponding space on the answer sheet.

1. Si tu as besoin d'argent, je pourrai t'en ...

    (A) emprunter   (C) prêter

    (B) acheter   (D) fabriquer

2. Tu seras gentil de descendre ma valise au ...

    (A) grenier   (C) rez-de-chaussée

    (B) toit   (D) plafond

3. Je ne suis pas d'accord. Ce n'est pas du tout ...

    (A) mon métier   (C) mon avis

    (B) ma chanson   (D) ma musique

4. Ils ne s'entendent pas. En effet, ils ne cessent jamais de ...

    (A) se rappeler   (C) se disputer

    (B) s'écrire   (D) s'embrasser

5. S'il y a trop de lumière, tu peux ... la lampe.

    (A) allumer   (C) atteindre

    (B) éteindre   (D) appuyer

6. A la fin du repas, on demande au garçon d'apporter ...

   (A) la monnaie   (C) l'addition

   (B) la carte   (D) les apéritifs

7. Pour prendre de l'essence, on va à ...

   (A) la station-service   (C) l'épicerie

   (B) la parfumerie   (D) l'église

8. L'évier est plein de verres et d'assiettes. Il faut ...

   (A) dîner tout de suite   (C) servir le vin

   (B) faire la lessive   (D) faire la vaisselle

9. Si vous avez froid aux mains, mettez vos ...

   (A) chaussettes   (C) gants

   (B) bottes   (D) bas

10. Si tu manges trop, tu vas ...

    (A) grandir   (C) élargir

    (B) maigrir   (D) grossir

11. Si vous voulez savoir à quelle heure arrivent tous les trains de Lyon, regardez ...

    (A) la pendule   (C) la caisse

    (B) le quai   (D) l'horaire

12. Mon grand-père a de la peine à lire sans ses ...

    (A) lunettes   (C) dents

    (B) pouces   (D) glaçons

13. Ces billets ont coûté très peu. Ils étaient assez ...

    (A) rares   (C) bon marché

    (B) chers   (D) pénibles

14. Si tu ne sais pas son numéro de téléphone, cherche-le dans …

    (A) l'annuaire   (C) le jeton

    (B) la poste   (D) l'appareil

15. Le facteur n'a pas encore apporté …

    (A) les sandwiches   (C) le courrier

    (B) les boissons   (D) les courses

16. Tu me le promets? — Oui, je te donne …

    (A) ma permission   (C) mon porte-monnaie

    (B) ma licence   (D) ma parole

17. Ridée et courbée par l'âge, elle a beaucoup …

    (A) rajeuni   (C) agi

    (B) vieilli   (D) vêtu

18. S'il y a beaucoup de monde, il faudra faire …

    (A) la line   (C) la file

    (B) la ligne   (D) la queue

19. Elle m'a donné son peigne parce que je n'avais rien pour …

    (A) me punir   (C) me réveiller

    (B) me coiffer   (D) me consoler

20. Depuis que François a perdu sa place à l'entreprise, il est …

    (A) en prison   (C) en premier

    (B) au chômage   (D) au commissariat

21. C'est une très bonne pièce de théâtre, mais je ne me rappelle pas le nom de tous les …

    (A) caractères   (C) morceaux

    (B) personnages   (D) gens

22. Il commence à faire frais. Mets ton pull, parce que je ne veux pas que tu attrappes ...

    (A) des abeilles

    (C) des fruits

    (B) un rhume

    (D) le climat

23. Ce type ne me plaît pas du tout. Je le trouve ...

    (A) impeccable

    (C) désagréable

    (B) sympathique

    (D) formidable

24. Chaque ... que je veux te voir, tu me dis que tu n'es pas libre.

    (A) temps

    (C) foi

    (B) heure

    (D) fois

25. Elle a l'air très triste. J'espère qu'elle ne va pas ...

    (A) plier

    (C) pleurer

    (B) prier

    (D) pleuvoir

26. J'aime les légumes cuits, mais je les préfère ...

    (A) verts

    (C) mûrs

    (B) crus

    (D) coupés

27. Il y avait beaucoup de monde à sa ... sur l'œuvre de Balzac.

    (A) lecture

    (C) conférence

    (B) porte-parole

    (D) manifestation

28. En France, à l'école, on apprend généralement deux ... étrangères.

    (A) classes

    (C) langues

    (B) leçons

    (D) langages

29. L'ascenseur ne marche pas. Il faut prendre ...

    (A) le trottoir

    (C) l'escalier

    (B) l'échelle

    (D) l'autobus

30. Fais attention et ... les conseils de ton père.

    (A) entends   (C) revois

    (B) regarde   (D) écoute

31. Si vous n'avez pas de voiture, je peux vous ... chez vous avec la mienne.

    (A) porter   (C) apporter

    (B) amener   (D) prendre

PART B

DIRECTIONS: In each of the sentences in this part of the test, one or more words are underlined. One of the four choices following each sentence can be correctly substituted for the underlined word(s) to form a grammatically correct statement or question. The new sentence may differ in meaning from the original example. Select the one choice which fits grammatically into the original sentence and blacken the corresponding space on the answer sheet.

32. Elle est allée voir son <u>frère</u>.

    (A) mère

    (B) sœur

    (C) amie

    (D) cousine

33. Téléphone-<u>moi</u> ce soir.

    (A) le

    (B) elle

    (C) te

    (D) lui

34. Cet <u>hôtel</u> est très connu.

    (A) restaurant

    (B) maison

    (C) jardin

    (D) immeuble

35. Il <u>ressemble</u> à sa soeur.

    (A) manque

    (B) se fâche

    (C) cherche

    (D) regarde

36. Ils ont une maison en <u>ville</u>.

    (A) Paris

    (B) campagne

    (C) France

    (D) Canada

37. Voilà <u>quelque chose</u> d'intéressant!

    (A) une conférence   (C) un retour

    (B) quelqu'un   (D) une question

38. Il est parti sans <u>Marie</u>.

    (A) la   (C) eux

    (B) nôtre   (D) le

39. Il s'est lavé <u>les dents</u>.

    (A) ses cheveux   (C) sa figure

    (B) la figure   (D) ses mains

40. <u>Puisque</u> je n'avais rien à faire, je me suis couché.

    (A) Malgré que   (C) Comme

    (B) A cause de   (D) Pour que

41. Il m'a dit de <u>ne pas partir</u>.

    (A) ne partir jamais   (C) ne jamais partir

    (B) ne partir plus   (D) ne partir pas

42. Il <u>nous</u> a promis de venir.

    (A) lui   (C) l'

    (B) les   (D) s'

43. Marie est contente <u>d'être venue</u>.

    (A) que vous êtes venu   (C) que vous viendriez

    (B) que vous soyez venu   (D) que vous viendrez

44. <u>Qui est-ce qui</u> vient?

    (A) Quoi   (C) Qui

    (B) Qu'est-ce que   (D) Pourquoi

45. Je n'aime pas les films italiens, mais j'ai bien aimé <u>le film</u> que nous avons vu hier soir.

    (A) ceux   (C) celui

    (B) ce   (D) cela

PART C

Est-ce ta voiture? — Non, _____ est garée derrière le camion

46. (A) mon

    (B) le mien

    (C) la tienne

    (D) la mienne

rouge _____ vous voyez là-bas.

47. (A) qui

    (B) quand

    (C) que

    (D) dont

As-tu demandé _____ Jean _____ venir? — Oui, je _____ ai dit que

48. (A) – –   49. (A) – –   50. (A) l'

    (B) à   (B) si   (B) le

    (C) de   (C) à   (C) lui

    (D) pour   (D) de   (D) les

nous _____ attendrions ici.

51. (A) vous

    (B) l'

    (C) lui

    (D) nous

Il est parti _____ je le sache. J'espère qu'il _____ fâché.

52. (A) après que   53. (A) n'a pas

    (B) sans que   (B) ne soit pas

    (C) dès que   (C) n'ait pas

    (D) depuis que   (D) n'est pas

S'il téléphone, _____-lui de revenir. Je voudrais _____ revoir.

54. (A) vous dites   55. (A) en

    (B) disiez   (B) le

    (C) dites   (C) y

    (D) dites-vous   (D) se

Maurice, _____ le père est américain, parle _____ anglais. Sa mère,

56. (A) de qui   57. (A) – –

    (B) dont   (B) un

    (C) duquel   (C) d'

    (D) que   (D) l'

_____ est française, parle plusieurs langues. Elle est

58. (A) qu'

    (B) qui

    (C) que

    (D) quelle

_____ professeur et elle aime _____ enseigner le français.

59.	(A)	– –		60.	(A)	– –
	(B)	un			(B)	à
	(C)	une			(C)	d'
	(D)	le			(D)	de l'

Si _____ à ta place, j'aurais fait la même chose. Je suis

61. (A) je suis

(B) je serais

(C) j'avais été

(D) j'ai été

certain que tout le monde _____ de mon avis.

62. (A) soient

(B) sera

(C) ait été

(D) soit

PART D

DIRECTIONS: Read the following passages carefully for comprehension. Each passage is followed by a number of questions or incomplete statements. Select the one answer or completion that is most appropriate according to the passage and blacken the corresponding space on the answer sheet.

Individualiste, entêté, frivole, instable, révolutionnaire: voilà seulement quelques-uns des adjectifs qu'on utilise pour caractériser les Français. Dans l'ensemble, ce sont des clichés sans trop de valeur.

Le Français moyen est tout aussi difficile à définir que l'Américain typique ou l'Italien ou l'Allemand moyen. On peut tout de même dégager certains traits. Le Français accorde un plus grand pourcentage de son budget familial et parallèlement une plus grande attention à la nourriture que ne le fait l'Américain. En même temps, il accorde une proportion plus réduite au logement. Pour la majorité des Français, les vacances sont sacrées et signifient une exode des villes vers les plages et les montagnes. En effet, près de 80% des Français partent annuellement en vacances.

63. Selon ce passage, les Français

    (A) ressemblent à des clichés sans trop de valeur

    (B) ne sont jamais ni frivoles ni instables

    (C) ne peuvent pas être caractérisés de façon définitive

    (D) sont tous révolutionnaires et individualistes

64. Le Français moyen

    (A) aime essayer de définir l'Allemand moyen

    (B) est plus difficile à définir que l'Américain typique

    (C) ne se prête pas facilement à une définition générale

    (D) trouve les Italiens très difficiles

65. En générale, pour les Français,

(A) les repas comptent plus que pour les Américains

(B) la nourriture ne demande pas beaucoup d'attention

(C) le budget familial est extrêmement grand

(D) la nourriture américaine a certains traits intéressants

66. Dans cette annonce, quelle est la plus courte durée possible d'un contrat proposé au client ?

(A) Cela peut varier en fonction du modèle désiré par le client

(B) 17 jours

(C) Cela dépend du type d'assurance pris par le client

(D) L'achat d'un véhicule neuf

67. Chacune des caractéristiques suivantes de ce service est citée sauf :

(A) La disponibilité de l'assistance routière

(B) Le type d'assurance proposé

(C) Quels modèles Peugeot sont offerts

(D) Le kilométrage

Annette Dujon est une femme mariée, mère de famille, qui travaille comme ouvrière dans une usine tout près de sa maison à Rennes. Son mari est ouvrier aussi. Comme vous pouvez imaginer, Annette a une vie très chargée. Elle travaille à l'usine de huit heures à quatre heures tous les jours de la semaine (sauf le samedi et le dimanche). En plus elle doit faire le ménage, le marché, la cuisine et la lessive. Et il ne faut pas oublier les enfants: elle essaie de leur consacrer un peu de temps chaque jour. Puisqu'elle est militante communiste, elle assiste à une réunion politique une fois par semaine, le jeudi soir. Quand Annette a un peu de loisir, elle aime lire un bon livre, tricoter, ou regarder la télévision.

68. Annette

   (A) est en congé le week-end

   (B) va à l'usine le samedi et le dimanche

   (C) travaille quatre jours par semaine

   (D) ne va à l'usine que le samedi et le dimanche

69. Elle

   (A) n'a pas du tout de temps pour ses enfants

   (B) a tendance à négliger ses enfants

   (C) préfère son travail à ses responsabilités de mère

   (D) essaie autant que possible de bien s'occuper de ses enfants

70. Elle

   (A) déteste les réunions politiques

   (B) s'intéresse à la politique

   (C) est féministe militante

   (D) est contre la politique

71. Dans son temps libre, elle

   (A) fait le ménage

   (B) reste à la maison

   (C) va en vacances à Rennes

   (D) achète des tricots

La général Bramble me pria de venir passer les fêtes de Noël à la campagne: "Je n'invite cette année que mon beau-frère et ma belle-sœur; ce ne sera donc pas bien gai et je m'en excuse; mais si vous ne craignez ni la solitude ni l'hiver anglais, je serai heureux de vous recevoir et de parler du bon vieux temps." Je savais que mon ami avait eu, au cours de l'année, le chagrin de perdre une fille de dix-huit ans, qui s'était tuée en tombant de cheval. Je le plaignais; je souhaitais le voir; j'acceptai.

72. Le général Bramble

   (A) avait décidé de passer les fêtes de Noël tout seul

   (B) n'a invité ni son beau-frère ni sa belle-sœur

   (C) s'est excusé de ne pas avoir invité le narrateur à passer Noël chez lui

   (D) a invité le narrateur à passer les fêtes de Noël à la campagne

73. Selon le général Bramble, les fêtes promettaient d'être

   (A) bien gaies   (C) très chaleureuses

   (B) un peu tristes   (D) effrayantes

74. Le général Bramble aime discuter

   (A) le climat   (C) le passé

   (B) sa famille   (D) le froid

75. Le narrateur

   (A) avait de la pitié pour son ami

   (B) avait peur de ses amis

   (C) craignait la solitude

   (D) se plaignait de l'hiver

76. Au cours de l'année, la fille du général Bramble

   (A) était morte dans un accident de cheval

   (B) était disparue pendant une chasse

   (C) s'était égarée en faisant du cheval

   (D) a tué son cheval

L'histoire des deux sœurs était attendrissante. On la citait au loin; elle avait fait pleurer bien des yeux.

Suzanne, l'aînée, avait été aimée follement, jadis, d'un jeune homme qu'elle aimait aussi. Ils furent fiancés et on n'attendait plus que le jour fixé pour le contrat, quand Henry de Sampierre était mort brusquement. Le désespoir de la jeune fille fut affreux, et elle jura de ne jamais se marier. Elle tint parole. Elle prit des habits de veuve qu'elle ne quitta plus.

Alors sa sœur, qui n'avait encore que douze ans, lui dit: "Je ne te quitterai jamais. Je resterai près de toi, toujours, toujours." Et elles vécurent ensemble tous les jours de leur existence.

77. L'histoire des deux sœurs était

(A) très exagérée   (C) assez inconnue

(B) un secret bien gardé   (D) très connue

78. Suzanne était

(A) plus aimable que sa sœur

(B) plus jeune que sa sœur

(C) plus âgée que sa sœur

(D) plus folle que sa sœur

79. Suzanne n'a pas épousé Henry de Sampierre parce qu'

(A) il ne voulait pas fixer le jour

(B) elle ne voulait pas faire un contrat

(C) elle attendait depuis trop longtemps

(D) il est mort

80. Elle a décidé

(A) de ne plus en parler

(B) de ne jamais se marier

(C) de ne jamais sortir de la maison

(D) d'entrer dans la religion

81. Sa sœur

    (A) avait encore douze ans à vivre

    (B) a essayé de libérer Suzanne de sa promesse

    (C) a promis de passer le reste de sa vie auprès de sa soeur

    (D) a promis d'aller la voir une fois par jour

Un beau dimanche de printemps, je regarde ma nièce, la lycéenne. Elle étudie, le nez dans ses livres, un oeil vers le ciel bleu.

On parle depuis des années de faire coïncider l'année scolaire avec l'année légale; elle commencerait en janvier et se terminerait avant Noël. Le débat continue, beaucoup d'enseignants et de parents n'étant pas persuadés de l'utilité d'une telle réforme. Ils doivent regarder en ce moment autour d'eux la mélancolie des élèves. Les révisions, si pénibles en mai-juin, s'accommoderaient certainement mieux du froid et du ciel gris de novembre-décembre. Bien sûr, nous avons tous connu cette situation au même âge. Les examens ont également empoisonné les beaux jours de notre adolescence. Est-ce une raison suffisante pour prolonger notre système éducatif? Il n'est pas raisonnable de demander aux élèves de fournir les plus gros efforts intellectuels au moment où, physiologiquement et psychologiquement, ils en ont le moins envie.

82. Le narrateur

    (A) travaille comme bouquiniste

    (B) est la tante d'une élève

    (C) est professeur

    (D) fait de la politique

83. Actuellement en France, l'année scolaire

    (A) ne finit pas en mai-juin

    (B) coincide avec l'année légale

    (C) finit à Noël

    (D) ne coincide pas avec l'année légale

84. La décision de changer l'année scolaire

    (A) n'est pas encore sur le point d'être prise

    (B) gagne en popularité

    (C) serait pénible pour les parents et les professeurs

    (D) est en plein mouvement

18ᵉ ARRONDISSEMENT

LA BONNE SOUPE

Bistrot gourmand
A deux pas de Montmartre,
le « bistrot »
français à connaître.
Que vous veniez pour un
repas sur le pouce ou pour
prendre votre temps, vous
trouverez votre bonheur
dans ce cadre rustique.
La Bonne Soupe célèbre
au mois de mars son
29ᵉ anniversaire.
Happy Birthday !
Ouvert de 11h30 à minuit.
28, rue Ordener - PARIS 18ᵉ
01 40 30 20 10

---

85. Qu'est-ce que ce restaurant est en train de célébrer ?

    (A) Des critiques favorables dans la presse

    (B) Un prix accordé par un jury

    (C) Presque 30 ans d'existence

    (D) L'ouverture d'un deuxième restaurant par le même propriétaire

86. On mentionne toutes les caractéristiques suivantes de ce service sauf :

    (A) Ses heures d'ouverture

    (B) Les noms des plats qui sont offerts

    (C) L'endroit où le restaurant se situe

    (D) Le style du décor

Un tyran éclairé: tel est apparu Armand Rohart aux jurés de la cour d'assises de Saint-Omer devant laquelle il répond du meurtre de sa femme. Maire de Peuplingues et gros propriétaire terrien, il gérait sa commune comme sa femme avec efficacité et dynamisme. Craint mais respecté, il régna jusqu'au jour où sa femme se noya alors qu'elle se baignait en sa compagnie. Il nie l'acte criminel qu'on lui reproche. Il plaide la thèse de l'accident tragique, ce que réfutent les experts et les deux médecins légistes qui ont été commis.

87. Armand Rohart a été accusé

   (A) d'être un tyran éclairé

   (B) d'avoir géré sa commune

   (C) d'avoir tué sa femme

   (D) d'avoir nié un acte criminel

88. Armand Rohart

   (A) est un homme craintif et respectueux

   (B) avait du pouvoir et de l'influence

   (C) voulait que sa femme soit efficace et dynamique

   (D) aimait se baigner avec sa femme

89. Il dit qu'il est

   (A) coupable

   (B) innocent

   (C) reproché

   (D) éclairé

90. Selon des experts,

   (A) il a été victime d'un accident tragique

   (B) deux médecins ont commis le crime

   (C) il a noyé sa femme

   (D) il était au travail quand l'accident a eu lieu

SAT II: French Subject Test
Test I

ANSWER KEY

1.	(C)	24.	(D)	47.	(C)	70.	(B)
2.	(C)	25.	(C)	48.	(B)	71.	(B)
3.	(C)	26.	(B)	49.	(D)	72.	(D)
4.	(C)	27.	(C)	50.	(C)	73.	(B)
5.	(B)	28.	(C)	51.	(B)	74.	(C)
6.	(C)	29.	(C)	52.	(B)	75.	(A)
7.	(A)	30.	(D)	53.	(D)	76.	(A)
8.	(D)	31.	(B)	54.	(C)	77.	(D)
9	(C)	32.	(C)	55.	(B)	78.	(C)
10.	(D)	33.	(D)	56.	(B)	79.	(D)
11.	(D)	34.	(D)	57.	(A)	80.	(B)
12.	(A)	35.	(A)	58.	(B)	81.	(C)
13.	(C)	36.	(C)	59.	(A)	82.	(B)
14.	(A)	37.	(B)	60.	(A)	83.	(D)
15.	(C)	38.	(C)	61.	(C)	84.	(A)
16.	(D)	39.	(B)	62.	(B)	85.	(C)
17.	(B)	40.	(C)	63.	(C)	86.	(B)
18.	(D)	41.	(C)	64.	(C)	87.	(C)
19.	(B)	42.	(A)	65.	(A)	88.	(B)
20.	(B)	43.	(B)	66.	(B)	89.	(B)
21.	(B)	44.	(C)	67.	(C)	90.	(C)
22.	(B)	45.	(C)	68.	(A)		
23.	(C)	46.	(D)	69.	(D)		

DETAILED EXPLANATIONS
OF ANSWERS

PRACTICE TEST I

1. **(C)**
    Prêter means to lend. Emprunter is the antonym, meaning to borrow. You also need to know the expression avoir besoin de, meaning to need.

2. **(C)**
    Le rez-de-chaussée is the first floor, and the only one of the choices to where someone could "take down a suitcase". Le grenier is the attic; le toit is the roof; le plafond is the ceiling.

3. **(C)**
    Je ne suis pas d'accord means I do not agree. Ce n'est pas du tout mon avis means That is not at all my opinion.

4. **(C)**
    S'entendre (avec quelqu'un) means to get along (with someone). Se disputer is the opposite, meaning to argue. They are both reflexive expressions. Cesser de means to stop (doing something).

5. **(B)**
    Eteindre means to extinguish, to turn off. Allumer is the opposite, meaning to light, to turn on (a light).

6. **(C)**
    At the end of a meal, you ask the waiter to bring the check.

7. **(A)**
    You need to know that l'essence is gasoline.

8. **(D)**
    If the sink (l'évier) is full of glasses and dishes, then you have to do the dishes (faire la vaisselle). Faire la lessive means to do the laundry.

9. **(C)**

If your hands are cold, you put on your <u>gloves</u>, not your <u>socks</u> (chaussettes), your <u>boots</u> (bottes), or your <u>stockings</u> (bas).

10. **(D)**

<u>Grossir</u> means <u>to get fat or fatter</u>. <u>Grandir</u> means <u>to grow</u> in the sense of <u>getting taller</u>; <u>élargir</u> means <u>to get wider</u>; <u>maigrir</u> means <u>to get thinner</u>.

11. **(D)**

If you want to know at what time all the trains arrive from Lyon, you look at <u>the schedule</u>, not the <u>clock (la pendule)</u>, <u>the cashier (la caisse)</u>, or <u>the platform (le quai)</u>.

12. **(A)**

<u>Avoir de la peine (à faire quelque chose)</u> means <u>to have difficulty (doing something)</u>. My grandfather has difficulty reading without his <u>glasses</u>.

13. **(C)**

Something that costs very little (<u>couter très peu</u>) is inexpensive (<u>bon marché</u>). The opposite is <u>cher</u>.

14. **(A)**

If you do not know a telephone number, then you look for it in <u>the telephone book</u>, not <u>the post office (la poste)</u>, <u>the token (le jeton)</u>, or <u>the phone itself (l'appareil)</u>.

15. **(C)**

<u>Le courrier</u> is the <u>mail</u>; <u>le facteur</u> is the <u>mailman</u>.

16. **(D)**

If you <u>promise</u> someone something, then you give your <u>word</u>.

17. **(B)**

<u>Vieillir</u> means <u>to age, to get old</u>. <u>Rajeunir</u> is the opposite; <u>agir</u> means <u>to act</u>. <u>Ridée et courbée par l'âge</u>, means <u>wrinkled and bent over with age</u>.

18. **(D)**

<u>Faire la queue</u> means <u>to wait in line</u>. If there is a crowd, a lot of people, then you will have to <u>wait in line</u>.

19. **(B)**

Se coiffer (reflexive verb) means to fix, arrange, style your hair. Un peigne is a comb. On se coiffe avec un peigne.

20. **(B)**

Etre au chômage means to be unemployed. Since François lost his position in the company (l'entreprise), he has been unemployed.

21. **(B)**

The word personnage always refers to characters in a novel, play, or movie. The word caractère means character in the sense of personal qualities and virtues. Do not confuse the two. They are not interchangeable.

22. **(B)**

Attraper un rhume means to catch a cold. Il commence à faire frais means It's beginning to be cool (weather).

23. **(C)**

Il me plaît means I like him, (literally, He is pleasing to me.) Ce type ne me plaît pas du tout means I do not like this guy at all.

24. **(D)**

Fois means time in the sense of an occasion or time in succession. Chaque fois means each time; trois fois means three times; la première fois means the first time. Temps refers to time as a general or abstract concept, as in Le temps passe vite.

25. **(C)**

Do not confuse pleurer, meaning to cry, with pleuvoir, meaning to rain. Il pleure means He is crying. Il pleut means It is raining.

26. **(B)**

The adjective cuit means cooked; the opposite is cru, or raw. Mûr means ripe.

27. **(C)**

Une conférence is a lecture, but the French word lecture means reading(s), and therefore is a "false friend" or "faux ami."

28. **(C)**

Langue means language, as in la langue française. Une langue étrangère is a foreign language. The French word langage refers to speech or useage, as in le langage des jeunes.

29. **(C)**

When the elevator (l'ascenseur) doesn't work, you take the stairs (l'escalier). The verb marcher in this sense means to operate, to function, to work properly.

30. **(D)**

Ecouter means to listen — actively and purposefully. Entendre means to hear, and not necessarily purposely. Conseils means advice.

31. **(B)**

When you want to express the idea of bringing or accompanying a person, use amener. When you want to express the idea of bringing a thing or object, use apporter. The two are not interchangeable.

32. **(C)**

This question tests possessive adjectives which agree in gender (feminine or masculine) and number (singular or plural) with the person or thing possessed, *not* the possessor. Although son modifies a singular masculine noun, it is also used before feminine nouns that begin with a vowel, like amie.

33. **(D)**

With an affirmative imperative, object pronouns immediately follow the verb and are connected to it with hyphens. Te and me become toi and moi.

Lui is the only correct choice because it is an indirect object pronoun. It is important to keep in mind that some common French verbs followed by à (téléphoner à, plaire à, offrir à, demander à, dire à) require an indirect object in French, but are not often introduced by to in English.

34. **(D)**

This question tests demonstrative adjectives (ce, cette, ces.) The alternate form cet is used before a masculine singular noun beginning with a vowel or a mute h.

35. **(A)**

The proposition à is the key to the correct answer. Ressembler à quelqu'un means to resemble someone. The expression manquer à quelqu'un is a construction that is different from the English equivalent.

Il manque à sa soeur means His sister misses him. Il manque à ses parents means His parents miss him. (In the French construction, the direct object becomes the subject and the subject becomes the indirect object, just as it did in the example Il me plaît.)

On se fâche <u>contre</u> quelqu'un. The verbs <u>chercher</u> (<u>to look for</u>) and <u>regarder</u> (<u>to look at</u>) are followed immediately by a direct object, with no preposition. Je cherche mes clefs. Nous regardons la télévision.

36. **(C)**
    The preposition <u>en</u> is the key to the correct answer. <u>En ville</u> is an adverbial expression that means <u>in town</u>, <u>in the city</u>. <u>En</u>, meaning <u>in</u>, <u>to</u>, or <u>at</u>, precedes most geographical locations (countries, provinces, and states) that end in <u>e</u> (and are consequently feminine.) Il va en France, en Italie, en Californie.
    The preposition <u>au</u> is used before masculine countries. Il va au Canada.
    The preposition <u>à</u> is used before cities. Il va à Paris, à Rome, à Boston.

37. **(B)**
    In order to modify the indefinite pronouns <u>quelque chose</u>, <u>quelqu'un</u>, <u>rien</u>, and <u>personne</u>, you use the masculine singular form of the adjective, preceded by the preposition <u>de</u>. <u>Quelqu'un d'intéressant</u> means <u>someone interesting</u>.

38. **(C)**
    <u>Disjunctive (or accentuated) pronouns</u> are used after prepositions like <u>de</u>, <u>avant</u>, <u>sans</u>, etc. The disjunctive pronouns are: <u>moi</u>, <u>toi</u>, <u>lui/elle</u>, <u>nous</u>, <u>vous</u>, <u>elles/eux</u>.

39. **(B)**
    When an action is performed by the subject on a part of his own body, a reflexive verb is used and the definite article is used instead of a possessive adjective.

40. **(C)**
    <u>Comme</u> and <u>puisque</u> are synonyms, both conjunctions meaning <u>since</u>, <u>as</u>. <u>Malgré que</u> and <u>pour que</u> are conjunctions that must be followed by the subjunctive. <u>A cause de</u> is a preposition.

41. **(C)**
    With the infinitive both parts of the negative precede it.

42. **(A)**
    <u>Nous</u> is the indirect object of <u>Il a promis</u>. <u>Lui</u> is the only one of the choices that can be an indirect object pronoun.

43. **(B)**

The expression <u>être content(e) que</u> must be followed by a clause with the verb in the subjunctive. It requires the subjunctive because it expresses an emotion.

44. **(C)**

<u>Qui</u> and <u>qui est-ce qui</u> are both interrogative pronouns meaning <u>who</u>? <u>Qui</u> is the short form.

45. **(C)**

This question tests <u>demonstrative pronouns</u>. <u>Celui</u>, meaning <u>the one</u>, replaces a masculine singular noun, a person, or a thing. The demonstrative pronouns are: <u>celui</u>, <u>celle</u>, <u>ceux</u>, <u>celles</u>. <u>Cela</u> is a demonstrative that replaces an entire sentence or idea.

46. **(D)**

This question tests <u>possessive pronouns</u>. <u>La mienne</u> replaces <u>ma voiture</u> in this sentence.

47. **(C)**

<u>Que</u> is a <u>relative pronoun</u>, meaning <u>that</u> and referring to <u>camion</u> as its antecedent. In the relative clause it introduces, it is the object of the verb <u>voyez</u>.

48. **(B)**

The preposition <u>à</u> here introduces the indirect object.

49. **(D)**

Some verbs require no preposition before a complementary infinitive (Je veux la voir); others require <u>de</u> before the infinitive (Il refuse <u>de</u> la voir); others require <u>à</u> before the infinitive (Il m'a invité <u>à</u> la voir). Verbs that govern the infinitive with <u>de</u> are by far the most numerous, but it is nevertheless a matter of memory for the student.

50. **(C)**

<u>Lui</u> is the indirect object of <u>dire</u>.

51. **(B)**

<u>L'</u> is the only choice that could be the direct object of <u>attendre</u>. It is important to remember that although <u>attendre</u> means to wait <u>for</u>, it is not followed by a preposition in French.

52. **(B)**

Sache is the subjunctive form of the verb savoir. Sans que is the only conjunction among the choices that requires the subjunctive.

53. **(D)**

The verb espérer in the affirmative is not followed by the subjunctive. Etre is used with se fâcher, not avoir.

54. **(C)**

Dites is the second person plural and the polite form of the imperative. The hyphen followed by the pronoun is a "clue" that only the imperative form could be correct here.

55. **(B)**

Le is the direct object pronoun. I would like to see him.

56. **(B)**

Dont is the relative pronoun used to express possession: whose, of whom.

57. **(A)**

Although a definite article is used before the names of languages (Nous apprenons le français), it is omitted after the verb parler.

58. **(B)**

Qui is the relative pronoun meaning who, and the subject of the relative clause that it introduces.

59. **(A)**

No article is used before a nationality or profession unless it is qualified by a more specific statement or description: Elle est professeur. C'est un bon professeur. Son père est médecin. Son oncle est un médecin très connu.

60. **(A)**

Aimer requires no preposition before a complementary infinitive. See #49.

61. **(C)**

This question tests the manipulation of verb tenses in hypothetical statements. Because the "result clause" (j'aurais fait le même chose) is in the past conditional, the "si clause," which is the clause that states the condition, must be in the pluperfect.

62. **(B)**

The indicative — not the subjunctive — is used after <u>être certain que</u> in the affirmative. It is only in the negative and interrogative (that create an expression of doubt) that it would be followed by the subjunctive.

63. **(C)**

"Les Français ne peuvent pas être caractérisés de façon définitive" is the general sense of the first seven lines. The clichés that are usually used are "sans trop de valeur" and the average French person is "difficile à définir."

64. **(C)**

This answer restates the same idea. The average French person is just as difficult to define ("tout aussi difficile à définir") as other nationalities.

65. **(A)**

The French allot a greater percentage of their family budget ("un plus grand pourcentage de son budget familial") and greater attention "une plus grande attention") to food than does the typical American. The <u>ne</u> in line 9 does not indicate a negative. It is an "expletive <u>ne</u>" that commonly appears after a comparative construction

66. **(B)**

(A) cannot be the answer because there is no mention of specific models the customer may want (<u>modèle souhaité par le client</u>) whatsoever in this ad. Choice (C) is also ruled out, since there is no mention of a relationship between the life of the contract and the insurance plan the customer may have chosen (<u>le type d'assurance pris par le client</u>) either. (D) cannot be true because this company leases vehicles to vacationers; it is not in the business of selling those vehicles (<u>L'achat d'un véhicule neuf</u>). The correct answer is therefore (B), 17 days (<u>17 jours</u>).

67. **(C)**

(A) is false because the ad does mention a roadside assistance plan (<u>Peugeot Assistance</u>). (B) is also false because there is mention of comprehensive insurance (<u>assurance tous risques</u>). (D) cannot be true because the ad specifically says that the mileage <u>kilométrage</u>) is unlimited (<u>illimité</u>). The correct answer is therefore (C), <u>Quels modèles Peugeot sont offerts</u> (which Peugeot models are available), since as stated previously the ad makes no mention of this.

68. **(A)**

Annette works every day of the week except Saturday and Sunday ("sauf le samedi et le dimanche"), so she is free ("en congé") on the weekend.

69. **(D)**

The answer is in line 7: "...elle essaie de leur consacrer un peu de temps chaque jour."

70. **(B)**

You can conclude that she is interested in politics because: 1. "...elle est militante communiste." 2. "...elle assiste à une réunion politique une fois par semaine."

71. **(B)**

Le loisir (free time) is a synonym for le temps libre. Her free time is spent doing things at home ("à la maison"): "lire un bon livre, tricoter, regarder la télévision."

72. **(D)**

The correct answer is in line 1: "Le général Bramble me pria de venir passer les fêtes de Noël à la campagne." Me pria is the equivalent of m'a demandé.

73. **(B)**

In line 3 Bramble says: "[C]e ne sera donc pas bien gai", which is the same thing as "un peu triste". The adjective chaleureux means warm. The adjective effrayant means frightful.

74. **(C)**

Bramble says: [J]e serai heureux ...de parler du bon vieux temps." It is reasonable to conclude that he likes to discuss the past.

75. **(A)**

"Je le plaignais" means "J'avais de la pitié pour lui."

76. **(A)**

Bramble a eu le chagrin (sorrow) de perdre sa fille. "Elle s'était tuée" means "Elle était morte." "Elle était disparue" means "She had disappeared." "Elle s'était égarée" would mean the same as "Elle s'était perdue." Se perdre — perdre used reflexively — means to get lost.

77. **(D)**

The story was well known ("très connue"). It was told far away ("On la citait au loin") and it had made many people cry ("Elle avait fait pleurer bien des yeux.")

78. **(C)**

Aînée means plus âgée.

79. **(D)**

The answer is in line 5. Il est mort. "[O]n n'attendait plus que le jour…" is not a negative but another example of ne…que. See #65.

80. **(B)**

The answer is in lines 5, 6, and 7. "[E]lle jura de ne jamais se marier."

81. **(C)**

The answer is in lines 9 and 10. "Je ne te quitterai jamais. Je resterai près de toi…" "[E]lle n'avait que douze ans" means "she was only twelve years old."

82. **(B)**

In line 2 the narrator says: "Je regarde ma nièce, la lycéenne." She is watching her niece, so she must be her aunt (tante).

83. **(D)**

The school year and the legal year do not coincide. "On parle depuis des années de faire coïncider…." means that "making them coincide has been discussed for years."

84. **(A)**

"Le débat continue" — the debate goes on, is another way of saying "la décision traîne" — the decision drags on, and therefore is not yet close to being made.

85. **(C)**

The ad makes no mention of favorable publicity in the press (des critiques favorables dans la presse), an award given by a jury (un prix accordé par un jury), or the opening of a second restaurant by the same owner (l'ouverture d'un deuxième restaurant par la même propriétaire). Choices (A), (B), and (D) are therefore eliminated. The correct answer is

(C), <u>Presque 30 ans d'existence</u> (Nearly 30 years of experience): <u>La Bonne Soupe célèbre [. . .] son 29 anniversaire</u> (29th anniversary).

86. (B)

The ad <u>does</u> tell us about the restaurant's business hours (<u>ses heures d'ouverture [11h30 à minuit]</u>), the area where the restaurant is located (<u>l'endroit où le restaurant se situe [28, rue Ordener]</u>), and the style of the decor (<u>le style du décor [rustique]</u>). This eliminates choices (A), (C), and (D) as valid answers. Answer (B) is correct, since the ad does not mention the names of the dishes that are served (<u>les noms des plats qui sont offerts</u>).

87. (C)

The answer is in line 2. "[I]l répond du meurtre (murder) de sa femme."

88. (B)

This answer is based on inference. Because he was the mayor (le maire) and a large property owner (gros propriétaire terrien) (line 3) and because he was feared, but respected, (craint mais respecté) and "reigned" until the death of his wife (line 5), it is reasonable to infer that he had power and influence.

89. (B)

"Il nie (denies) l'acte criminel... Il plaide (pleads) la thèse de l'accident tragique."

90. (C)

"Les experts refutent sa thèse de l'accident tragique." The implication is that they support the charge that he killed her.

SAT II:
SUBJECT TEST IN
FRENCH

PRACTICE
TEST II

FRENCH TEST II

PART A

Time: 1 Hour
90 Questions

DIRECTIONS: This part consists of a number of incomplete statements, each followed by four suggested completions. Select the most appropriate completion and blacken the corresponding space on the answer sheet.

1. Il est quatre heures ...

    (A) à la salle à manger

    (B) au grenier

    (C) à la pendule

    (D) au goûter

2. Le jeune homme marchait les mains ...

    (A) sur la plage

    (B) sur la route

    (C) sur la table

    (D) dans les poches

3. Il fait tout très promptement, c'est-à-dire qu'il le fait ...

    (A) sur-le-champ

    (B) inutilement

    (C) sobrement

    (D) d'une façon ennuyeuse

4. Le balcon saillait de la façade; cela veut dire qu'il ...

    (A) était en arrière

    (B) avançait

    (C) était rétracté

    (D) était caché

5. Abattre un arbre c'est le ...

    (A) couper

    (B) battre

    (C) combattre

    (D) casser

6. Quand on coud un vêtement on ...

   (A) le corps

   (B) le porte

   (C) l'assemble

   (D) le coupe

7. Dans l'adversité souvent les liens de l'amitié ...

   (A) se remettent

   (B) se resservent

   (C) s'attachent

   (D) se resserrent

8. Elle était sur le sable, la peau toute brûlée par ...

   (A) la mer

   (B) le ciel

   (C) le soleil

   (D) le sable

9. C'étaient les derniers jours d'école; bientôt ils seraient ...

   (A) en vadrouille

   (B) en vacances

   (C) en virevolte

   (D) en virée

10. A côté de chez nous il y avait une bonne famille; ils étaient ...

    (A) des bons voisins

    (B) des personnes riches

    (C) des bons vivants

    (D) des bons oncles et tantes

11. Nous nous avons trouvés tout à coup dans l'obscurité lorsque le coucher de soleil nous ...

    (A) a souris

    (B) a frappés

    (C) a battus

    (D) a surpris

12. Il y a un grand ... d'étudiants qui participent à la manifestation devant la mairie.

    (A) nom

    (B) nombre

    (C) numéro

    (D) néant

13. L'hiver était terrible et la neige abondante, et les petits oiseaux n'avaient ...

    (A) plus rien à chanter

    (B) personne à regarder

    (C) plus qu'à manger

    (D) rien à manger

14. Dans ce silence impressionnant on n'entendait que les cœurs …

   (A) battre
   (C) se gonfler

   (B) disparaître
   (D) se dégoûter

15. Nous fûmes reçus … , c'est-à-dire qu'on nous fit un accueil fantastique.

   (A) à bouche ouverte
   (C) à bras ouverts

   (B) à mains ouvertes
   (D) dans la salle à manger

16. Je lui avais choisi des livres avec …

   (A) un grand charme
   (C) grand son

   (B) beaucoup d'argent
   (D) grand soin

17. La nuit est tombée, il n'y a plus …

   (A) de bruit
   (C) d'air

   (B) rien
   (D) d'argent

18. Quand on s'habille, on met … dans les manches des vêtements.

   (A) les pieds
   (C) les genoux

   (B) les bras
   (D) les jambes

19. Le tonnerre s'était vite rapproché; l'orage faisait des pas …

   (A) de géant
   (C) réguliers

   (B) de loup
   (D) perdus

20. Pourquoi fallait-il nous dépêcher? Eh bien, tout simplement parce que nous étions …

   (A) à l'heure
   (C) pressés

   (B) en avance
   (D) déprimés

21. La verdure pousse … ; elle a en peu de temps gagné les bosquets.

   (A) dans la forêt
   (C) à vue d'œil

   (B) au lointain
   (D) à perte de vue

22. Au plafond de la cuisine pendaient ... car tous ces paysans avaient bon appétit.

    (A) des jambons et des saucissons

    (B) des chaussettes

    (C) des étoiles

    (D) des paniers

23. Le coucher de soleil était écarlate et il semblait que le ciel était ...

    (A) en feu   (C) sur nos têtes

    (B) sur la terre   (D) dans le lointain

24. Cette année-là les autorités avaient décidé d'assécher ...

    (A) la montagne   (C) la neige

    (B) les marais   (D) la plage

25. Les acrobates faisaient de la gymnastique ou ils jonglaient ...

    (A) avec finesse   (C) avec force

    (B) sans fin   (D) dangereusement

26. Les feuilles mortes tournoient ... sur le sol.

    (A) en s'élevant   (C) en tombant

    (B) en tremblant   (D) pour tomber

27. L'été dernier, quand nous étions à la montagne, il faisait souvent de l'orage, et ...

    (A) nous faisions du ski

    (B) le soleil brillait

    (C) nous avions très peur

    (D) nous descendions les torrents en kayak

PART B

DIRECTIONS: In each of the sentences in this part of the test, one or more words are underlined. One of the four choices following each sentence can be correctly substituted for the underlined word(s) to form a grammatically correct statement or question. The new sentence may differ in meaning from the original example. Select the one choice which fits grammatically into the original sentence and blacken the corresponding space on the answer sheet.

---

28. Regardez comme cette petite fille est belle.

    (A) image

    (B) printemps

    (C) ciel

    (D) profil

29. Son père le lui a dit.

    (A) m'

    (B) nous

    (C) leur

    (D) vous

30. Venez avec nous.

    (A) lui

    (B) leur

    (C) vous

    (D) tu

31. Jacqueline veut y aller sans lui.

    (A) leur

    (B) il

    (C) tu

    (D) eux

32. Après avoir raconté son histoire, elle s'en est allée.

    (A) l'avoir racontée

    (B) la avoir racontée

    (C) le avoir raconté

    (D) l'avoir raconté

33. Pouvez-vous <u>me</u> dire l'heure qu'il est?

    (A) te   (C) le

    (B) lui   (D) il

34. Avec <u>son</u> professeur de biologie <u>il</u> fait un meilleur travail.

    (A) ton   ...   lui

    (B) notre   ...   se

    (C) notre   ...   elle

    (D) ce   ...   leur

35. <u>C'</u> est mon oncle qui <u>m'</u> a donné cette montre.

    (A) Il   ...   l'

    (B) C'   ...   lui

    (C) Il   ...   c'

    (D) C'   ...   sa

36. <u>Qu'est-ce que</u> vous voulez que je <u>lui</u> dise?

    (A) Qu'est-ce qui   ...   nous

    (B) Qu'est-ce qu'   ...   leur

    (C) Qui est-ce qui   ...   te

    (D) Qu'est-ce que   ...   vous

37. A Paris, en été, il y a toujours <u>un grand nombre de</u> touristes.

    (A) nombreux   (C) beaucoup des

    (B) très nombreux   (D) beaucoup de

38. Pendant que j'étais dans le garage, j'ai trouvé <u>ceci</u>.

    (A) ceux   (C) ce

    (B) l'   (D) cela

39. On a défendu que cela <u>se fasse</u> à l'école.

    (A) se passe   (C) se décident

    (B) se fassent   (D) se prenne

40. Savez-vous jouer <u>de la clarinette</u>?

    (A) le piano   (C) de la raquette

    (B) au tennis   (D) au violon

41. Mon oncle <u>nous</u> faisait lire tous les soirs.

    (A) notre   (C) il

    (B) se   (D) les

42. Il ne savait pas très bien <u>l'anglais</u>.

    (A) en français   (C) le russe

    (B) en anglais   (D) la chinoise

43. <u>Pas un</u> étudiant <u>n'</u> a répondu à ma question.

    (A) Aucuns   ...   n'

    (B) Nul   ...   —

    (C) Nulle   ...   —

    (D) Aucun   ...   n'

44. Nous avons fait <u>plusieurs</u> robes.

    (A) quelques   (C) quelques-unes

    (B) beaucoup   (D) quelque

45. Il a dit: "Je voudrais <u>te</u> voir."

    (A) se   (C) leur

    (B) la   (D) toi

PART C

Ce matin Roberta _____ de bonne heure. Elle _____,

46. (A) s'est levé
    (B) s'a levée
    (C) s'est levée
    (D) se levait

47. (A) s'a baignée
    (B) s'est baigné
    (C) s'est baignée
    (D) se baignait

puis elle _____, et elle _____ au travail.

48. (A) a déjeuné
    (B) est déjeuné
    (C) a déjeunée
    (D) s'est déjeunée

49. (A) a quitté
    (B) s'est quittée
    (C) a partie
    (D) est partie

Roberta _____ à huit heures moins dix,

50. (A) arrivait
    (B) est arrivée
    (C) a arrivé
    (D) a arrivée

et le chef de service _____ le

51. (A) ont distribué

(B) a distribuée

(C) a distribué

(D) distribuera

travail à huit heures. A midi tout le monde _____.

52. (A) avait fini

(B) aura fini

(C) eut fini

(D) finira

Cet après-midi quand Pierre _____ le stade _____;

53. (A) a quitté

(B) est allée

(C) a parti

(D) est parti

54. (A) il pleuvait

(B) il pleuvra

(C) il pleuvrait

(D) il a plu

mais comme il _____ son imperméable, il _____.

55. (A) avait

(B) a eu

(C) avait eu

(D) aurait eu

56. (A) ne pas se mouiller

(B) n'était pas mouillé

(C) n'a pas été mouillé

(D) n'a pas eu mouillé

_____ devant une boulangerie il _____

57. (A) À marcher

(B) En passant

(C) Après avoir marché

(D) En allant

58. (A) voyait

(B) a vus

(C) a vues

(D) a vu

des petits pains au chocolat. Il _____ deux, et puis

59. (A) y a achetés

    (B) en a acheté

    (C) en a achetés

    (D) a acheté

il _____ pour ne pas arriver en retard chez lui.

60. (A) se dépêchaient

    (B) s'est dépêchée

    (C) s'est dépêché

    (D) se serait dépêché

Si tu était à Paris, tu _____ Notre-Dame,

61. (A) voyais

    (B) vois

    (C) verrais

    (D) aurais vu

la Tour Eiffel et le Louvre. Tu _____ à l'Opera,

62. (A) allais

    (B) vas

    (C) irais

    (D) serais allé(e)

tu _____ le métro, etc., etc.; il y a tant

63. (A) prenais

    (B) prends

    (C) prendrais

    (D) aurais pris

de choses à faire quand on est à Paris!

PART D

DIRECTIONS: Read the following passages carefully for comprehension. Each passage is followed by a number of questions or incomplete statements. Select the one answer or completion that is most appropriate according to the passage and blacken the corresponding space on the answer sheet.

Quand il entra, il s'approcha de moi et tout de suite je remarquai que son sourire habituel était absent; en effet, son visage paraissait bouleversé et il me dit: "Pourquoi pensez-vous que je sois venu vous voir? Il s'agit d'une question très sérieuse et il faut faire quelque chose. J'ai eu affaire à une canaille; voyez plutôt!" Il me remit une liasse de documents qui m'indiquèrent que le pauvre Roland venait d'acheter une maison à la campagne, une maison qui était en partie effondrée mais pour laquelle il avait payée fort cher; et pourtant elle était inhabitable. Il ne pouvait plus rien faire à ce qu'il me semblait, car les signatures avaient été apposées au bas des documents. Il avait tout simplement fait confiance au courtier, ce qui est souvent dangereux. Mais Roland me confia que les choses n'allaient pas se passer "comme ça", qu'il allait consulter un avocat, mais que je devais lui faire le grand plaisir de lui prêter l'argent dont il avait besoin. Je le lui refusai sur l'instant, me souvenant de l'adage selon lequel on perd ses amis quand on leur prête de l'argent. Et c'est à cette minute même que je m'aperçus que Roland n'était pas vraiment un ami car il se fâcha. Il devint tellement violent, ce qui était tout à fait contraire à ses habitudes, que je dus même m'échapper pour éviter ses coups.

64. Dans ce passage nous pouvons présumer que les deux personnages

    (A) sont à la mairie

    (B) communiquent par téléphone

    (C) sont dans la maison du narrateur

    (D) sont dans un tribunal

65. Dès l'entrée de Roland le narrateur s'est aperçu, selon l'aspect de son visage,

(A) que quelque chose le chagrinait

(B) que tout allait pour le mieux dans le meilleur des mondes

(C) qu'il était venu le voir pour rien

(D) qu'il était très affairé

66. Encore tout surpris de ce qui lui était arrivé, Roland a dit au narrateur

(A) qu'il avait peur

(B) qu'il était sérieux

(C) qu'il ne voulait pas sourire

(D) qu'il avait été trompé

67. Roland vient d'acheter une maison à la campagne, une maison dont le prix

(A) est trop élevé

(B) est établi par le narrateur

(C) a été publié

(D) a été augmenté

68. Roland a dit à son ami, le narrateur, qu'il a fait l'acquisition de cette maison de campagne, mais

(A) que c'est une canaille

(B) que le courtier est dangereux

(C) qu'il a été victime d'une malhonnêteté

(D) que cette maison est trop spacieuse

69. Roland ne peut pas accepter cette affaire malheureuse et donc il décide d'aller demander conseil

(A) au maire de la ville

(B) à son ami

(C) à un avocat

(D) à ses parents

DÉMÉNAGEMENT

DEMENAGEMENTS LOCAUX ET INTERNATIONAUX
Transports maritimes et aériens • Envoi de voitures Bureaux
à Paris et à Londres
MEMBRE DU HHGFAA

Tel: 02 99 88 77 66   FAX: 02 99 88 66 77
Email : delmovblue@aol.com
http://www.delmovblue.com

70. Cette annonce s'adresse surtout à :

(A) Des hommes d'affaires

(B) Toutes personnes souhaitant déménager

(C) Des étudiants

(D) Une clientèle basée à Londres

71. Laquelle des caractéristiques suivantes n'est pas mentionnée dans cette annonce ?

(A) La disponibilité du transport maritime

(B) Les tarifs

(C) Le statut professionnel de cette société

(D) Le transport de véhicules pour usage professionnel

J'arrivai au milieu de la nuit dans le petit village de Hangau; tout était sombre partout. Je me demandais si c'était bien la gare où je devais descendre; il n'y avait personne autour de moi. Le train était reparti et il s'était perdu dans la nuit, mais je pouvais encore voir la petite lumière rouge du fourgon là-bas dans la courbe. Il faisait déjà froid et pourtant ce n'était pas encore l'automne. Apparemment, le chef de gare n'était pas à son poste pour accueillir ce train et s'assurer que tout était en ordre pour son départ. Soudain, quelqu'un déboucha de la salle d'attente; c'était une femme qui portait des vêtements d'homme et qui marchait d'un pas assuré mais lourd. Elle était cachée dans l'obscurité, mais arrivé près d'elle son visage m'apparut; elle me regarda de ses yeux très bleus, fatigués et infiniment tristes. Ses mains étaient gonflées non pas par le froid mais par le travail. Elle bredouillait mais je ne pouvais pas la comprendre. C'était peut-être une étrangère qui ne parlait pas allemand, peut-être parlait-elle un dialecte, ou peut-être encore était-elle à bout de forces et son état était tel que son esprit refusait de fonctionner. Elle était donc incohérente, ou peut-être déçue. Elle s'éloigna.

Jamais je ne reverrais cette solide paysanne sans âge, sans forme, sans expression et peut-être aussi sans moyens.

72. Dans ce texte le narrateur

    (A) aime les voyages

    (B) va visiter les musées et l'Opéra de Hangau

    (C) se demande s'il est à sa destination

    (D) n'aime pas la nuit

73. Quand il descend du train, le voyageur constate

    (A) qu'il y a beaucoup de lumière partout

    (B) que c'est bien la gare où il devait descendre

    (C) qu'il s'est perdu dans la nuit

    (D) qu'il n'y a guère de gens autour de lui

74. Le train est arrivé en gare et il est reparti

    (A) sans l'assistance du chef de gare

    (B) sans le fourgon

    (C) fonçant tout droit dans la nuit

    (D) sans lumières

75. La narrateur se sent abandonné mais tout à coup

    (A) il voit le chef de gare

    (B) il voit une femme habillée en homme

    (C) il voit le train qui démarre

    (D) il voit le ciel sombre

76. La personne que le voyageur rencontre donne l'impression

    (A) d'être courageuse

    (B) d'être joyeuse

    (C) d'être assez riche

    (D) d'être extrêmement fatiguée

77. Cette personne dont il est question dans le texte

    (A) s'exprime avec difficulté

    (B) parle allemand couramment, ou peut-être un dialecte

    (C) a l'esprit ailleurs

    (D) est sourde et muette

78. En quelle saison sommes-nous dans cette histoire?

    (A) nous sommes en hiver

    (B) nous sommes en automne

    (C) nous sommes en été

    (D) nous sommes au printemps

Winnie était une petite femme bien sympathique et pourtant peu de gens l'aimaient. Pourquoi? Personne ne le saura jamais; les gens sont parfois bizarres. Cependant Winnie me donnait bonne impression. Avec ses bons petits yeux noirs au regard vif et intelligent qui trahissaient sa bonté, elle avait su me séduire. Ces yeux ressemblaient à ceux qu'ont les nounours, comme les appellent les petits enfants, ces ours que l'on vend dans les magasins de jouets et qui souvent ont des yeux noirs, ronds, brillants, ces yeux qui nous attirent et qui nous font aimer ces petits animaux en peluche.

Winnie devait être écossaise, ou peut-être irlandaise; venue en Amérique bien jeune, elle n'avait jamais beaucoup fréquenté l'école. Elle venait de perdre son mari quand j'ai fait sa connaissance. Elle était éplorée mais elle aimait son fils, un bon à rien de seize ans.

Et petit à petit, à chacune de nos rencontres fortuites, j'essayais de définir pourquoi on laissait Winnie de côté. Je découvris qu'elle avait le visage tellement rouge qu'il en était légèrement bleu, et Winnie parlait trop. En fait elle ne cessait jamais de parler, mais la voix de Winnie était douce et plaisante.

Les gens sont drôles, pensais-je un jour. Pauvre Winnie, son visage bleu indique tout simplement qu'elle a le cœur malade, et si elle parle tellement de sa propre condition c'est parce que les gens ne s'intéressent pas à elle et qu'elle se sent toujours abandonnée à elle-même.

79. Bien que très peu cultivée Winnie était une personne

    (A) agréable   (C) déplaisante

    (B) malveillante   (D) discrète

80. L'auteur du passage semble avoir de la compassion pour Winnie parce qu'elle était

    (A) seule   (C) délaissée par son mari

    (B) veuve   (D) mariée

81. Elle avait des yeux qui

    (A) étaient grands et ronds

    (B) faisaient penser à ceux des ours en peluche qu'on achète aux enfants

    (C) étaient verts comme ceux de beaucoup d'Irlandais

    (D) suggéraient la méchanceté

82. Elle avait un fils de seize ans qu'elle aimait et qui était

    (A) étudiant

    (B) cardiaque

    (C) indispensable

    (D) inutile

83. Winnie était laissée sans affection, délaissée par les gens

(A) à cause de son chagrin

(B) parce qu'elle parlait trop

(C) parce qu'elle n'avait pas d'éducation

(D) parce que son fils était un bon à rien

Monsieur Demonchaux, en sa qualité d'architecte et d'ingénieur-constructeur, un amoureux de la nature, fut chargé de la tâche énorme de développer le tourisme dans cette région des Alpes du Sud. Ce n'était pas très loin de Nice et il y était venu souvent au cours de ses vacances. On lui demanda de faire des plans et de les soumettre tant au gouvernement français qu'au préfet du département et qu'au maire de chacune des municipalités (villes, villages et hameaux) sur le territoire en question. On allait travailler dans le but unique de voir les jeunes, garçons et filles, rester au pays en leur donnant du travail et de les voir prospérer, ce qui était extrêmement important et urgent, car il faut bien le dire que les jeunes abandonnent les campagnes pour chercher dans les grandes villes un travail durable et lucratif qu'ils peuvent tenir de janvier à décembre. Il s'agissait aussi de donner du travail aux femmes, qui travaillent partout dans le monde aujourd'hui pour, à ce qu'il semble, améliorer le sort de la famille.

Par le truchement des emprunts internationaux, on donna à Monsieur Demonchaux plusieurs millions de francs français afin d'entreprendre la construction d'hôtels, de campings, de gîtes ruraux, de centres d'accueil et de récréation (courts de tennis, piscines, etc.) qui seraient utilisés pendant la saison d'été puisqu'il y a là un lac de bonne dimension et que les plages artificielles y abondent, de même que la pratique du ski nautique, du kayak, et du deltaplane. En hiver on y fait du ski, ski de fond ou nordique et ski alpin, mais tout cela se fait à une toute petite échelle actuellement et donc cette région était un choix excellent, et il fallait y développer les possibilités d'un tourisme d'hiver plus étendu.

Les travaux sont en cours mais déjà quelques difficultés entravent la bonne marche des choses. D'abord, en montagne les terrains ne sont pas toujours stables et il faut les renforcer ou tout simplement s'abstenir d'y construire quoi que ce soit. De plus, certaines routes importantes doivent être déviées, ce qui n'est pas facile à faire à cause de la lenteur administrative.

84. M. Demonchaux, architecte et ingénieur-constructeur,

(A) n'a pas assez d'expérience pour faire ce travail

(B) ne connaît pas la région où il va opérer

    (C) a refusé de faire les plans nécessaires

    (D) a accepté de faire le travail monumental dont on l'a chargé

85. Ce projet de développement touristique intéressait

    (A) tout le monde sauf le gouvernement français

    (B) les maires seulement

    (C) le maire de chaque municipalité, le préfet, et le gouvernement français

    (D) le département seulement

86. Il était important et urgent de développer le tourisme dans cette région

    (A) parce que les jeunes quittent la campagne pour trouver un travail plus assuré dans les grandes villes

    (B) parce que les femmes ne veulent plus travailler de janvier à décembre

    (C) parce qu'il n'y a là du travail qu'en été

    (D) parce que plus personne ne veut monter à l'échelle

87. On a trouvé les premiers millions de francs français pour commencer les travaux

    (A) par le truchement des emprunts nationaux

    (B) par l'entremise des maires et du préfet

    (C) par l'intermédiaire des riches financiers étrangers

    (D) par un prêt offert par des sociétés locales

88. Les hôtels, campings, gîtes ruraux, centres d'accueil et de récréation

    (A) ne seront en service qu'en été

    (B) ne seront que pour ceux qui savent faire du ski, de fond ou alpin

    (C) ne serviront qu'à ceux qui savent faire du ski nautique, du kayak ou du deltaplane

    (D) doivent être construits de façon à satisfaire le touriste toute l'année

89. En lisant cette annonce, on peut déduire que :

    (A) Ce cabinet se spécialise dans les procès contre les fautes professionnelles dans le secteur médical

    (B) Les tarifs de ce cabinet sont comparables à ceux de la concurrence

    (C) Les tarifs de ce cabinet sont plus bas que ceux de la concurrence

    (D) La plupart des clients de ce cabinet habitent en région marseillaise

90. Selon cette annonce, on peut aussi déduire que les avocats qui font partie de ce cabinet :

    (A) Ont tous obtenus leurs diplômes dans les meilleures universités

    (B) Proposent des tarifs réduits pour les étudiants et les personnes âgées

    (C) Ont les compétences nécéssaires pour traiter plusieurs sortes de dossiers

    (D) Travaillent sept jours sur sept

SAT II: French Subject Test
Test II

ANSWER KEY

1.	(C)	24.	(B)	47.	(C)	70.	(B)
2.	(D)	25.	(A)	48.	(A)	71.	(B)
3.	(A)	26.	(C)	49.	(D)	72.	(C)
4.	(B)	27.	(C)	50.	(B)	73.	(D)
5.	(A)	28.	(A)	51.	(C)	74.	(A)
6.	(C)	29.	(C)	52.	(A)	75.	(B)
7.	(D)	30.	(A)	53.	(A)	76.	(D)
8.	(C)	31.	(D)	54.	(A)	77.	(A)
9	(B)	32.	(A)	55.	(A)	78.	(C)
10.	(A)	33.	(B)	56.	(C)	79.	(A)
11.	(D)	34.	(C)	57.	(B)	80.	(B)
12.	(B)	35.	(B)	58.	(D)	81.	(B)
13.	(D)	36.	(D)	59.	(B)	82.	(D)
14.	(A)	37.	(D)	60.	(C)	83.	(B)
15.	(C)	38.	(D)	61.	(C)	84.	(D)
16.	(D)	39.	(A)	62.	(C)	85.	(C)
17.	(A)	40.	(B)	63.	(C)	86.	(A)
18.	(B)	41.	(D)	64.	(C)	87.	(C)
19.	(A)	42.	(C)	65.	(A)	88.	(D)
20.	(C)	43.	(D)	66.	(D)	89.	(D)
21.	(C)	44.	(A)	67.	(A)	90.	(C)
22.	(A)	45.	(B)	68.	(C)		
23.	(A)	46.	(C)	69.	(C)		

DETAILED EXPLANATIONS
OF ANSWERS

PRACTICE TEST II

1. **(C)**
   is the correct answer for only a clock (<u>une pendule</u>) can give the time. Granted, there could also be a clock in the dining room (<u>la salle à manger</u>) or in the attic (<u>le grenier</u>); and it is also true that most French families have a <u>goûter</u> (afternoon snack) at four o'clock in the afternoon; however, logic must be applied here and (A), (B), and (D) will be eliminated.

2. **(D)**
   is the correct answer for the young man was walking with his hands in his pockets (<u>dans les poches</u>), not (A) on the beach, (B) on the road, nor (C) on the table.

3. **(A)**
   is the correct answer; <u>sur-le-champ</u> is an expression which means "at once", and "promptly" is a synonym of "at once"; therefore, (B), (C), and (D) are understandably eliminated since they mean (B) needlessly, (C) moderately, and (D) in a tiresome manner, which clearly do not fit this situation.

4. **(B)**
   is the correct answer; one must know the meaning of the verb <u>saillir</u> (<u>saillait</u>) in order to find the answer. <u>Saillir</u> means "to stand out", "to jut out", "project" or "protrude", therefore, <u>avancer</u> (<u>avançait</u>) evokes the idea of <u>going forward</u> and it fits this sentence. (A) <u>en arrière</u> meaning "behind" or "backward", (C) was retracted (backward motion), and (D) hidden, are out of place here.

5. **(A)**
   is the correct form; <u>abattre</u> means "to knock down", "to pull down", "to chop off" (a tree), "cut off" (a tree); therefore, <u>couper un arbre</u> and <u>abattre un arbre</u> are synonyms. (B) to beat, (C) to combat, and (D) to break, are not the completions we need here.

6. **(C)**

   is the correct answer because <u>coudre</u> means "to sew", "to stitch, or join together", therefore, <u>assembler</u> is definitely what is needed here, for both <u>coudre</u> and <u>assembler</u> are synonyms; that is why (A) body, (B) to wear, and (D) to cut, must be eliminated.

7. **(D)**

   is the correct answer because <u>se resserrer means</u> "to become tighter"; <u>les liens de l'amitié</u> means the ties, or bond, of friendship. And it is correct that friendship becomes stronger (tighter) in difficult times, misfortune or calamity, that is: adversity. (A) to get back to the way it was, (B) to serve again, and (C) to do up, fasten, are not what is needed here.

8. **(C)**

   is the correct answer since it is the sun (<u>le soleil</u>) that burns (<u>brûler</u>) someone's skin (<u>la peau</u>). (A) the sea, (B) the sky, and (D) the sand are simply other words related to or associated with the beach.

9. **(B)**

   is the correct answer since we know that these are the last days of school; therefore, a vacation (<u>les vacances</u>) is coming. (A) to roam, i.e., to travel without a fixed goal, (C) quick circling, of a dancer for example, and (D) to go on a trip, are not what is needed here.

10. **(A)**

   is the correct answer since <u>les voisins</u> are people who live next door (<u>à côté de chez nous</u>). The neighbors may very well be (B) rich people, (C) jolly good fellows, people who enjoy life, and (D) good uncles and aunts, but the absolutely correct answer is (A).

11. **(D)**

   is the correct answer for the sunset (<u>le coucher du soleil</u>) falling suddenly (<u>tout à coup</u>) may indeed cause someone a surprise (<u>une surprise</u>) — the verb is <u>surprendre</u> and the past participle of that verb is <u>surpris</u>. (A) smiled, (B) hit, and (C) to strike, hit, or beat, do not fit this situation.

12. **(B)**

   is the correct answer since <u>nombre</u> suggests a quantity, whereas (C) <u>numéro</u> signifies a particular number or numeral, and is therefore incorrect. (A) <u>nom</u>, a name or a noun, and (D) <u>néant</u>, meaning nothing or nothingness, would not make sense in this context.

13. **(D)**
is the correct answer; the winter was terrible and the snow was abundant, and the birds had (D) nothing to eat, which is the only correct answer. (A) nothing to sing, (B) nobody to look at, and (C) nothing to do but eat, are incorrect.

14. **(A)**
is the correct answer for les cœurs (the hearts) do beat (battre), and one could easily hear (entendait) those heartbeats. You cannot hear hearts (B) disappear, (C) become distended, or swollen, (D) get disgusted; therefore, these last three are incorrect.

15. **(C)**
is the correct answer because in this context, recevoir means the same as faire accueil à, and étre reçus à bras ouverts means to be received with open arms, which is a synonym of faire un accueil fantastique. (A) with open mouth, (B) with open hands, and (D) in the dining room, are out of the picture here.

16. **(D)**
is the correct answer for indeed one chooses books with (D) great care, not (A) great charm, (B) a lot of money, or (C) a great sound.

17. **(A)**
is the correct answer for it is true that when the night (la nuit) has fallen (est tombée) noise becomes muffled. But it is not true that when the night has come about there is (B) nothing, (C) no more air, and (D) no more money.

18. **(B)**
is the correct answer because it is our arms (les bras) that we place into the sleeves (les manches) of our clothes (les vêtements). (A) the feet, (C) the knees, and (D) the legs, are therefore incorrect.

19. **(A)**
is the correct answer for se rapprocher vite (to get rapidly nearer) and faire des pas de géant (giant's steps) are synonyms. (B) des pas de loup are silent steps, (C) réguliers are regular, and (D) des pas perdus are said of people who are waiting endlessly in a room, and who walk to kill time.

20. **(C)**
is the correct answer because people hurry (se dépêcher) when they are in a hurry (pressés). It is simple logic. They do not hurry when they are

(A) à l'heure (on time), (B) en avance (early, or ahead of time) nor (D) déprimés (depressed).

21. **(C)**

is the correct answer because à vue d'œil and en peu de temps mean "rapidly"; had we chosen (A) dans la forêt (in the forest), (B) au lointain (in the distance), or (D) à perte de vue (as far as the eye can reach), we would have been incorrect because the meaning would have been lost in this particular context.

22. **(A)**

is the correct answer; indeed only hams and sausages (des jambons et des saucissons) can be eaten. (B) socks (des chaussettes), (C) stars (des étoiles), and (D) baskets (des paniers), are not edible items.

23. **(A)**

is the correct answer since fire (le feu) is écarlate (scarlet); again we have synonyms here; le ciel (the sky) may indeed appear to be on fire (en feu) when showing off with a magnificent sunset; it will not be (B) on earth, or (C) on our heads, and (D) dans le lointain (in the distance) does not fit here since it had to equate the idea of redness.

24. **(B)**

is the correct answer for assécher means "to dry" or "to drain"; one does not dry (A) a mountain, (C) the snow, nor (D) the beach. Only les marais (swamps or marshes) are dried, or drained, presumably to build upon.

25. **(A)**

is the correct answer, for we may very well equate jugglery with finesse. (B) sans fin (endlessly), (C) avec force (firmly), and (D) dangereusement (dangerously), are incorrect.

26. **(C)**

is the correct answer because one can easily visualize the dead leaves (les feuilles mortes) falling from the trees, which turn round and round (tournoyer) before reaching the ground (le sol). En tombant is a gérondif (a gerund) which means "while falling", therefore it is correct. (A) en s'élevant (while going up), (B) en tremblant (while shaking), and (D) pour tomber (for the purpose of falling), are wrong.

27. **(C)**

is the correct answer; indeed anyone who has witnessed a storm in the mountains knows that the thunder is much louder there than anywhere else; therefore, it causes fear (<u>la peur</u>). Let us now recognize that (A) one does not ski in the summer, (B) the sun does not shine during a storm, and (D) no one would take a trip by kayak (or canoe) over the torrents during a storm, consequently, (A), (B), and (D) are incorrect.

28. **(A)**

is the correct answer for it is the only noun among these four which is feminine; consequently, it agrees in gender and number with (1) the demonstrative adjective <u>cette</u> and (2) the adjective <u>belle</u>. (B) <u>printemps</u> (spring), (C) <u>ciel</u> (sky), and (D) <u>profil</u> (profile) are masculine, thus, they do not fit grammatically.

29. **(C)**

is the correct answer, for <u>leur</u> (to them) can very well be substituted for <u>lui</u> (to him or to her). (A) <u>m'</u>, (B) <u>nous</u>, and (D) <u>vous</u>, being direct object pronouns which directly follow the subject, cannot be correct in this sentence.

30. **(A)**

is the correct answer because only <u>moi</u>, <u>toi</u>, <u>lui</u>, <u>elle</u>, <u>nous</u>, <u>vous</u>, <u>eux</u>, <u>elles</u>, called "stressed" subject pronouns, follow a preposition, such as <u>avec</u> (with). Granted, (C) <u>vous</u> is present in the list of choices but it cannot be used here since the sentence would mean "Come with you (yourself, yourselves)", which would make no sense.

31. **(D)**

is the correct answer. <u>Sans</u> (without) being a preposition (please see explanation in #29) cannot be followed by an indirect object pronoun such as (A) <u>leur</u>, nor by subject pronouns such as (B) <u>il</u> and (C) <u>tu</u>.

32. **(A)**

is the correct answer because the direct object pronoun <u>l'</u> is positioned in front of the infinitive <u>avoir</u>; <u>l'</u> is called for since <u>avoir</u> starts with a vowel; in addition, the noun <u>histoire</u> (story), being feminine and the direct object of <u>avoir racontée</u>, is now in front of that verb; therefore, the past participle <u>racontée</u> must agree in gender and number with it.

33. **(B)**

is the correct answer for <u>lui</u> (to him or to her), an indirect object pronoun, may very well be a susbstitution for <u>me</u>. (A) <u>te</u> (to you, to yourself), (C) <u>le</u> (it, him), and (D) <u>il</u> (he, it), could not serve as a substitution in this situation.

34. **(C)**

    is the correct answer, for <u>il</u> being a subject pronoun must be replaced by another subject pronoun; in the list of choices only (C) <u>je</u> is a subject pronoun, and the possessive adjective <u>notre</u> (our) is also correct since <u>elle</u> (she) — <u>son</u> (her) — is part of it.

35. **(B)**

    is the correct answer because a determiner always announces a noun (<u>mon</u>, possessive adjective, is one of them); therefore, <u>c'est</u> is the form to be used here; <u>il</u> does not belong in this situation for the simple reason that <u>il</u> is modified by an adjective (as in <u>il est gentil</u>) or by a noun used adjectivally (as in <u>il est capitaine</u>) — as opposed to <u>c'est le capitaine du bateau</u>), which is especially true of professions (occupations) and nationalities (an example of this is <u>il est américain</u> — as opposed to <u>c'est un Américain</u>). N.B. Unlike English, only nouns of nationalities are capitalized in French, not the adjectives. <u>Lui</u> of (B) is correct because it is the only form which is able to replace <u>m'</u> of the sentence since both <u>lui</u> and <u>m'</u> are indirect object pronouns.

36. **(D)**

    is the correct answer because <u>qu'</u> and <u>que</u> of this interrogative pronoun are both the direct objects of the verb <u>vous voulez</u> (main clause); and (D) <u>vous</u> is also correct because even if (A) <u>nous</u> (B) <u>leur</u>, and (C) <u>te</u> are indirect object pronouns, as (D) <u>vous</u>, they have to be eliminated since the interrogative pronouns that go with them are incorrect.

37. **(D)**

    is the correct answer since <u>un grand nombre de</u> is a synonym of <u>beaucoup de</u>, thus eliminating (A), (B), and (C).

38. **(D)**

    is the correct answer because <u>cela</u> can be used instead of <u>ceci</u>; they both are demonstrative pronouns and they refer to something which remains unnamed; they stand by themselves. (A) <u>ceux</u> and (C) <u>ce</u> are also demonstrative pronouns but they refer to someone who, or something that, has already been named, and they cannot stand by themselves. (B) is a direct object pronoun, not a demonstrative pronoun.

39. **(A)**

    is the only possible replacement for <u>se fasse</u> because (B) and (C) are in the plural, and (D) makes no sense.

40. **(B)**

is the correct answer because in French one plays of a (<u>du</u>, <u>de la</u>, <u>de l'</u>) musical instrument and <u>at a</u> (<u>au</u>, <u>à la</u>, <u>à l'</u>) sport, thus eliminating (A), (C), and (D).

41. **(D)**

is the correct answer because "my uncle made (caused — causative verb <u>faire</u>) us (<u>nous</u>) or them (<u>les</u>) — both direct object pronouns — (to) read". (A) a possessive adjective, (B) a reflexive pronoun, and (C), a subject pronoun, cannot fit here.

42. **(C)**

is the correct answer because when speaking of a language only a definite article (<u>le</u>, <u>l'</u>) is used, which is the case with (C). The use of the preposition <u>en</u> in (A) and (B) is incorrect. (D) means the Chinese woman, which would require the verb <u>connaître</u> (<u>connait</u>) instead of <u>savoir</u> (<u>savait</u>) since it involves a person. <u>Le chinois</u> is the Chinese language.

43. **(D)**

is the correct answer because <u>pas un</u> and <u>aucun</u> are synonyms. In addition, it must be noted that if careless French speaking people tend sometimes to forget the form <u>ne</u> (in the written and the spoken traditions) it is incorrect; <u>ne</u> (<u>n'</u>) is part of the negation in French, and it must be expressed. This eliminates (B) and (C), which indeed delete <u>n'</u>; and (A) is also incorrect because <u>aucun</u> is here in the plural; <u>aucun(e)</u>, being specifically singular, cannot ever be in the plural.

44. **(A)**

is the correct answer because the indefinite adjectives <u>plusieurs</u> and <u>quelques</u> are interchangeable in this context. (B) <u>beaucoup</u> alone cannot function when it modifies, or precedes, a noun where it must be followed by the preposition <u>de</u> since it is a partitive situation; (C) <u>quelques-unes</u>, an indefinite pronoun, cannot modify the noun <u>robes</u>, and (D) <u>quelque</u>, being singular, cannot modify a plural noun, <u>robes</u>.

45. **(B)**

is the correct answer since <u>la</u> means "her". I want to see you (<u>te</u>) / I want to see her (<u>la</u>). (A) being a reflexive pronoun, (C) an indirect object pronoun, and (D) a so-called "stressed" personal pronoun, used also in the affirmative imperative, do not fit in this sentence.

The correct answers to numbers 46, 47, 48, 49, 50, 51, and 52 are as follows:

46. **(C)**,   47. **(C)**,   48. **(A)**,   49. **(D)**,   50. **(B)**,   51. **(C)**, 52. **(A)**

The verbs in numbers 46, 47, 48, 49, 50, and 51 must be conjugated in the *passé composé* because the adverbial phrase ce matin indicates *when* each one of these actions occurred.

Numbers 46 and 47 are reflexive verbs: se lever (to get up) and se baigner (to take a bath). Notice that 46 (C) and 47 (C) are the correct answers because reflexive verbs are conjugated with the auxiliary être in their compound tenses, and their past participles agree in gender and number with the direct object of those verbs. (Remember that être NEVER has an indirect object). In both instances: 46, elle s'est levée and 47, elle s'est baignée the direct object is s'; and since they both precede the verb, the past participles levée and baignée agree in gender and number with s', which stands for Roberta, feminine and singular. Since (A), (B), and (D) do not follow the important rules described above, they must be eliminated.

The verbs of clauses 48, déjeuner (to have breakfast) and 51, distribuer (to distribute) are verbs conjugated with the auxiliary avoir; here again, the direct object must be found to see if it is positioned in front of or after the verb so that the past participles déjeuné and distribué will agree. 48 has no direct object, therefore, the past participle remains neutral, i.e., it does not change; the correct answer to 48 is (A). 48 (B) is conjugated with être, (C) the past participle is misspelled, (D) is conjugated as a reflexive verb, which déjeuner is not. Therefore, (B), (C), and (D) are incorrect.

On the other hand, in 51, distribuer has a direct object: le travail, which follows the verb: il a distribué le travail; therefore, it does not have any effect upon the past participle; thus, the past participle distribué remains neutral. The correct answer to 51 is (C).

49 (D) is the correct answer because partir takes the preposition à (and sometimes de); quitter does not. Partir is never followed by a noun; quitter must be followed by a determiner and the noun which it modifies; (examples: quitter la maison, quitter sa ville, etc.); these two verbs are synonyms, but they must be handled with care so that there is no mistake made. Thus, Roberta est partie au travail; partir, being an action verb, is conjugated with the auxiliary être, and its past participle, partie, must agree in gender and in number with its subject: Roberta. Hence, (A) and (B) are eliminated because quitter does not fit here, and (C) conjugating partir with the auxiliary avoir is also wrong.

50 (B) is the correct answer since <u>arriver</u>, being an action verb, is also conjugated with the auxiliary <u>être</u>, and as such its past participle, <u>arrivée</u>, agrees with its subject: Roberta. (A) is in the imperfect, and in (C) and (D) <u>arriver</u> is conjugated with <u>avoir</u>; therefore, they are incorrect.

52 (A) is the correct answer because it means "By noon everyone had finished his (or her) work," which is perfectly correct in both French and English. (B) and (D), using a future form, and (C), in the *passé antérieur,* are wrong.

The correct answers to numbers 53, 54, 55, 56, 57, 58, 59 and 60 are as follows:

53. **(A)**, 54. **(A)**, 55. **(A)**, 56. **(C)**, 57. **(B)**, 58. **(D)**, 59. **(B)**, 60. **(C)**

Again the verbs of clauses numbers 53, 54, 55, 56, 57, 58, 59 and 60 deal with a series of successive actions which occurred in the past, except for two of them (54 and 55) which are *descriptions*; therefore, they cannot be conjugated in the *passé composé*, which is the tense of narration. Descriptions are given in the imperfect.

53 (A) is the correct answer because the action of leaving (<u>a quitté</u>) occurred once in the past and has ended (please see explanation to number 49 above; see also why number 53 (B), (C), and (D) are incorrect).

54 (A) is correct for, as stated above, this situation is a *description,* therefore, the imperfect is required here. (B) using the future, (C) the present conditional, and (D) the *passé composé*, are incorrect.

55 (A) is the correct answer for the same reason stated in number 54 (B) using the *passé composé,* (C) the pluperfect, and (D) the past conditional, are wrong.

56 (C) is the correct answer because the fact that "Pierre did not get wet" (<u>il n'a pas été mouillé</u>) shows a finished action and therefore, the *passé composé* must be used.

57 (B) is the correct answer because <u>en passant</u>, a gerund, means "while passing by". (A), (C), and (D) have different meanings; therefore, they are incorrect.

58 (D) is the correct answer because <u>he saw</u> (<u>il a vu</u>) some <u>petits pains</u>; the action of seeing is a finished action, therefore, the *passé composé* is called for, not the imperfect, as in (A). In both (B) and (C), the past participle is incorrect. In this sentence the direct object is positioned after the verb; therefore, there is no agreement with the past participle.

59 (B) is the correct answer in spite of the fact that <u>en</u>, an adverbial pronoun (quantity), is found in front of the verb, and stands for <u>les petits pains</u>; the reason the agreement cannot take place between <u>en</u> and the past

participle <u>acheté</u> is that <u>en</u> is an adverb; and adverbs have neither gender nor number. (A) <u>y,</u> not being an adverb of quantity, (C) having a plural past participle, and (D) ignoring the adverb <u>en</u>, are all three incorrect.

60 (C) is the correct answer because the rules for conjugating a reflexive verb are followed. <u>Se dépêcher</u>, being a pronominal verb, must be conjugated with the auxiliary <u>être</u>, and the past participle <u>dépêché</u> must agree with <u>s'</u>, since <u>s'</u> is the direct object of the verb. (A) being in the plural, (B) in the feminine, and (D) in the past conditional, are incorrect.

61. **(C)**, 62. **(C)**, 63. **(C)**

are the correct answers because we are dealing with a conditional sentence here. The verb of the "if" (<u>si</u>) clause is in the imperfect, therefore, the present conditional must be used for the verbs of the "result" clause; this is an example of what is called "sequence of tenses".

61 (A), 62 (A), and 63 (A) are incorrect because the imperfect cannot be used in the "result" clause of a conditional sentence.

61 (B), 62 (B), and 63 (B) are incorrect because they use the present indicative. 61 (D), 62 (D), and 63 (D) are eliminated because the verbs are in the past conditional, which would require the <u>si</u> clause to be in the pluperfect tense.

64. **(C)**

is the correct answer because it is the only plausible one. Roland is visiting the narrator. Nothing leads us to believe that the narrator and Roland are in (A) the city hall (<u>à la mairie</u>) or (D) in a court house (<u>dans un tribunal</u>); and they are not (B) talking on the phone (<u>au téléphone</u>).

65. **(A)**

is the correct answer; indeed as soon as he entered the door the narrator saw that (A) something was troubling Roland (<u>chagriner</u>). No, (B) everything was not for the best in the best of worlds. It is also untrue that (C) he had come to see the narrator for nothing; and (D) is also incorrect, for Roland was not "very busy" (<u>très affairé</u>); he was simply worried.

66. **(D)**

is the correct answer; he said he had been deceived, cheated. No, (A) he did not say that he was afraid, nor that he was (B) serious; (C) is also incorrect because nowhere in the text is there any indication stating that he was not willing to smile.

67. **(A)**

is the correct answer: <u>un prix élevé</u> (a high price) is referred to in the text as "une maison ... pour laquelle il avait payée fort cher" (a very expensive house). (B) the price of the house was set by the narrator, (C) the price was published, and (D) was increased, are incorrect.

68. **(C)**

is the correct answer, for indeed this man (Roland) did say he had been a victim of dishonesty, of a fraud. No, the house is not (A) a scoundrel, and no, Roland did not <u>say</u> that (B) the agent is dangerous, nor that (D) the house is too spacious.

69. **(C)**

is the correct answer for indeed he declares that he will seek the help of a lawyer (<u>un avocat</u>). He will not ask the assistance of either (A) the mayor (<u>la maire</u>), (B) his friend (<u>son ami</u>) or (D) his parents (<u>ses parents</u>).

70. **(B)**

This ad primarily concerns (<u>cette annonce s'adresse surtout à</u>) anyone looking to move (<u>toute personne cherchant à déménager</u>). (B) is therefore the correct answer. There is nothing in the ad which would give us reason to believe that this service is particularly geared towards businesspeople (<u>les hommes d'affaires</u>), students (<u>les étudiants</u>), or a client base located in London (<u>une clientèle basée à Londres</u>), since that city is only mentioned to indicate that it is one of the locations to which company cars can be sent; Paris is also mentioned for that same reason.

71. **(B)**

There is no mention at all of rates (<u>les tarifs</u>). Even without knowing the precise meaning of that word, its resemblance to the English word "tariff" indicates that it is in all likelihood a financial term. No such terms appear anywhere in this ad. (B) is therefore the correct answer. <u>Le transport maritime</u> (shipping) is mentioned, as is <u>le statut professionnel de cette société</u> (this company's status [<u>membre du HHGFAA</u>]). Likewise, the transportation of company vehicles is also mentioned (<u>l'envoi de voitures Bureaux</u>).

72. **(C)**

is the correct answer; yes, he is wondering if he really is where he was supposed to end his trip; everything seems so strange to him! (A) is incorrect because the text does not mention that he likes to travel. (B) is also incorrect because the narrator never mentions what he is going to do in the (fictitious) village of Hangau. (D) is incorrect, for the narrator does not say that he does not like the night.

73. **(D)**

is the correct answer; indeed when he gets off the train he does not see a soul around him (il n'y a guère de gens and il n'y a personne are synonyms). (A) cannot be correct since it indicates that the station and its surroundings were well lit. (B) shows that the narrator is absolutely sure that this was the station where he was to get off, which is incorrect, and (C) says that the narrator got lost in the night, which is incorrect.

74. **(A)**

is the correct answer for indeed the station master (le chef de gare) was totally absent from the picture, both when the train arrived and when it departed. The others are incorrect because the train did not leave (B) without the boxcar, (C) tearing straight ahead into the night, nor (D) without lights (since a red light is indicated).

75. **(B)**

is the correct answer, for it is true that he thought he was completely alone, and all of a sudden (tout à coup) he saw a woman who was wearing man's clothes. No, it is not true, the narrator did not suddenly see (A) the train master, (B) the train move off, nor (D) the dark sky; therefore, they are incorrect.

76. **(D)**

is the correct answer; the lady appeared to be exhausted (extrêmement fatiguée); she did not appear (A) brave, (B) joyful, nor (C) quite rich; therefore, (A), (B), (C) are incorrect.

77. **(A)**

is the correct answer because it is true that the narrator did not understand what the lady said to him (elle bredouillait — she was mumbling). No, she does not (B) speak German fluently; how can the narrator say that she does since he did not understand her? (C) her thoughts were elsewhere; who can ascertain this? There was no contact whatsoever between the narrator and the lady. And (D) she was deaf-and-dumb is indicated nowhere in the text. Therefore, all three are incorrect.

78. **(C)**

is the correct answer; correct, it is cold but it is still summer (ce n'était pas encore l'automne — it was not autumn yet); therefore, even if it is the end of summer, it is still summer. (A) winter, (B) fall, and (D) spring are wrong.

79. **(A)**
    is the correct answer; it is true that although Winnie was not very much of an educated person still she was pleasant (agréable). No, she was not (B) ill-willed, (C) unpleasant, nor (D) discreet. (B), (C), and (D) are incorrect.

80. **(B)**
    is the correct answer; Winnie was a widow (une veuve). And she was not (A) alone (since she has a son whom she loves); nor was she (C) abandoned by her husband, nor (D) married (since her husband had just passed away) therefore, (A), (C), and (D) are incorrect.

81. **(B)**
    is the correct answer; her eyes, mentioned in the text, were evocative of those of the teddy-bears (les nounours, les ours en peluche) that children like so much. No, her eyes were not (A) large and round, nor (C) green like those of many Irish people, and they were not (D) suggesting wickedness, for Winnie is a good person; therefore, (A), (C), and (D) are incorrect.

82. **(D)**
    is the correct answer because bon à rien (good-for-nothing) and inutile (useless or of no use) are synonyms. (A) étudiant (student) is incorrect because nowhere in the text can we find that he is going to school; (B) cardiaque (a heart patient) is also incorrect; and (C) indispensable is not correct either since this young man is a good-for-nothing. (A), (B), and (C) are incorrect.

83. **(B)**
    is the correct answer for it is true that people did not like Winnie because she talked too much. No, it was not because of her (A) grief, nor was it because (C) she was uneducated, nor because (D) her son was a good-for-nothing. (A), (C), and (D) are wrong.

84. **(D)**
    is the correct answer; yes, he has accepted to do the colossal job which is very much in demand in that region. (A) is not true because Mr. Demonchaux is an architect and a builder, therefore, he has experience. (B) is incorrect because he came to visit that region during periods of vacation. (C) is also incorrect because he did not refuse to make the blueprint of the project. Hence, (A), (B), and (C) are eliminated.

85. **(C)**

is the correct answer for everyone (the mayor of each municipality, the préfet, and the French government) is involved in this development. (A), (B), and (D), ignoring one or the other, are incorrect.

86. **(A)**

is the correct answer because the primary (fundamental) reason for developing tourism in that region was to provide jobs at home for the young people so that they would not leave the area to find jobs in large cities; therefore, jobs had to be created, good jobs, lucrative jobs, which they could hold all year around; jobs for women too, which is very important these days. Thus, (B) saying that women no longer want to work from January through December, (C) indicating that there are only jobs there in the summer, which is not true since there is a small ski resort there (en hiver on y fait du ski ... mais à une toute petite échelle), and (D) saying that no one is willing to climb the ladder anymore, are all incorrect.

87. **(C)**

is the correct answer, for it is true that foreign money (des emprunts internationaux) allowed this project to get started. It is not (A) national loans, (B) through the intervention of the mayors and the préfet, (D) through a loan from local companies, that this was made possible; therefore, (A), (B), and (D) must be eliminated.

88. **(D)**

is the correct answer. Tourism must go on all year round in this region so that everyone has a job from January 1 to December 31; this is feasible since they can offer anything the tourist likes to do while on vacation, in all seasons. (A) considering only the summer, (B) considering only those who can ski, and (C) only those who know how to water-ski, kayak, or deltaplane, must be eliminated.

89. **(D)**

The answer is (D), la plupart des clients [. . .] habitent en région marseillaise (Most of this law firm's clients live in the Marseille area). There is no mention of medical malpractice (les fautes professionnelles dans le secteur médical), so the answer cannot be (A). Likewise, no information is provided about the rates (les tarifs), which eliminates choices (B) and (C).

90. **(C)**

The answer is (C). According to this ad, we can deduce that this firm's lawyers (<u>on peut [. . .] déduire que les clients de ce cabinet</u>) are qualified to deal with several different types of cases (<u>ont les compétences nécéssaires pour traiter plusieurs sortes de dossiers</u>). There is no mention whatsoever of degrees (<u>les diplômes</u>), reduced rates for students and senior citizens (<u>tarifs réduits pour les étudiants et les personnes agées</u>), or working seven days a week (<u>travaillent sept jours sur sept</u>), which eliminates choices (A), (B), and (D), respectively.

SAT II:
SUBJECT TEST IN
FRENCH

PRACTICE
TEST III

FRENCH TEST III

PART A

Time: 1 Hour
          90 Questions

DIRECTIONS: This part consists of a number of incomplete statements, each followed by four suggested completions. Select the most appropriate completion and blacken the corresponding space on the answer sheet.

1. Allô? Ce n'est pas le 32-34-53? Excusez-moi, j'ai fait un faux ...

    (A) addition   (C) nombre

    (B) numéro   (D) adresse

2. Quelle heure est-il? Ma montre ne ... pas.

    (A) travaille   (C) voit

    (B) marche   (D) recule

3. Donne-moi des clous et un marteau. Je vais ... la porte.

    (A) repartir   (C) détruire

    (B) réparer   (D) repeindre

4. A cette réunion je voudrais ... mes parents et ma sœur.

    (A) apporter   (C) amener

    (B) prendre   (D) connaître

5. Il est ... de se baigner sur cette plage. C'est trop dangereux.

    (A) exige   (C) invraisemblable

    (B) insolite   (D) interdit

6. Ce potage est trop chaud. Je me suis brûlé …

    (A) la langue   (C) l'assiette

    (B) les pieds   (D) la cuillière

7. Pour payer, vous devez passer …

    (A) à la caisse   (C) à l'argent

    (B) au front   (D) à l'agent

8. Ce soir, nous allons manger …

    (A) du poison   (C) du poisson

    (B) du désert   (D) du péché

9. Si la fête de l'Indépendance tombe un lundi, on aura trois jours de …

    (A) congé   (C) congrès

    (B) congelé   (D) comblé

10. Je me suis levé tard parce que mon … n'a pas sonné.

    (A) réveil   (C) timbre

    (B) jouet   (D) matin

11. Où est Jacques? — Retourne-toi! Il est juste … toi.

    (A) avant   (C) devant

    (B) derrière   (D) après

12. C'est la deuxième … que tu as fait cette faute!

    (A) temps   (C) heure

    (B) fois   (D) époque

13. N'ayez pas peur. Il n'y a aucun …

    (A) chance   (C) remords

    (B) hasard   (D) danger

14. Si tu manges tous ces desserts, tu vas …

   (A) rétrécir   (C) maigrir

   (B) grossir   (D) grandir

15. Tout ce linge sale! Bon, alors samedi je ferai …

   (A) la lessive   (C) une plainte

   (B) la grasse matinée (D) la vaisselle

16. Quelle bonne … ! Tu as les joues toutes roses!

   (A) fleur   (C) mine

   (B) jardinière   (D) recette

17. Prends ton parapluie. Il va certainement …

   (A) pleurer   (C) plaire

   (B) pleuvoir   (D) prier

18. Je n'ai pas pu aller à …

   (A) la conférence   (C) l'étoile

   (B) la lecture   (D) l'évêque

19. Julien ne paie pas parce que le spectacle est … pour les enfants de moins de dix ans.

   (A) résumé   (C) volé

   (B) gratuit   (D) ennuyeux

20. Il a l'air fâché. Il doit être encore …

   (A) ennuyeux   (C) amusant

   (B) ennuyé   (D) amusé

21. C'est … . Ses frères sont plus jeunes que lui.

   (A) l'aîné   (C) un jumeau

   (B) un nouveau-né   (D) le cadet

22. Elle n'a pas pu ... à la messe parce qu'elle était malade.

    (A) attendre
    (B) manger
    (C) assister
    (D) nettoyer

23. On l'a accusé à tort. Il n'était pas ...

    (A) blessé
    (B) coupable
    (C) avocat
    (D) innocent

24. Il faut ... une décision.

    (A) prendre
    (B) faire
    (C) couper
    (D) conter

25. Maintenant, il ... sa faute.

    (A) ressort
    (B) repart
    (C) réalise
    (D) se rend compte de

26. Ils se disputent rarement. En général, ils ...

    (A) se battent
    (B) s'entendent bien
    (C) se rappellent
    (D) s'assemblent bien

27. Aprés un repas au restaurant, on laisse ... pour le garçon.

    (A) une carte
    (B) un tuyau
    (C) une nappe
    (D) un pourboire

28. Je faisais attention, mais je ne pouvais pas ...

    (A) décrire
    (B) écouter
    (C) entendre
    (D) découvrir

29. Nous avons besoin de café. Je vais en acheter chez ...

    (A) l'épicier
    (B) le fermier
    (C) le boucher
    (D) le voisin

30. Je n'ai pas le temps de bavarder. Je suis …

    (A) vieilli   (C) arriéré

    (B) pressé   (D) vite

PART B

DIRECTIONS: In each of the sentences in this part of the test, one or more words are underlined. One of the four choices following each sentence can be correctly substituted for the underlined word(s) to form a grammatically correct statement or question. The new sentence may differ in meaning from the original example. Select the one choice which fits grammatically into the original sentence and blacken the corresponding space on the answer sheet.

31. Cet enfant <u>obéit</u> à sa mère.

(A) regarde   (C) écoute

(B) ressemble   (D) attend

32. Ils vont voyager en <u>Europe</u>.

(A) Japon   (C) Etats-Unis

(B) Canada   (D) Angleterre

33. Mon frère <u>manque</u> d'argent.

(A) prête   (C) a besoin

(B) gagne   (D) demande

34. Donnez-les-<u>lui</u>!

(A) te   (C) la

(B) me   (D) moi

35. Il est parti sans <u>Margot</u>.

(A) eux   (C) vôtre

(B) la   (D) vos

36. <u>Qui est-ce qui</u> a dit cela?

    (A) Qu'est-ce que   (C) De quoi

    (B) Qui   (D) Quoi

37. C'est un <u>vieil</u> ouvrier.

    (A) gentille   (C) belle

    (B) grande   (D) nouvel

38. Je me suis cassé <u>la jambe</u>.

    (A) ma jambe   (C) le bras

    (B) la vase   (D) mon nez

39. Voilà la robe que j'ai <u>vue</u> hier.

    (A) essayé   (C) achetée

    (B) déchiré   (D) cousu

40. Je regrette <u>de partir</u>.

    (A) que vous partez   (C) que vous partiez

    (B) que vous partirez   (D) êtes partis

41. Il faut <u>nous</u> dire la vérité.

    (A) les   (C) leurs

    (B) leur   (D) vos

42. Je vous conseille de <u>ne pas fumer</u>.

    (A) ne fumer plus   (C) ne fumer encore

    (B) ne jamais fumer   (D) ne fumer pas

43. Cette maison est à eux? Oui, c'est <u>leur maison</u>.

    (A) la sienne   (C) la leur

    (B) la leurs   (D) leurs

44. De toutes ces photos, je préfère <u>la photo</u> de Marc.

    (A) cela   (C) celui

    (B) celle   (D) celui-là

PART C

Aussitôt que tu _____ le temps, j'espère que tu me téléphoneras.

45. (A) as

    (B) auras

    (C) as eu

    (D) avais

Si tu _____, nous irons au cinéma. Il y a un bon film _____

46. (A) voulais   47. (A) qui

    (B) voudras   (B) que

    (C) veux   (C) dont

    (D) voudrais   (D) lequel

passe maintenant au Cinéma Rex _____ j'aimerais _____ voir.

48. (A) dont   49. (A) – –

    (B) que   (B) à

    (C) qui   (C) du

    (D) lequel   (D) de

C'est possible qu'il _____ en italien, parce que c'est un film

50. (A) sera

   (B) soit

   (C) est

   (D) serait

de Rosselini. Mais je suis sûr qu'il y _____ des sous-titres.

51. (A) ait

   (B) aura

   (C) auront

   (D) ait eu

J'ai envie _____ le voir, parce que c'est un film _____ tout le

52. (A) – –   53. (A) auquel

   (B) de   (B) duquel

   (C) a   (C) que

   (D) du   (D) dont

monde parle.

Tu aimes _____ vin? — Non, je n'aime pas _____ vin.

54. (A) – –   55. (A) – –

   (B) le   (B) du

   (C) du   (C) de

   (D) de   (D) le

Mais, pourquoi voulez-vous _____ savoir? — Parce que hier

56. (A) – –

   (B) à

   (C) de

   (D) vous

soir, nous _____ au restaurant, et nous avons commandé une

57. (A) sommes allé

    (B) avons allé

    (C) sommes allés

    (D) avons allés

bouteille _____ vin français qui était extraordinaire. Je

58. (A) – –

    (B) du

    (C) au

    (D) de

prends toujours _____ vin avec le dîner, alors, moi, je m'y

59. (A) – –

    (B) du

    (C) le

    (D) de

connais en vin! C'est dommage que tu _____ apprécier un bon vin!

60. (A) ne peux pas

    (B) n'a pas pu

    (C) ne puisses pas

    (D) ne pourras pas

PART D

DIRECTIONS: Read the following passages carefully for comprehension. Each passage is followed by a number of questions or incomplete statements. Select the one answer or completion that is most appropriate according to the passage and blacken the corresponding space on the answer sheet.

Qu'est-ce que la France? Pour beaucoup de touristes étrangers, la France, c'est Paris, et Paris seulement la nuit!

Monsieur Smith, ingénieur américain, arrive à Paris un jeudi soir en octobre. Fatigué par son voyage, il prend un taxi et va directement à son hôtel. Il a juste le temps de dormir un peu avant de partir à la conquête de Paris. A 21 heures, il monte dans un grand autobus spécial pour les touristes, et la visite de Paris commence. Chaque soir 2.000 étrangers comme Monsieur Smith visitent Paris en autobus. Premier arrêt: une boîte de nuit.

61. Est-ce que beaucoup de touristes connaissent bien la France?

(A) Oui, car Paris, c'est la France.

(B) Non, parce que la plupart du temps ils ne visitent que Paris.

(C) Non, parce qu'il faut connaître Paris la nuit.

(D) Oui, parce que Paris ne change jamais.

62. Monsieur Smith

(A) est typique de beaucoup de touristes.

(B) a toujours besoin de dormir un peu.

(C) connaît très bien Paris.

(D) revient souvent à Paris.

63. L'autobus qu'il prend à 21 heures

(A) a 2.000 places.

(B) est uniquement pour les touristes.

(C) est le moyen de transport de plus de 2.000 Parisiens.

(D) est une boîte de nuit.

Quand j'avais dix ans mon père est mort. Il avait accumulé des dettes, et nous nous sommes trouvés très pauvres, sans un sou. Alors, nous avons dû quitter le grand appartement où j'étais né et dont je garde encore un très beau souvenir.

Notre nouveau logis était plus étroit et moins confortable. Il était sans eau courante; ma mère vidait chaque jour la lourde lessive installée sous le lavabo. Il n'y avait pas de chauffage; en hiver, l'appartement était glacé. La chambre que je partageais avec mon frère était trop petite pour y mettre un pupitre. J'ai appris à faire mes devoirs dans le brouhaha des voix, mais il m'était pénible de ne jamais pouvoir m'isoler.

64. Pourquoi est-ce que la famille du narrateur a déménagé?

(A) Parce qu'il fallait accumuler des dettes.

(B) Parce que le narrateur n'avait que dix ans.

(C) Parce qu'il fallait trouver un appartement moins cher.

(D) Parce que la mère était trop triste pour y rester après la mort de son mari.

65. Comment savez-vous que le narrateur était assez heureux dans le grand appartement?

(A) Il était plus jeune à cette époque-là.

(B) Il s'entendait très bien avec son père.

(C) Il en garde de beaux souvenirs.

(D) Il était sans un sou.

66. Pourquoi est-ce qu'il faisait froid dans l'appartement en hiver?

(A) Parce qu'il n'y avait pas de place pour mettre un pupitre.

(B) A cause de la brouhaha des voix.

(C) Le climat était très rude.

(D) Parce qu'il n'y avait pas de chauffage.

SÉCURITÉ MAXIMUM

Bosch lance une nouvelle génération d'appareils de froid qui maintiennent une réfrigération ventilée. Équipé du système Multiflux, le réfrigérateur-congélateur KSU 40600 assure une circulation complète de l'air et une température constante à tous les niveaux. Très fonctionnel et d'une grande capacité, il est doté de nombreux aménagements, dont un compartiment maxi-frais pour les aliments délicats et d'une fonction de sondes électroniques capables de déceler et de corriger les variations de température. Des spécificités qui diminuent considérablement les risques bactériologiques, comme la listéria. Et si le froid ne peut détruire cette bactérie, quelques règles d'hygiène alimentaire permettent de limiter son développement.

4 790 FF
Service consommateur :
01 49 48 31 31

67. Selon l'annonce, quels sont les principaux avantages de ce modèle ?

(A) Son ergonomie ultramoderne et le fait qu'il consomme peu d'électricité

(B) Il fait partie des modèles les moins chers du marché

(C) Il fait très peu de bruit et tout est contrôlé par ordinateur

(D) Il est spacieux et assure un excellent niveau de propreté

68. Qu'est-ce que cette annonce affirme à propos de l'hygiène ?

(A) Qu'il ne faut pas craindre les bactéries

(B) Qu'avec ce modèle, il n'y a plus aucun risque en ce qui concerne l'hygiène

(C) Qu'une basse température et quelques précautions alimentaires réduisent les risques de façon considérable

(D) Que ce modèle est le plus efficace pour réduire ce genre de risque

Le problème auquel se heurtent la plupart des villes françaises, c'est comment alléger le centre-ville des embouteillages, sans diminuer le nombre de personnes venues y faire des emplettes. La ville de Montpellier a répondu au problème d'une façon originale en inaugurant l'été dernier un système d'autobus gratuits. Ces bus font le tour des parkings en bordure du centre-ville toutes les dix minutes de 7h30 à 19 heures.

Après six mois d'expérience, les résultats sont fort encourageants. Le système fonctionne à 76% de sa capacité. Les habitués les plus nombreux sont les étudiants et les lycéens, suivis par les retraités. De tous les usagers, 26% reconnaissent ne plus prendre leur voiture dans le centre-ville.

69. La circulation et les embouteillages

    (A) sont un problème unique à Montpellier.

    (B) posent un problème à la plupart des villes françaises.

    (C) permettent aux gens de faire des emplettes.

    (D) inaugurent la saison d'été à Montpellier.

70. Comment est-ce que la ville de Montpellier a répondu au problème?

    (A) Ils ont inauguré un système de parkings gratuits en bordure du centre-ville.

    (B) Ils ont réduit le nombre de personnes venues en ville pour faire des courses.

    (C) Ils ont fait construire des routes en dehors de la ville.

    (D) Ils ont inauguré un système d'autobus gratuits qui font le tour des parkings en bordure du centre-ville.

71. Après six mois d'expérience, ils ont trouvé

    (A) qu'il n'y a que 76% des bus qui marchent.

    (B) que les retraités aiment suivre les routes des autobus.

    (C) que ce sont les étudiants et les lycéens que s'en servent le plus.

    (D) que 26% des habitués oublient où ils ont laissé leurs voiture.

Le 5 mai 1789, l'assemblée des états généraux se réunissait à Versailles en séance solennelle. A l'exception possible d'une infime minorité, personne ne souhaitait ni même ne prévoyait une révolution. Le tiers état, cependant, était unanime à réclamer une constitution garantissant l'égalité avec les deux autres ordres: la noblesse et le clergé. Le Roi avait résolu que les états voteraient par assemblée, ce qui devait mettre le tiers en minorité. L'assemblée du tiers état, affirmant qu'elle représentait 96 pour cent de la population, s'est déclarée "L'Assemblée des représentants de la nation."

Trois jours plus tard, dans un nouveau défi à la puissance royale, les députés du tiers état ont juré de ne pas se séparer avant d'avoir une constitution: c'est le célèbre serment du Jeu de Paume.

72. Dans l'assemblée des états généraux, "le tiers état"

(A) était un groupe de propriétaires qui réclamaient la terre du Roi.

(B) représentait la justice et les lois du pays.

(C) était chargé par la population de promulguer de nouvelles lois.

(D) était composé de tous ceux qui n'étaient ni de la noblesse ni du clergé.

73. Au début de la séance de l'assemblée des états généraux, qui prédisait une révolution?

(A) Personne que le Roi.

(B) La noblesse et le clergé la garantissaient.

(C) Le tiers état était unanime.

(D) Une très petite minorité.

74. Pourquoi le Roi voulait-il que les états votent ensemble par assemblée?

(A) Parce qu'il était résolu à créer un nouveau défi.

(B) Parce qu'il voulait mettre le tiers état en minorité.

(C) Parce qu'il voulait affirmer le droit du tiers état de représenter le peuple.

(D) Parce qu'il voulait insister sur l'égalité des trois ordres.

75. Dans le serment du Jeu de Paume, les députés du tiers état ont promis

(A) de se réunir avec la puissance royale.

(B) d'insister sur une constitution pour toute la France.

(C) de ne jamais se séparer de l'église.

(D) de se déclarer au-dessus des lois de la cour.

Henri Langlois était un homme jovial, affable, et peu élégant, mais c'était un des hommes les plus respectés du cinéma. Ce n'était pourtant ni un acteur, ni un scénariste, ni un réalisateur, ni un producteur. Henri Langlois était un collectionneur de films.

Pendant trente ans il en avait accumulé près de 50.000 qu'il conservait précieusement dans sa "Cinémathèque", véritable musée du cinéma. Voilà pourquoi il était connu dans le monde entier, et peut-être plus à l'étranger qu'en France. On lui téléphonait de partout pour lui demander s'il avait tel ou tel film. La réponse était presque toujours "oui".

En 1930, en effet, un grand nombre de films avaient déjà disparu. Certains avaient été détruits. Il fallait absolument préserver les premières manifestations d'un art qui venait de naître. Henri Langlois s'est attaché à sa mission avec une patience de détective et d'archéologue. Si nous connaissons aujourd'hui l'histoire de la première époque du cinéma, c'est grâce à lui.

76. Henri Langlois était un des hommes les plus respectés du cinéma

   (A) parce qu'il n'avait rien à faire ni avec les acteurs ni avec la production des films.

   (B) parce qu'il ne refusait jamais de prêter ses films.

   (C) parce qu'il a conservé des milliers de films qui autrement auraient disparu.

   (D) parce qu'il était toujours jovial et affable.

77. Dans sa "Cinémathèque," il

   (A) conservait tous les films qu'il avait collectionnés.

   (B) détruisait un grand nombre de films.

   (C) vendait à l'étranger aussi bien qu'en France des films précieux.

   (D) a caché des films pendant trente ans.

78. En 1930, le cinéma

   (A) était un art en train de disparaître.

   (B) était un art plus connu à l'étranger.

   (C) était encore un assez nouvel art.

   (D) était un art méprisé.

79. Henri Langlois a réussi parce qu'il

    (A) avait des contacts importants à l'étranger.

    (B) avait beaucoup de patience.

    (C) savait reconstruire les films disparus.

    (D) savait reconnaître le vrai talent.

80. Henri Langlois est un exemple

    (A) de l'archéologue parfait.

    (B) d'un homme raffiné et cultivé.

    (C) d'un homme qui s'est attaché à sa mission et qui l'a poursuivie.

    (D) d'un homme pieux et généreux.

"Je voudrais passionnément, déclarait Georges Pompidou (ancien Président de la République), que Paris possède un centre culturel qui soit à la fois un musée, un centre de création, où les arts plastiques voisineraient avec la musique, le cinéma, les livres, la recherche audio-visuelle." C'était en 1969.

Le 31 janvier 1977, le rêve de M. Pompidou est devenu réalité et le Président Giscard d'Estaing a inauguré un centre national d'art et de culture, le Centre Georges-Pompidou. On l'appelle familièrement "Beaubourg," du nom du vieux quartier médiéval situé près des Halles, le marché central de Paris, maintenant disparu. Aujourd'hui, le Centre est submergé. Pendant la première année, il a reçu 6 millions de visiteurs, c'est-à-dire, autant que le Louvre, le château de Versailles et la Tour Eiffel réunis.

Ce "paquebot" de la culture est 150 mètres de long, 60 mètres de large, et 42 mètres de haut. Les amoureux du vieux Paris poussent toujours des cris d'horreur devant cette boîte d'acier et de verre qui se dresse sur le plateau Beaubourg, entre Montmartre et Belleville. 800 personnes y travaillent en permanence. Dix milles visiteurs par jour ne réussissent pas à créer un embouteillage.

81. Qu'est-ce qui est arrivé le 31 janvier 1977?

    (A) Giscard d'Estaing est devenu Président.

    (B) Georges Pompidou, ancien Président, a eu un rêve prémonitoire.

    (C) Le Centre Georges-Pompidou s'est ouvert.

    (D) Le mérite des arts plastiques a été reconnu pour la première fois.

82. Qu'est-ce qu'on appelle familièrement "Beaubourg"?

    (A) le marché central de Paris

    (B) le Centre Georges-Pompidou

    (C) les Halles

    (D) tous les monuments réunis: le Louvre, etc.

83. Le Centre Georges-Pompidou se trouve

    (A) près de la Tour Eiffel

    (B) dans le marché central

    (C) dans les meilleurs rêves des hommes politiques

    (D) entre Montmartre et Belleville

84. Pendant sa première année,

    (A) le Centre a reçu autant de visiteurs que le Louvre, le château de Versailles et la Tour Eiffel réunis.

    (B) 800 personnes y sont perdus.

    (C) 10.000 personnes par jour ont créé des embouteillages.

    (D) le Centre a reçu 6 millions de visiteurs, moins que les autres musées.

85. En général, quelle en est l'opinion des amoureux du vieux Paris?

    (A) Ils trouvent que le Centre a créé des embouteillages.

    (B) Ils en ont très peur.

    (C) Ils ne l'aiment pas du tout.

    (D) Ils se dressent sur le plateau Beaubourg.

Lorsque j'y arrivai, je le trouvai assis, parmi les autres. Tous les anciens étaient là. Avec le chef Mbaka, cela faisait sept personnes … sept anciens du village pour me parler de mon cas. Les sept visages noirs prirent leur air des grandes occasions, renforcé par la pénombre de la pièce où se tenait la réunion. On me fit asseoir au milieu du groupe, et l'on me parla. Ce fut le chef lui-même qui parla le premier.

"Ecoute, fils," me dit-il, "je dois te dire que l'esprit de ton père est ici, avec nous, en ce moment même. Sache donc que nous ne faisons rien qui aille contre sa volonté. D'ailleurs, même s'il était encore vivant, il nous laisserait faire, car il avait confiance aux anciens."

Puis, il continua: "Nous allons te marier. C'est notre devoir de te marier. Mais, si à l'exemple de certains jeunes gens d'aujourd'hui, tu crois que tu peux mener à bien, tout seul, les affaires de ton propre mariage, nous sommes prêts à te laisser les mains libres et à ne plus nous occuper de toi dans ce domaine-là. Tu es libre de choisir ton propre chemin."

Je compris. Je devais choisir en toute liberté ce que je voulais faire, ou laisser faire. Liberté toute théorique d'ailleurs, car les anciens savaient bien que je ne pouvais pas choisir de vivre sans eux.

86. Pour quelle raison est-ce que tous les anciens du village se sont réunis?

(A) Pour ajouter une huitième personne à leur groupe.

(B) Pour prendre de l'air ensemble pendant la nuit.

(C) Pour discuter le mariage du narrateur.

(D) Pour conseiller au narrateur de s'enfuir avant l'aube.

87. Le père du narrateur

(A) était assis parmi les autres.

(B) était mort.

(C) était le chef Mbaka.

(D) n'était pas d'accord avec les anciens.

88. Pourquoi le groupe d'anciens voulait s'occuper des affaires du narrateur?

(A) Parce qu'ils aimaient les grandes occasions.

(B) Parce qu'ils voulaient le faire sentir la présence des esprits.

(C) Parce que c'était leur devoir.

(D) Pour montrer l'exemple aux jeunes gens du tribu.

L'EUROPE AU FIL DE L'EAU

Spécialiste du tourisme fluvial haut de gamme, **Athenæum** propose chaque année de prestigieuses croisières sur les fleuves européens. Ponctuées d'escales, où se succèdent représentations musicales, soirées de gala ou encore visites privées de palais et musées, elles sont riches en découvertes et en émotions. Ainsi, au printemps, embarquez pour trois destinations privilégiées : l'Elbe (du 08 au 16 mai 2002), le Danube (du 25 mai au 1ᵉʳ juin) ou encore une magnifique croisière thématique (du 19 au 30 juin), qui vous mènera des ors du Kremlin aux palais de Saint-Pétersbourg, pour des "Nuits Blanches" et mélodieuses en perspective.

Croisière au fil de l'Elbe à partir de 3 020 €
Croisière au fil du Danube à partir de 2 560 €
Croisière musicale des Nuits Blanches à partir de 3 570 €
Renseignements au : 01 58 36 08 36

89. Cette annonce souligne surtout :

(A) La proximité des destinations

(B) La durée des croisières

(C) Le luxe et l'exotisme des croisières

(D) La réputation de la société Athenæum

90. Laquelle des descriptions suivantes correspond le mieux à ces croisières selon cette annonce ?

(A) Animation et ambiance de fête

(B) Haute cuisine et méditation

(C) Divertissement pour toute la famille

(D) Scènes pastorales et cours de danse

SAT II: French Subject Test
Test III

ANSWER KEY

1.	(B)	24.	(A)	47.	(A)	70.	(D)
2.	(B)	25.	(D)	48.	(B)	71.	(C)
3.	(B)	26.	(B)	49.	(A)	72.	(D)
4.	(C)	27.	(D)	50.	(B)	73.	(D)
5.	(D)	28.	(C)	51.	(B)	74.	(B)
6.	(A)	29.	(A)	52.	(B)	75.	(B)
7.	(A)	30.	(B)	53.	(D)	76.	(C)
8.	(C)	31.	(B)	54.	(B)	77.	(A)
9	(A)	32.	(D)	55.	(D)	78.	(C)
10.	(A)	33.	(C)	56.	(A)	79.	(B)
11.	(B)	34.	(D)	57.	(C)	80.	(C)
12.	(B)	35.	(A)	58.	(D)	81.	(C)
13.	(D)	36.	(B)	59.	(B)	82.	(B)
14.	(B)	37.	(D)	60.	(C)	83.	(D)
15.	(A)	38.	(C)	61.	(B)	84.	(A)
16.	(C)	39.	(C)	62.	(A)	85.	(C)
17.	(B)	40.	(C)	63.	(B)	86.	(C)
18.	(A)	41.	(B)	64.	(C)	87.	(B)
19.	(B)	42.	(B)	65.	(C)	88.	(C)
20.	(B)	43.	(C)	66.	(D)	89.	(C)
21.	(A)	44.	(B)	67.	(D)	90.	(A)
22.	(C)	45.	(B)	68.	(C)		
23.	(B)	46.	(C)	69.	(B)		

DETAILED EXPLANATIONS
OF ANSWERS

PRACTICE TEST III

1. **(B)**
   Numéro (de téléphone) is the word for telephone number. Although numéro and nombre both mean number, the word numéro is used to refer to numbers in the sense of digits, alone or in succession. Nombre is usually used in a collective sense, as in "un grand nombre de personnes".

2. **(B)**
   Marcher means to work, in the sense of to operate properly, to be in working order. Travailler is never used in this sense.

3. **(B)**
   You need to recognize the words clous (nails), marteau (hammer) to select réparer (to repair).

4. **(C)**
   The idea of bringing or accompanying a person is expressed by the verb amener. The idea of bringing a thing or object is expressed by apporter. The two are never interchangeable. The verb prendre is not used with a person.

5. **(D)**
   Interdit means prohibited.

6. **(A)**
   If the soup (potage) was too hot, you would burn (se brûler) your tongue (la langue).

7. **(A)**
   La caisse means cash register and also cashier's post or check-out. Passer à la caisse means to go through the check-out. Le front is a false cognate; it means forehead.

8. **(C)**

Poisson means <u>fish</u>. <u>Poison</u> is a cognate meaning <u>poison</u>. <u>Aller à la pêche</u> means <u>to go fishing</u>, but the word <u>péché</u> means <u>sin</u>. Le <u>désert</u> (the desert) is not what you eat after a meal (le dessert).

9. **(A)**

<u>Un jour de congé</u> is <u>a day off</u> or <u>a holiday from work or school</u>.

10. **(A)**

<u>Mon réveil</u> is <u>my alarm clock</u>. <u>Se lever tard</u> means <u>to get up late</u>.

11. **(B)**

<u>Derrière</u> is a preposition meaning physically situated <u>behind, in back of</u>. <u>Devant</u> is the opposite, meaning <u>in front of</u>. <u>Avant</u> means <u>before, ahead of</u>. The opposite is <u>après</u>, meaning <u>after</u>. (Le professeur est <u>devant</u> la classe. Il part <u>après</u> les élèves, mais <u>avant</u> le Directeur.)

12. **(B)**

<u>Fois</u> means <u>time</u> in the sense of an occasion or time in succession. <u>Chaque fois</u> means <u>each time</u>; <u>la deuxième fois</u> means <u>the second time</u>; <u>trois fois</u> means <u>three times</u>. <u>Temps</u> refers to <u>time</u> as a general or abstract concept, as in "Il a beaucoup de temps libre." <u>Époque</u> refers to time in the sense of <u>era</u>, as in "à l'époque de Louis XVI".

13. **(D)**

If there is no <u>danger</u>, you need not <u>fear, be afraid</u> (avoir peur). <u>Le hasard</u> is a false cognate. It means <u>random chance, luck</u>.

14. **(B)**

<u>Grossir</u> means <u>to get fatter</u>. <u>Maigrir</u> is the opposite, <u>to get thinner</u>. When the subject is a person, <u>grandir</u> means <u>to get bigger in the sense of taller</u>.

15. **(A)**

<u>Le linge sale</u> is <u>the dirty laundry</u>. <u>Faire la lessive</u> is <u>to do the laundry</u>.

16. **(C)**

<u>Quelle bonne mine!</u> is a complimentary expression that means <u>You are looking healthy</u>. <u>La mine</u> refers to the aspect of the face. <u>Avoir les joues roses</u> means <u>to have pink cheeks</u>.

17. **(B)**
Un parapluie is an umbrella. Do not confuse pleuvoir with pleurer. Il pleut means it is raining. Il pleure means he is crying.

18. **(A)**
La lecture is a false congate; it always refers to a reading in French. Une conférence is the equivalent of the English word lecture.

19. **(B)**
Gratuit means free, at no cost.

20. **(B)**
The adjective ennuyé(e) means annoyed. The opposite is amusé(e). Ennuyeux (euse) means boring. The opposite is amusant(e). Avoir l'air fâché means look or seem angry.

21. **(A)**
L'aîné is the oldest child in a family; le cadet is the youngest. Un nouveau-né is a newborn. Un jumeau is a twin.

22. **(C)**
Assister à la messe means to go to mass. Assister is a false cognate; it means to attend, to be present at. Attendre is also a false cognate; it means to wait for. (J'ai attendu l'autobus pendant une heure.)

23. **(B)**
A tort is an adverbial locution meaning wrongly, incorrectly. Coupable is the opposite of innocent.

24. **(A)**
Prendre une décision is an idiomatic expression meaning to make a decision. Faire cannot be correct here.

25. **(D)**
Se rendre compte de means to realize, to understand. The verb réaliser in French means to realize in the sense to make real, as in "Il a réalisé son rêve" or "Il a réalisé une fortune."

26. **(B)**
S'entendre bien is an expression meaning to get along well (together). It is the opposite of se disputer (to argue) and also of se battre (to fight, in a physical, combative way).

27. **(D)**

Un pourboire is a tip. Un tuyau is a slang expression meaning a tip, as in a hint or a piece of advice. In a French restaurant, la nappe is the tablecloth, and la carte is the menu.

28. **(C)**

Do not confuse écouter (which refers to the activity of listening) with entendre (which means to hear). "J'ai écouté, mais je n'ai pas bien entendu."

29. **(A)**

L'épicier is the merchant who runs une épicerie, a small grocery store. One would not buy coffee from a neighbor, (voisin), a farmer (fermier), or a butcher (boucher).

30. **(B)**

Etre pressé means to be in a hurry. Le temps de bavarder means the time to chat. Arriéré means either mentally retarded or out-of-date.

31. **(B)**

The preposition à is the key to the correct answer. Obéir and ressembler (unlike their equivalents in English) are followed by an indirect object, introduced by à. Regarder, écouter, and attendre take a direct object, not preceded by a preposition.

32. **(D)**

The preposition en is the key to the correct answer. En, meaning in, to, or at precedes the names of geographical locations (continents, countries, provinces, and states) that are feminine. The preposition au is used before countries that are masculine. "Il va au Canada. Elle va au Japon."

33. **(C)**

No article is used after verbal or adjectival expressions that end in de, such as avoir besoin de (to need) and manquer de (to lack). The verbs prêter, gagner, and demander in this sentence would require a partitive article to express the idea of some. "Il demande de l'argent."

34. **(D)**

In the affirmative imperative, the indirect object pronoun me becomes moi when it is in the final position. "Donnez-le-moi!" but "Donnez-m'en!"

35. **(A)**

Disjunctive (or accentuated) pronouns refer to persons and are used after prepositions (<u>avec</u>, <u>sans</u>, <u>chez</u>, etc.) The disjunctive pronouns are: <u>moi</u>, <u>toi</u>, <u>lui/elle</u>, <u>nous</u>, <u>vous</u>, <u>eux/elles</u>.

36. **(B)**

<u>Qui</u> and <u>Qu'est-ce qui</u> are interrogative pronouns meaning <u>Who?</u> <u>Qui</u> is the short form.

37. **(D)**

The adjectives <u>beau</u>, <u>fou</u>, <u>mou</u>, <u>nouveau</u>, and <u>vieux</u> have a second masculine form, used before nouns beginning with a vowel or a mute h: <u>bel</u>, <u>fol</u>, <u>mol</u>, <u>nouvel</u>, and <u>vieil</u>.

38. **(C)**

When an action is performed by the subject on a part of his own body, a reflexive verb is usually used, and a definite article is used, not a possessive adjective, as in English. Je me suis cassé <u>le</u> bras, <u>la</u> cheville, <u>la</u> jambe, <u>le</u> nez, etc. When an object such as <u>la vase</u>, is broken, the action is not reflexive and the auxiliary verb <u>avoir</u> is used in the <u>passé composé</u>.

39. **(C)**

The past participle agrees in number and in gender with a direct object that precedes it. <u>Vue</u> agrees with <u>robe</u>, which is feminine singular.

40. **(C)**

<u>Regretter que</u> (which expresses the emotion of regret) requires the subjunctive in the dependent clause that follows.

41. **(B)**

<u>Nous</u> is the indirect object of <u>dire</u>. It answers the question: <u>A qui</u> faut-il dire la vérité? <u>Leur</u> is the only choice that is an indirect object pronoun.

42. **(B)**

Both parts of the negation (<u>ne + pas</u>, <u>ne + jamais</u>, <u>ne + plus</u>) are placed before the present infinitive.

43. **(C)**

This question tests possessive pronouns. <u>La leur</u> (theirs) replaces <u>leur maison</u> (their house). It agrees in gender (feminine) and number (singular) with the noun it replaces.

44. **(B)**

This question tests demonstrative pronouns. <u>Celle</u>, meaning <u>the one</u>, <u>this one</u>, replaces the singular feminine noun <u>photo</u>. The demonstrative pronouns are: <u>celui</u>, <u>celle</u>, <u>ceux</u>, and <u>celles</u>. <u>Cela</u> is a demonstrative pronoun that replaces an entire sentence or idea. "Qu'est-ce que tu penses de cela?"

45. **(B)**

Unlike English, the future tense is always used in French after <u>quand</u>, <u>lorsque</u>, (which mean <u>when</u>) and <u>aussitôt que</u> and <u>dès que</u> (which mean <u>as soon as</u>) when the verb expresses an action or condition that will occur in the future.

46. **(C)**

This question tests the manipulation of verb tenses in hypothetical statements. Because the verb of the result clause (<u>nous irons au cinéma</u>) is in the future tense, the verb of the "si clause" (the clause that states the condition) must be in the present tense.

47. **(A)**

<u>Qui</u> is the relative pronoun that functions as the subject in a relative clause. In this sentence, it is the subject of <u>passe</u>; <u>un bon film</u> is the antecedent.

48. **(B)**

<u>Que</u> is the relative pronoun that functions as a direct object in a relative clause. In this sentence, it is the direct object of <u>j'aimerais voir</u>; <u>un bon film</u> is the antecedent of this relative pronoun, also.

49. **(A)**

<u>Aimer</u> requires no preposition before its complementary infinitive.

50. **(B)**

<u>C'est possible que</u> requires the subjunctive in the dependent clause that follows.

51. **(B)**

<u>Etre sûr que</u> and its synonym <u>être certain que</u> are followed by the indicative mood. It is only when these expressions are in the negative or interrogative that they are followed by the subjunctive. <u>Auront</u> is incorrect because <u>il y a</u> is a fixed expression and must be in the singular in all tenses and moods.

52. **(B)**

The preposition <u>de</u> is part of the expression <u>avoir envie de</u>, meaning <u>to want</u>.

53. **(D)**

<u>Dont</u> is the relative pronoun that "absorbs" the preposition <u>de</u>. "C'est un film" + "Tout le monde parle <u>de</u> ce film" = "C'est un film <u>dont</u> tout le monde parle."

54. **(B)**

The definitive article is used in French (but omitted in English) before nouns used in a general or abstract sense. "<u>La</u> vie est difficile." "<u>Les</u> hommes sont aussi intelligents que <u>les</u> femmes." Since the direct objects of verbs like <u>aimer</u>, <u>préférer</u>, <u>détester</u>, are usually understood in a general sense, the definite article will commonly be used after these verbs. "J'aime le vin mais je déteste la bière."

55. **(D)**

The definite article (see #54 above) does not change in the negative.

56. **(A)**

<u>Vouloir</u> requires no preposition before its complementary infinitive.

57. **(C)**

Two rules of the <u>passé composé</u> apply here. 1.) Intransitive verbs like <u>aller</u> are conjugated with the auxiliary verb <u>être</u>, and 2.) the past participle of verbs conjugated with <u>être</u> agree with the subject.

58. **(D)**

After expressions of quantity such as <u>beaucoup de</u>, <u>trop de</u>, <u>peu de</u>, <u>un verre de</u>, <u>un kilo de</u>, <u>un sac de</u>, and <u>une bouteille de</u>, no article is used. Note that the preposition <u>de</u> is part of these expressions of quantity.

59. **(B)**

The partitive article expresses an unspecified amount or quantity.

60. **(C)**

<u>C'est dommage que</u> requires the subjunctive in the dependent clause that follows.

61. **(B)**

The answer is in lines 1 and 2. The sentence "Pour beaucoup de touristes étrangers, la France, c'est Paris" implies that Paris is the only part of France they ever visit or know. (A) is not the correct choice because it is only the <u>opinion</u> of many tourists.

62. **(A)**

The idea that Monsieur Smith is typical of many tourists is explicitly expressed in the phrase: "Chaque soir 2.000 étrangers comme Monsieur Smith …"

63. **(B)**

The answer is found in line 6: "…un grand autobus spécial pour les touristes."

64. **(C)**

<u>Alors</u>, meaning <u>and so</u> connects the idea of: "nous nous sommes trouvés très pauvres" with "nous avons dû quitter l'appartement."

65. **(C)**

You can infer that he was "happy" in the former apartment because he still has pleasant memories of it. "/Il/ en garde encore un très beau souvenir."

66. **(D)**

Even if you were not sure of the meaning of <u>glacé</u>, you might have guessed that it means <u>très froid</u>. You need to know or conclude that <u>chauffage</u> means <u>heat, heating system</u>. (Chaud means <u>warm</u>, <u>la chaleur</u> means <u>warmth</u>, and <u>chauffer</u> means <u>to warm</u>.)

67. **(D)**

There is no mention of this refrigerator's ultra-modern ergonomics or its limited consumption of electricity (<u>son ergonomie ultramoderne et le fait qu'il consomme peu d'électricité</u>). Nor is there any indication that it is one of the cheapest models on the market (<u>il fait partie des modèles les moins chers du marché</u>), which eliminates (A) and (B), respectively. Answer (C) cannot be right, because there is nothing in this ad about this model not making much noise and everything being computerized (<u>il fait très peu de bruit et tout est contrôlé par ordinateur</u>).

68. **(C)**

The answer is (C). This ad simply claims that its cool temperature (<u>le</u>

froid) and some basic precautions pertaining to food (<u>quelques règles d'hygiène alimentaire</u>) make it possible to limit the development of bacteria (<u>limiter son développement</u>). It does not claim that one need not fear bacteria (<u>il ne faut pas craindre les bactéries</u>), that this model completely eliminates all risks of this nature (<u>avec ce modèle, il n'y a plus aucun risque [. . .]</u>), or that this model is the most efficent at reducing such risks (<u>ce modèle est le plus efficace pour réduire ce genre de risque</u>), which eliminates choices (A), (B), and (D), respectively.

69. **(B)**
The answer is found in the first two lines. Although the sentence may present some difficult syntax and vocabulary, the meaning can be worked out. <u>Se heurter à</u> means <u>to come up against</u>, a meaning you might deduce from the word <u>problème</u> and the general context. The "problem" itself is defined after <u>C'est</u>; it is "comment alléger le centre-ville des embouteillages..." You may not know immediately that <u>alléger</u> means <u>to lighten</u>, but you probably do know that <u>léger, légère</u> means <u>light</u>. <u>Embouteillage</u> means <u>traffic bottleneck</u>; note that <u>bouteille</u> is embedded in the word.

70. **(D)**
The answer is taken directly from the last two lines of the first paragraph. Note that it is <u>les autobus</u>, and not <u>les parkings</u>, that are free (<u>gratuits</u>).

71. **(C)**
<u>Se servir de</u> means <u>to use</u>. "Les étudiants et les lycéens s'en servent le plus" is another way of saying "Les habitués les plus nombreux sont les étudiants et les lycéens."

72. **(D)**
Despite the difficult, and perhaps unfamiliar, subject matter of this text, it is a very straightforward and factual account. The key is to identify the correct portion of text that responds to each question asked. If the other two estates (les deux autres ordres) consisted of the nobility and the clerics, then you can conclude that <u>le tiers état</u> must have included everyone else, or those who were neither from the nobility nor from the clergy.

73. **(D)**
The answer is in the sentence: "A l'exception possible d'une infime (très petite) minorité, personne ne souhaitait ni prévoyait une révolution." You might deduce that <u>prévoir</u> is to <u>foresee</u> and that <u>prédire</u> is to <u>foretell</u>.

74. **(B)**

  The answer is in the sentence: "Le Roi ... ce qui devait mettre le tiers en minorité."

75. **(B)**

  The answer is in the last two lines: "Les députés ont juré de ne pas se séparer ... serment du Jeu de Paume."

76. **(C)**

  He was "un collectionneur de films" (last line of first paragraph) who had accumulated almost 50,000 films (first line of second paragraph.) A great number of films had already disappeared (first line of third paragraph.)

77. **(A)**

  His "Cinémathèque" is described as a kind of "museum" (<u>musée</u>) where he kept and preserved (<u>conserver</u>) his collection of films.

78. **(C)**

  The answer is in the last paragraph that describes the cinema as "un art qui venait de naître", and was in other words, "a relatively recent or new art."

79. **(B)**

  He pursued his goal with the patience of a detective and an archeologist, two professions that require a great deal of patience.

80. **(C)**

  <u>Poursuivre</u> ("il l'a poursuivie") means <u>to pursue</u>, <u>follow through</u>. He was not an archeologist; he only had the patience of one. No information in the text tells you that he was either "refined and cultivated" or "pious and generous."

81. **(C)**

  The answer is in the first sentence of the second paragraph. "Le 31 janvier 1977, ...le Président Giscard d'Estaing a inauguré ... le Centre Georges-Pompidou."

82. **(B)**

  In the sentence: "On l'appelle familièrement "Beaubourg", the <u>l'</u> refers to the noun that is closest to it in the preceding sentence, which is le Centre Pompidou.

83. **(D)**
The answer is in the second sentence of the last paragraph. "[C]ette boîte d'acier et de verre" refers to le Centre Pompidou, which rises (se dresser) "sur le plateau Beaubourg, entre Montmartre et Belleville."

84. **(A)**
The answer is taken directly from the first sentence of the second paragraph.

85. **(C)**
"[Ils] poussent toujours des cris d'horreur" is a vivid way to say: "Ils ne l'aiment pas du tout."

86. **(C)**
You need to put together two pieces of information. 1.) From the first paragraph, that the seven elders of the village had assembled to talk to the narrator about his "case" ([son] cas), and 2.) from the third paragraph, the statement of Mbaka to the narrator: "Nous allons te marier."

87. **(B)**
In the second paragraph, the phrase "même s'il était encore vivant" makes it clear that the narrator's father is dead.

88. **(C)**
The answer is in the words of Mbaka to the narrator: "C'est notre devoir de te marier."

89. **(C)**
The answer is (C). This ad primarily stresses (cette annonce souligne surtout) the luxury and exoticism of the cruises (le luxe at l'exotisme des croisières). Travel to nearby destinations (la proximité des destinations) is not the central idea being conveyed here, which eliminates choice (A). Although the length of the cruises is mentioned in the form of excursion dates in May and June, this is clearly not the main selling point here. Thus, (B) cannot be the answer either. Likewise, although the name of the company (Athenæum) and a brief description of what it offers (préstigieuses croisières sur les fleuves européens) are of course mentioned, the reputation of the Athenæum company cannot be said to be the key point being made here.

90. **(A)**

Although it would not be unreasonable to assume that fine cuisine (<u>la haute cuisine</u>) is served on these cruises, it is not mentioned, and nor is meditation (<u>la méditation</u>), which therefore eliminates answer (B). Likewise, since no mention is made of activities specifically geared towards children or teenagers, entertainment for the whole family (<u>Divertissement pour toute la famille</u>) is not a logical assumption based on the information provided, hence (C) cannot be the answer. As for (D), there is neither anything in this ad about pastoral scenes (<u>les scènes pastorales</u>) nor about dance lessons (<u>les cours de danse</u>), which leaves (A) animation and a festive atmosphere (<u>animation et une ambiance de fête</u>) as the only logical answer.

SAT II: SUBJECT TEST IN

FRENCH

PRACTICE TEST IV

FRENCH TEST IV

PART A

Time: 1 Hour
         90 Questions

DIRECTIONS: This part consists of a number of incomplete statements, each followed by four suggested completions. Select the most appropriate completion and blacken the corresponding space on the answer sheet.

1. Si tu veux voyager en Europe l'été prochain, il faut faire ...

    (A) des fautes   (C) des bêtises

    (B) des économies   (D) du sauvetage

2. Jean roule trop vite. Il ... mal aujourd'hui.

    (A) marche   (C) danse

    (B) joue   (D) conduit

3. Quand j'ai ..., je me couche.

    (A) faim   (C) sommeil

    (B) honte   (D) chaud

4. On emploie un pinceau pour faire ...

    (A) un essai   (C) une table

    (B) un tableau   (D) un roman

5. Marc essaie de ... à ses examens.

    (A) réussir   (C) passer

    (B) succéder   (D) organiser

6. Il pleut maintenant et Louise est fâchée parce qu'elle a oublié son ...

   (A) patin

   (B) pourboire

   (C) papier

   (D) parapluie

7. "Un ancien ami" veut dire ...

   (A) un vieil ami

   (B) un ami qu'on ne voit plus

   (C) un ennemi

   (D) un copain

8. Simone est ... chez elle à minuit.

   (A) rencontré

   (B) rentrée

   (C) rendue

   (D) raconté

9. Céleste adore parler. Sa mère dit qu'elle est trop ...

   (A) brave

   (B) parlant

   (C) bavarde

   (D) bruyant

10. Les jeunes Français aiment assister aux ... américains.

    (A) films

    (B) disques

    (C) vêtements

    (D) travaux

11. Quand vous rencontrez Monsieur Dupont, vous lui ... la main.

    (A) saurez

    (B) serez

    (C) serrez

    (D) seriez

12. Pierre achète ... avec son argent de poche.

    (A) un magazine

    (B) un yacht

    (C) une maison

    (D) un magasin

13. On porte un maillot de bain ...

    (A) à l'opéra

    (B) au désert

    (C) à la salle de bains

    (D) à la plage

14. François déteste travailler parce qu'il est très …

    (A) sportif   (C) paresseux

    (B) ambitieux   (D) pareil

15. Avant de se lever le matin, il faut …

    (A) se laver   (C) se raser

    (B) s'habiller   (D) se réveiller

16. A cause d'une panne d'essence nous avons …

    (A) marché à la station-service

    (B) préparé un autre sandwich

    (C) écrit au président

    (D) acheté du parfum élégant

17. Si vous souriez beaucoup, vous êtes généralement …

    (A) souffrant   (C) triste

    (B) heureux   (D) déprimé

18. Paul est fauché cette semaine. Il …

    (A) n'a pas d'argent (C) ne dit pas la vérité

    (B) est en colère   (D) est très riche

19. Elle était entourée, juste … de la foule.

    (A) au dehors   (C) à côté

    (B) au milieu   (D) une lieue

20. "Actuellement" veut dire …

    (A) en réalité   (C) maintenant

    (B) par une action   (D) véritablement

21. Avant le concert nous faisons … pour acheter nos billets.

    (A) la moue   (C) la quiche

    (B) la ligne   (D) la queue

22. Pour maigrir il faut ...

    (A) ne pas trop parler   (C) dormir huit heures

    (B) suivre un régime   (D) suivre son chemin

23. Si nous ne gagnons pas le match, nous ...

    (A) serons déçus   (C) allons sauter de joie

    (B) ne fumerons plus   (D) serons contents

24. On fabrique du tissu dans ...

    (A) une ferme   (C) un facteur

    (B) une facture   (D) une usine

25. Selon le proverbe, "Mieux vaut ... que jamais."

    (A) tôt   (C) tard

    (B) toujours   (D) tant

26. Parce que Georges est enrhumé, il a mal ...

    (A) à la cheville   (C) au poignet

    (B) à la gorge   (D) au pied

27. Un exemple d'un fruit de mer est ...

    (A) un bateau   (C) une pomme

    (B) un poison   (D) un poisson

PART B

DIRECTIONS: In each of the sentences in this part of the test, one or more words are underlined. One of the four choices following each sentence can be correctly substituted for the underlined word(s) to form a grammatically correct statement or question. The new sentence may differ in meaning from the original example. Select the one choice which fits grammatically into the original sentence and blacken the corresponding space on the answer sheet.

28. Nous nous <u>amusons</u> le dimanche.

    (A) promenons

    (B) mangeons

    (C) dormons

    (D) souvenons

29. Patrice <u>écoute</u> souvent ses amis.

    (A) obéit

    (B) téléphone

    (C) invite

    (D) écrit

30. Il est préférable que nous <u>mangions</u> ensemble.

    (A) voyageons

    (B) voyagerions

    (C) travaillons

    (D) travaillions

31. <u>Sous</u> la table, il y avait beaucoup de livres.

    (A) avant

    (B) près

    (C) devant

    (D) parmi

32. Nous comptons passer une soirée agréable chez <u>Laurent</u>.

    (A) leur

    (B) les

    (C) ils

    (D) eux

33. Cet homme est une <u>victime</u> pitoyable.

   (A) personne   (C) être

   (B) individu   (D) type

34. Le nouvel <u>appartement</u> est très beau.

   (A) arbre   (C) adresse

   (B) auto   (D) amie

35. Voulez-vous que Paul <u>sorte</u> avec nous ce week-end?

   (A) va   (C) ira

   (B) aille   (D) allait

36. On dit que cette femme est <u>riche</u>.

   (A) naïf   (C) content

   (B) bel   (D) nerveuse

37. En <u>parlant</u> à Maurice, Yvette a souri.

   (A) regardant   (C) téléphonant

   (B) écoutant   (D) entendant

38. Je <u>me reposerais</u> si j'étais à Hawaii.

   (A) m'amuserais   (C) me souvenais

   (B) me rappelais   (D) m'endormais

39. Quand Henri <u>sera</u> à Rome, il nous écrira.

   (A) est   (C) arrive

   (B) arrivera   (D) va

40. Que <u>désire</u>-t-elle faire ce soir?

   (A) veut   (C) vient

   (B) voudrait   (D) va

41. C'est la <u>troisième</u> fois que je lis ce livre.

    (A) premier

    (C) dernier

    (B) première

    (D) cinq

42. Il fallait que nous <u>sachions</u> la vérité.

    (A) disons

    (C) dirons

    (B) dirions

    (D) disions

43. Pauline est partie sans <u>nous</u> écrire.

    (A) avoir

    (C) la

    (B) toi

    (D) leur

44. Quel est ton <u>disque</u> préféré?

    (A) couleur

    (C) cours

    (B) saison

    (D) peinture

45. Je sais <u>son numéro de téléphone</u>.

    (A) le nom de cet homme

    (C) une femme célèbre

    (B) un bon restaurant

    (D) cette belle ville

PART C

Samedi dernier Paul et Margot _____ ensemble et ils _____ au cinéma

46. (A) ont sorti   47. (A) iraient

   (B) sortaient   (B) sont allés

   (C) sont sortis   (C) étaient allés

   (D) sont sorties   (D) allaient

où ils _____ Marie et Jeanne, _____ bonnes amies.

48. (A) ont vus   49. (A) leurs

   (B) ont vues   (B) leur

   (C) voyaient   (C) ses

   (D) ont vu   (D) sa

Après le film, tout le monde _____ faim, mais malheureusement,

50. (A) avaient

   (B) a eu

   (C) avait

   (D) ont eu

_____ les restaurants étaient fermés. "Venez chez moi," a dit Jeanne.

51. (A) tout

    (B) toute

    (C) toutes

    (D) tous

"J'ai _____ de préparer une omelette pour nous tous."

52. (A) honte

    (B) envie

    (C) mal

    (D) peur

Georges et Gertrude sont _____ bons copains qui aiment _____ faire

53. (A) – –   54. (A) – –

    (B) des   (B) de

    (C) de   (C) à

    (D) les   (D) que

beaucoup _____ choses ensemble. Ils _____ ensemble, ils sortent

55. (A) – –   56. (A) étudient

    (B) des   (B) études

    (C) les   (C) étudiaient

    (D) de   (D) ont étudié

ensemble, et ils se parlent au téléphone chaque soir. La mère de Georges et le père de Gertrude demandent: "Mais _____ est-ce que

57. (A) que

    (B) qu'

    (C) qui

    (D) quoi

vous avez à vous dire? Vous vous voyez _____ la journée et vous

58. (A) tout

    (B) tous

    (C) toutes

    (D) toute

vous parlez chaque soir!" Les parents ne _____ pas que le téléphone

59. (A) voulaient

    (B) voudrons

    (C) veulent

    (D) veuillent

_____ occupé quand ils sont chez _____ parce qu'ils s'attendent

60. (A) être   61. (A) ils

    (B) soit   (B) leurs

    (C) sera   (C) elles

    (D) est   (D) eux

souvent à des coups de téléphone. Alors les jeunes
gens _____ ont promis _____ ne pas parler au

62. (A) leur   63. (A) − −

    (B) les   (B) à

    (C) leurs   (C) de

    (D) lui   (D) que

téléphone plus de quinze minutes par jour. Les croyez-vous?

PART D

Le mois de juillet est le mois du Tour de France, le plus grand, le plus difficile, et le plus célèbre concours de vélo qui existe au monde. Chaque matin on lit les nouvelles des "géants de la route", on discute leur progrès et leurs problèmes. Chaque soir on regarde la télé afin de suivre les étapes de ce voyage de 23 jours — "la grande boucle," qui traverse villes, villages, montagnes et plaines et qui finit dans les rues de Paris.

En 1986, devant une foule de 250.000 personnes, un nouveau champion arriva aux Champs-Elysées et reçut des mains du Premier Ministre Jacques Chirac le célèbre "maillot jaune," symbole précieux du gagnant. Le Tour de 1986 (le 73ème) marqua un moment historique: pour la première fois, un Américain emporta la victoire et gagna non seulement le maillot célèbre mais aussi plusieurs prix importants. Le conquérant, Greg Lemond, avait participé au Tour en 1984 et en 1985, et sa victoire fut prévue par la majorité des dévots du concours.

64. Le Tour de France se réfère à

   (A) un monument célèbre de Paris

   (B) un concours difficile

   (C) un concert international

   (D) un voyage tranquille

65. Le Tour de France existe depuis

   (A) le 19ème siècle

   (B) 1973

   (C) plus de soixante-dix ans

   (D) le Moyen-Age

66. Les "géants de la route" sont

   (A) des montagnes énormes

   (B) les gens qui parlent à la télé

   (C) des grands arbres à la campagne

   (D) les cyclistes du Tour

Couronne et fond vissés - 100 heures de réserve de marche - 100 mètres étanche - 100 jours de contrôle

DEPUIS 1735 IL N'EXISTE PAS DE MONTRE BLANCPAIN
À QUARTZ. ET IL N'Y EN AURA JAMAIS.

En 1994, Blancpain présente en première mondiale un nouveau concept de montre.

Réalisée avec le savoir-faire que Blancpain perpétue depuis 1735, aussi élégante que fonctionnelle, cette montre symbolise un art de vivre conciliant des traditions et culture actuelle, et peut se porter en toutes circonstances.

PARIS: Arfan - Bry - Buccellati -
O.J. Perrin - Royal Quartz - Wempe

En hommage à son fondateur Jehan-Jacques Blancpain et aux générations de maîtres-horlogers qui lui ont succédé depuis le Siècle des Lumières, Blancpain célèbre l'avènement du nouveau millénaire par un chef-d'oeuvre qui, du 18e au 21 siècle, scelle une alliance tricentenaire.

Montre 2100 de Blancpain
L'alliance des siècles

67. Pour donner une image de classe et de luxe à cette montre, la société Blancpain mise surtout sur :

   (A) Le rapport qualité-prix

   (B) La tradition que représente le nom Blancpain

   (C) Le fait qu'elle est vendue dans de nombreuses grandes villes

   (D) Le quartz

68. On peut supposer que la société Blancpain s'adresse avant tout à une clientèle :

   (A) Pragmatique

   (B) Rurale

   (C) Fine

   (D) Modeste

Nicolas entraîna Marise au deuxième étage du musée, tout impatient de lui montrer la splendide toile de Vermeer qu'il admirait tant. Il fallait se dépêcher parce qu'il faisait déjà tard et l'on allait bientôt fermer les portes du bâtiment.

— Vite, suis-moi! s'écria Nicolas. Tu vas voir pourquoi je travaille depuis six mois sur ma copie de cette peinture formidable. Étudiant d'art, le jeune homme avait du talent mais était assez difficile à vivre.

— Laisse-moi respirer un moment! pria Marise, épuisée. Nous ne faisons que courir comme des fous depuis une demi-heure! Et elle s'arrêta devant une grande sculpture.

— Bon, bon, repose-toi un peu, répondit le jeune homme impatient. Mais après un instant, il lui prit la main.

— Écoute, il se fait tard; on va bientôt nous mettre à la porte. Viens!

Fatiguée, Marise se mit à courir encore une fois le long du couloir, à côté de son ami. Enfin, ils arrivèrent dans une salle où se trouvait la célèbre "Dentellière" du maître hollandais Jan Vermeer. Malgré l'heure tardive, il s'y trouvait une grande foule de touristes et d'étudiants. Les gens remplissaient la salle et empêchaient les deux amis de voir la peinture. Et, pour combler leur déception, immédiatement après leur arrivée on signala la fermeture du musée.

— Zut! dit Nicolas, énervé. On doit retourner demain. Mais cette fois-ci, sois prête quand j'arriverai!

69. On peut dire que ce jour-là Nicolas était

   (A) assez ennuyeux

   (B) détendu

   (C) fatigué

   (D) agité

70. Une personne qui est "difficile à vivre"

   (A) est gravement malade

   (B) s'impatiente facilement

   (C) fait toujours plaisir aux autres

   (D) ne s'énerve jamais

71. Le "maître hollandais" se réfère à

    (A) un peintre célèbre

    (B) une peinture fameuse

    (C) un cigare coûteux

    (D) un professeur d'art

72. Nicolas fait une copie de la toile parce qu'il

    (A) veut la vendre

    (B) peut faire mieux

    (C) veut la montrer à ses amis

    (D) est étudiant d'art

73. Les deux amis sont déçus parce qu(e)

    (A) la peinture n'est pas visible

    (B) le musée est vide

    (C) le tableau n'est pas bon

    (D) ils sont fatigués

74. "Zut!" est une expression de

    (A) joie   (C) surprise

    (B) tristesse   (D) colère

A la fin du 17ème siècle, Jean de La Bruyère publia Les Caractères, une série de portraits des gens de la cour et de la ville. L'aspect critique de cet œuvre créa beaucoup d'hostilité envers l'auteur, et plusieurs de ses ennemis montèrent une campagne amère contre lui au moment de son élection à l'Académie française. Néanmoins, le public aimait bien l'œuvre et tout le monde essayait de deviner les identités des personnes y dépeintes. Contre les protestations de La Bruyère, on circulait même des "clefs" qui prétendaient révéler les modèles de ces descriptions incisives.

Dans un de ses portraits célèbres, La Bruyère décrit Giton, un individu cru, impoli, d'une intelligence médiocre, mais d'une vanité extrême. Cet homme a des habitudes choquantes: il déploie un grand mouchoir en public et se mouche bruyamment; il crache loin et éternue haut; quand une autre personne parle, il ne l'écoute pas; quand il s'ennuie, même en compagnie, il s'endort et ronfle. Malgré ces traits peu admirables, plusieurs gens entourent Giton, l'écoutent attentivement et se trouvent toujours d'accord avec tout ce qu'il dit. On rit quand il rit, on croit ce qu'il raconte; s'il marche, on marche, s'il s'arrête, on s'arrête.

Pourquoi fait-on la cour à ce monstre mal élevé? La raison en est très simple, nous dit La Bruyère: il est riche.

75. Jean de La Bruyère fut

   (A) écrivain

   (B) peintre

   (C) compositeur

   (D) dramaturge

76. Dans Les Caractères, il s'agit

   (A) d'une pièce de théâtre

   (B) d'un roman historique

   (C) des contes de fée

   (D) des images de la société

77. On essaya d'empêcher

   (A) la publication de l'œuvre

   (B) l'élection de l'auteur à l'Académie française

   (C) l'identification des personnages

   (D) la vente des portraits

78. L'œuvre de La Bruyère fut populaire parce qu(e)

   (A) elle dépeignit des personnes réelles

   (B) les lecteurs reconnaissaient les personnages

   (C) l'auteur publia des "clefs" pour identifier les gens

   (D) l'auteur avait beaucoup d'amis dans la société

79. Giton est "peu admirable" parce qu(e)

    (A) tout le monde l'imite

    (B) il dort beaucoup

    (C) il n'aime pas l'exercice

    (D) il ne respecte personne

80. La conclusion de cet extrait

    (A) implique que les riches sont impolis

    (B) explique pourquoi Giton est toléré

    (C) montre les problèmes de Giton

    (D) est une déclaration basée sur les faits

Barbara et Frédéric étudiaient le français au lycée et essayaient toujours de parler la langue quand ils étaient ensemble. Quelquefois les gens dans la rue les prenaient pour des Français — une situation qui rendait les deux amis très contents. Dans la petite ville où ils habitaient, les touristes européens étaient rares. Alors Barbara et "Frédo" (comme elle l'appelait) aimaient jouer le rôle de "Parisiens." Ils portaient souvent le costume populaire des jeunes gens français: le blue-jean bien serré, un pullover, un veston en cuir noir et, naturellement, des lunettes de soleil "super cool."

Un jour, les copains eurent la bonne fortune d'aller à Chicago, la plus grande ville de la région, pour célébrer l'anniversaire de Barbara. A midi, ils sont allés dans un bon petit restaurant français. (Le père de Frédo lui avait prêté assez d'argent pour inviter Barbara.) Les amis étaient fiers de pouvoir commander leur déjeuner en français et ils bavardaient avec le serveur, un jeune homme amical qui les félicita de leur bonne prononciation. Comme font les Français, on a commencé avec des hors-d'œuvre variés, suivis d'une bonne soupe à l'oignon, puis du coq-au-vin avec des carottes vichy et enfin, de la salade. C'était un repas délicieux.

Enfin il fallait commander le dessert. Très confiante, Barbara a dit au serveur, "Je voudrais un mousse au chocolat, s'il vous plaît." Le serveur a éclaté de rire! "En êtes-vous certaine, mademoiselle?" demanda-t-il. Un peu embarrassée, Barbara a répondu, "Mais oui. Je l'aime beaucoup." Encore une fois le serveur a ri et la jeune femme se trouvait confondue. Ni elle ni Frédo ne savaient pourquoi il riait.

Rentrée chez elle, Barbara chercha "mousse" au dictionnaire. Quelle surprise! Le mot existait au masculin et au féminin!

"Ah, s'est-elle dit, je vois maintenant pourquoi il a ri quand j'ai commandé "un mousse." J'ai commandé "un jeune garçon qui travaille sur un bateau!"

81. Barbara et Frédo parlent français

    (A) seulement en cours

    (B) pour impressionner leurs parents

    (C) quand ils sont ensemble

    (D) à la maison

82. On porte un "veston"

    (A) quand il fait frais

    (B) quand il fait chaud

    (C) pour se baigner

    (D) quand on se couche

83. Les passants pensent que les amis sont de la France parce qu(e)

    (A) ils accompagnent des touristes

    (B) tout le monde parle français dans la ville

    (C) ils portent des lunettes de soleil

    (D) ils essaient d'avoir l'air français

84. L'expression "super cool" est un exemple

    (A) du "franglais"

    (B) de l'ancien français

    (C) de l'influence italienne

    (D) du français formel

85. Barbara et Frédo vont à Chicago

    (A) pour rencontrer des touristes

    (B) pour visiter la grande ville

    (C) pour fêter l'anniversaire de Barbara

    (D) pour acheter des vêtements français

86. Au restaurant, Barbara et Frédo

    (A) sont un peu perdus

    (B) sont ravis de pouvoir parler français

    (C) ont des gros problèmes avec le serveur

    (D) ne savent pas ce qu'il faut faire

87. Les Français prennent leur salade

    (A) avant le repas

    (B) comme entrée

    (C) avec le plat principal

    (D) après le plat principal

88. Frédo peut payer l'addition parce qu(e)

    (A) il prend de l'argent de Barbara

    (B) c'est l'anniversaire de son amie

    (C) son père lui a donné assez d'argent

    (D) il a une carte de crédit

89. Cet immeuble appartient à :

    (A) Un particulier qui loue des chambres

    (B) Une famille nombreuse

    (C) La ville de Paris

    (D) Une société privée

90. Ce qui rend « Le Kennedy » exceptionnel, c'est :

    (A) Un barème de prix pour accomoder les riches et les moins riches

    (B) Le fait qu'il se situe à côté d'un parc tout en étant à deux pas de
         la Tour Eiffel

    (C) Sa proximité des transports publics

    (D) Le fait que son espace de vente est ouvert le mercredi

SAT II: French Subject Test
Test IV

ANSWER KEY

1.	(B)	24.	(D)	47.	(B)	70.	(B)
2.	(D)	25.	(C)	48.	(D)	71.	(A)
3.	(C)	26.	(B)	49.	(A)	72.	(D)
4.	(B)	27.	(D)	50.	(C)	73.	(A)
5.	(A)	28.	(A)	51.	(D)	74.	(D)
6.	(D)	29.	(C)	52.	(B)	75.	(A)
7.	(B)	30.	(D)	53.	(C)	76.	(D)
8.	(B)	31.	(C)	54.	(A)	77.	(B)
9	(C)	32.	(D)	55.	(D)	78.	(A)
10.	(A)	33.	(A)	56.	(A)	79.	(D)
11.	(C)	34.	(A)	57.	(B)	80.	(B)
12.	(A)	35.	(B)	58.	(D)	81.	(C)
13.	(D)	36.	(D)	59.	(C)	82.	(A)
14.	(C)	37.	(C)	60.	(B)	83.	(D)
15.	(D)	38.	(A)	61.	(D)	84.	(A)
16.	(A)	39.	(B)	62.	(A)	85.	(C)
17.	(B)	40.	(D)	63.	(C)	86.	(B)
18.	(A)	41.	(B)	64.	(B)	87.	(D)
19.	(B)	42.	(D)	65.	(C)	88.	(C)
20.	(C)	43.	(D)	66.	(D)	89.	(D)
21.	(D)	44.	(C)	67.	(B)	90.	(B)
22.	(B)	45.	(A)	68.	(C)		
23.	(A)	46.	(C)	69.	(D)		

DETAILED EXPLANATIONS
OF ANSWERS
PRACTICE TEST IV

1. **(B)**
    This question tests your understanding of idiomatic expressions based on "faire." In the context, you must <u>save money</u>, "faire des économies," if you are to go to Europe next summer. (A) "faire des fautes" = to make mistakes; and (C) "faire des bêtises" = to do foolish things, are incorrect. (D) "faire du sauvetage," while it may look somewhat like the English "saving," refers to saving lives. Thus, (B) is the only correct response.

2. **(D)**
    Since the verb of the example is "roule," we are talking about the movement of a car ("goes" or "runs"). The only logical answer must deal with driving. Neither (B) "joue" = plays, nor (C) "danse" = dances, is possible. (A) "marche," = goes, "doing" (# of m.p.h.), while used to describe motors and cars, is not logical in this context, since we are referring to John and not his car. Only (D) "conduit" = drives, is acceptable.

3. **(C)**
    Logically, I go to bed when I'm sleepy (C) "j'ai sommeil," rather than when (A) "j'ai faim" = I'm hungry, (B) "j'ai honte" = I'm ashamed, or (D) "j'ai chaud" = I'm warm. French uses "avoir" to express many personal feelings and conditions, both physical and emotional, whereas English uses "to be" for these descriptions.

4. **(B)**
    You use a paintbrush, "pinceau," to make (B) "un tableau" = a painting. Although (C) "une table" looks and sounds similar to "tableau," it means table. (A) "un essai" = an essay and (D) "un roman" = a novel, would not be written with a paintbrush.

5. **(A)**
    Three of the four verbs given as choices do not take "à" before an infinitive, while "réussir" does. (B) "Succéder" = to follow, or to succeed, to come after, as in "The prince will succeed his mother, the queen, to the throne." Be careful of this *faux ami*. (C) "passer" un examen = to take an

exam, not necessarily to pass it, is another trap for the unwary; (D) "organiser" is obviously incorrect.

6. **(D)**

Although all four nouns begin with "p," that is all they have in common lexically. (A) un "patin" = a skate; (B) "pourboire" = a tip (left for a waiter); (C) "papier" is an English cognate which makes no sense in the context of Louise's being angry because she forgot her umbrella (D) "parapluie", and is now getting wet in the rain.

7. **(B)**

A few adjectives in French change meaning according to whether they precede or follow the noun: "ancien" before the noun = former; following the noun, it means old. Therefore, (B) "un ami qu' on ne voit plus" = a friend whom one no longer sees, is the best choice. (A) "un vieil ami" = an elderly friend, (C) "un ennemi," and (D) "un copain" = a pal, are all incorrect.

8. **(B)**

Although all choices begin with "r," neither (A) "rencontré" = met, (C) "rendue" = gave back, returned (not for a person coming back to a place, but for an object being returned), nor (D) "raconté" = told (a story, etc.) is possible in this context. In addition, "rencontré," "rendue" and "raconté" all take "avoir," not "être," in the *passé composé*. Only (B) "rentrée" = to return home, is correct.

9. **(C)**

The correct answer (C) "bavarde" = talkative, is the most logical choice. While Céleste may be (A) "brave" = courageous or nice, this is irrelevant to the fact that she loves to talk = "adore parler." (B) "parlant" = speaking, seems possible at first glance, since it is related to "parler," but this present participle is generally used after "en" to mean "while speaking," and is therefore incorrect. (D) "bruyant" = noisy, which is not necessarily true of someone who talks a lot; it is also masculine and therefore not possible either.

10. **(A)**

"Assister" is a *faux ami* which does not mean "to assist" or "to help," but rather "to attend." Thus (A) "films" is the only possible answer. (B) "disques" = records and (C) "vêtements" = clothing, are not "attendable" events. (D) "travaux" = works (plural of "travail") is also incorrect in this context.

11. **(C)**
This example tests your verb skills as well as your grasp of vocabulary. Since "rencontrer" = to meet, keep in mind the custom of shaking hands. (A) "saurez" = you will know, (B) "serez" = you will be, and (D) "seriez" = you would be (conditional), are not appropriate. Only (C) "serrez" is logical because "serrer la main" is an idiomatic expression meaning "to shake hands."

12. **(A)**
"Argent de poche" = pocket money, and is therefore sufficient to buy only small items, such as (A) "un magazine." (B) "yacht," (C) "maison" = house, and (D) "magasin" = store, are incorrect, because they are all too expensive to buy with pocket money.

13. **(D)**
One wears a "maillot de bain" = a swimsuit, at the beach, (D) "la plage." Neither (A) "à l'opéra," (B) "au désert," nor (C) "à la salle de bains" = to the bathroom," is correct.

14. **(C)**
Since François doesn't like to work ("travailler"), it is logical to consider him (C) "paresseux" = lazy, rather than (A) "sportif" = athletic, or (B) "ambitieux." (D) "pareil" = the same, begins like "paresseux" but makes no sense in this example.

15. **(D)**
These reflexive verbs are all involved with early morning actions, but you must remember that "se lever" means to get up (out of bed). Thus, in order to get washed (A) "se laver," dressed (B) "s'habiller," or shaved (C) "se raser," it is first necessary to (D) "se réveiller" = to wake up. Don't confuse "se lever" with "se laver" or "se réveiller."

16. **(A)**
"Une panne d'essence" = a lack of gas; "panne" is also used for other forms of mechanical breakdown, e.g., "une panne d'électricité." It has nothing to do with "pain" = bread, however. Therefore, although (B) "preparé un autre sandwich," (C) "écrit au président," and (D) "acheté du parfum élégant," are all perfectly acceptable actions, they do not logically follow from being stranded in a car which is out of gas. Only (A) "marché à la station-service" would help the situation.

17. **(B)**
Although you smile ("souriez") for different reasons, one is generally

"heureux" (B) = happy, rather than (A) "souffrant" = not well, (C) "triste" = sad, or (D) "déprimé" = depressed, when one smiles.

18. **(A)**

"Fauché" = without any money, or "broke," and should not be confused with "fâché." (B) "est en colère" = (he) is angry, and (D) "est très riche," are therefore incorrect. While Paul may not tell the truth (C) "ne dit pas la vérité," this is not a logical reply. Only (A) "n'a pas d'argent" is correct.

19. **(B)**

She was encircled or surrounded, therefore she was (B) "au milieu" = in the middle "de la foule" = of the crowd, not (A) "au dehors" = on the outside, (C) "à coté" = next to, nor (D) "une lieue" = a league (from) the crowd.

20. **(C)**

Another *faux ami:* despite its appearance, "actuellement" = now, at the present time. Therefore (A) "en réalité" = really, in reality, (B) "par une action" = by an action, and (D) "véritablement" = truly, are all incorrect.

21. **(D)**

"Faire la queue" (D) is an idiomatic expression meaning "to stand in line." (A) "faire la moue" = to make a face, to pout. (B) "faire la ligne" is a common mistake, since it is similar to the English expression, but is incorrect and (D) "faire la quiche" is obviously wrong.

22. **(B)**

This example deals with "maigrir" = to become thin, or to lose weight, for which goal it is usually necessary to (B) "suivre un régime" = to go on a diet. (A) "ne pas trop parler" will not help lose weight, nor will (C) "dormir huit heures." (D) "suivre son chemin" = to go one's way, is also incorrect in this context.

23. **(A)**

Although "déçus" looks like the English "deceived," it is another *faux ami*, since it really means "disappointed." It is therefore the most logical response to "not winning the match." (B) "ne fumerons plus" = we'll quit smoking, does not follow logically from the given statement. (C) "allons sauter de joie" = we'll jump for joy, and (D) "serons contents" = we'll be happy, make no sense under the circumstances.

24. **(D)**
    "Tissu" = cloth is manufactured in (D) "une usine" = a factory. The raw materials for the cloth may come from (A) "une ferme" = a farm, but the cloth itself is not manufactured there. (B) "une facture" = a bill and (C) "un facteur" = a mailman, are included as choices because of their similarity to the English word "factory."

25. **(C)**
    The English equivalent of this proverb is "Better late than never." Therefore, although all the choices begin with "t," it is (C) "tard" = late, which is correct. (A) "tôt" = early (antonym of "tard"); (B) "toujours" = always, is the opposite of "jamais," and therefore tempting. (D) "tant" = so much, so many, is incorrect.

26. **(B)**
    The example tests your knowledge of "enrhumé" = to have a cold, and parts of the body. With a cold, one is more likely to have a sore throat = "mal à la gorge" (B) than a sore ankle = "la cheville" (A), wrist = "le poignet" (C), or foot = "le pied" (D). Note that French does not use the possessive adjective to express parts of the body, but rather the definite article.

27. **(D)**
    "Un poisson" = a fish (D), is an example of "un fruit de mer" = seafood. (B) "un poison" is an English cognate. (A) "un bateau" = a boat and (C) "une pomme" = an apple, are incorrect.

28. **(A)**
    Since there are two "nous" in the sentence, a reflexive verb is needed. Although (D) "souvenons" (from "se souvenir" = to recall), is such a verb, it takes "de" after it and there is no "de" given. (B) "mangeons" and (C) "dormons" are not reflexive, and therefore are incorrect. "Promenons" (from "se promener" = to take a walk), is the only possible answer here.

29. **(C)**
    A direct object follows "écoute." Thus, (A) "obéit," (B) "téléphone," and (D) "écrit," all of which require "à" before an object, are incorrect. Only (C) "invite" is possible: "inviter quelqu'un à faire quelque chose."

30. **(D)**
    The subjunctive is required after "Il est préférable que." The only subjunctive form given is (D) "travaillions," which is the correct answer. (A) "voyageons" is the present indicative; (B) "voyagerions" = (we)

would voyage (the conditional tense); (C) "travaillons" is also the present indicative.

31. **(C)**
This example tests your knowledge of prepositions. (A) "avant" = before, (in time only) is often confused with (C) "devant" = in front of, before (physically), which is the correct choice. (B) "près" requires "de" after it to = near, and (D) "parmi" = among, makes no sense in this context.

32. **(D)**
After the preposition "avec," you must use the disjunctive pronoun, "eux" = them (D). The other choices, (A) "leur" = to them or (possessive) their, (B) "les" = them (direct object pronoun or the plural definite article), and (C) "ils," subject pronoun, are all incorrect.

33. **(A)**
This example is based on the gender of "victime," which is always feminine, even though you may be describing a male subject (such as "Cet homme"). The only other feminine noun given is (A) "personne" = person, which is also always feminine. (B) "individu" = individual, is masculine, as are (C) "être" = [human] being, and (D) "type" = "guy" (slang).

34. **(A)**
Since (B) "auto," (C) "adresse," and (D) "amie," are all feminine nouns, the only correct answer is (A) "arbre," which is masculine. The form "nouvel" (rather than "nouveau") is required before a masculine noun which begins with a vowel or an "h."

35. **(B)**
After "Voulez-vous que Paul..." the subjunctive is required because there are two different subjects; "vouloir" expresses an emotion, and the two clauses are joined by "que." Thus (A) "va" = (he) goes, (C) "ira" = (he) will go, and (D) "allait" = (he) used to go, was going, went (imperfect) are all incorrect, since they are all in the indicative mood. Only (B) "aille" is the subjunctive form, and therefore correct.

36. **(D)**
A feminine adjective is required to replace "riche," since it is describing a woman. Only (D) "nerveuse" is correct, since the other choices are in the masculine form: (A) "naïf" = naive; (B) "bel" = beautiful (for a masculine noun having an initial vowel or "h"), and "content" = happy.

37. **(C)**

This example deals with the present participle form "En parlant" = by or while talking. (A) "regardant" = looking at, (B) "écoutant" = listening to, and (D) "entendant" = hearing, all take direct objects in French and therefore are not followed by "à." (C) "téléphonant" = phoning or calling, takes an indirect object, indicated by "à," and is therefore the only possible correct answer.

38. **(A)**

Since the conditional form "me reposerais" must be substituted by another conditional form, only (A) "m'amuserais" = would enjoy myself, is possible. (B) "me rappelais" = used to remember, was remembering, is in the imperfect, as are (C) "me souvenais" [de] = used to recall, was recalling, and (D) "m'endormais" = was falling asleep or used to fall asleep. Be careful not to confuse the imperfect with the conditional; they both have the same endings (— ais, ais, ait, etc.), but the conditional always has an "r" before those endings, since its stem is the infinitive form of the verb.

39. **(B)**

After "quand" = when, is used to express future time, French requires that the verb be in the future tense (unlike English, which uses the present tense for this structure). Thus, only (B) "arrivera" = will arrive, is possible, since (A) "est," (C) "arrive," and (D) "va," are all in the present tense.

40. **(D)**

With a question in the inverted form (verb-subject), be careful of the verb ending before third person pronouns (il, elle). In order to avoid two vowels coming together, you must add a "t" (for sound only — no meaning), e.g., parle-t-il? donne-t-elle? If there is already a "t" in the verb, another "t" is not needed. Therefore, neither (A) "veut," (B) "voudrait," nor (C) "vient," is correct, since they do not require a "t," as does the example. Only (D) "va" needs a "t" to avoid "va-elle?"

41. **(B)**

Of the four choices given, only (B) "première" = first, is correct. (A) "premier" and (C) "dernier" are masculine, while (D) "cinq" is a cardinal number = five, rather than an ordinal number = fifth ("cinquième"), which is required before "fois" = time (in a series of action: first time, tenth time, etc.).

42. **(D)**

After "Il fallait que" the subjunctive is required, so (D) "disions", the subjunctive of the "nous" form of "dire" is the correct answer. (A) "disons" = (we) say, is the present indicative; (B) "dirions" = (we) would say, is the conditional, and (C) "dirons" = (we) will say, is the future indicative. Only (D) is possible in this example.

43. **(D)**

(A) "avoir" may be used in the expression "sans avoir écrit," but is incorrect in this sentence because the final verb must be a past participle, not an infinitive ("écrit," not "écrire"). (B) "toi" = you (familiar), is either a reflexive pronoun ("leve-toi!") or a disjunctive pronoun ("je vais avec toi.") and cannot be used as an indirect object pronoun ("te") as "nous" is used in the example. Although a direct object may fit grammatically into the sentence, changing its meaning, (C) "la" is incorrect because "écrire," beginning with a vowel, must be preceded by a consonant; as "l'" or "les." (D) "leur" = to them, in this context is an indirect object and therefore correct.

44. **(C)**

"Disque" = record, despite its "e" ending, is masculine and must be replaced by a masculine noun. (A) "couleur" = color, is feminine, as are (B) "saison" = season, and (D) "peinture" = painting. The correct choice is (C) "cours" = class, course, which is masculine (and singular, despite its plural-looking ending).

45. **(A)**

The difference between "savoir" and "connaître" = to know, is more or less the difference in the way knowledge is gained. "Savoir" refers to knowing through study or learning: "L'enfant sait lire. Il sait que l'alphabet a 26 lettres et où se trouve la bibliothèque." After "connaître" you cannot use the infinitive or "que," "qui," or "où." Also, "connaître" is used to indicate knowing or being familiar with people, places, things, i.e., works of art — all learned about through your senses or by experience: "Je connais Paris et ses rues. Nous connaissons la musique de Jacques Brel et les peintures de Picasso," etc. In our example, "Je sais son numéro de téléphone" = I know his phone number, I know a fact because I have learned it. Only (A) "le nom de cet homme" = this man's name, is a similar form of knowing. (B) "un bon restaurant," (C) "une femme célèbre" = a famous woman, and (D) "cette belle ville" = this lovely city, all require "connaître," rather than "savoir."

46. **(C)**

"Sortir" takes "être" in the *passé composé*, when it is an intransitive verb, i.e., it has no object. It takes "avoir" in a transitive sense: "J'ai sorti le crayon de mon sac." However, this structure (A) "ont sorti" = they took out, is not appropriate because there is no object in this example. (B) "sortaient" = were going out, used to go out, the imperfect, is also incorrect, since a definite time is given, within which the action took place. (D) "sont sorties" = they went out (fem.), does not apply to "Paul et Margot." The correct answer is (C) "sont sortis."

47. **(B)**

(A) "iraient" = conditional, they would go, (C) "étaient allés" = the pluperfect, they had gone (used to describe one past action which preceded a more recent past action), and (D) "allaient" = imperfect, they were going, they used to go, are all incorrect. We are speaking of "samedi dernier," which requires the *passé composé*, (B) "sont allés" = they went.

48. **(D)**

Again, the *passé composé* is required and since there is no direct object preceding the verb, there is no need for "accord" (agreement), as reflected in (A) "ont vus" (preceding masc. plural direct object) and (B) "ont vues" (preceding fem. plural direct object). (C) "voyaient" = they were seeing, used to see (imperfect), is the wrong tense for describing an action completed within a given time. The correct answer is (D) "ont vu" = they saw.

49. **(A)**

The possessive adjective is tested here; it is necessary to have agreement between the adjective and the noun (with the thing possessed, and not with the possessor, as in English). (B) "leur" = their, used to describe several owners of a singular thing, (C) "ses" = his, her things, (D) "sa" = his or her thing (fem.), are all incorrect. Since we are describing the "bonnes amies" = good friends (plural), of two people, (A) "leurs" is the correct answer.

50. **(C)**

"Tout le monde" takes the third person singular form of the verb, so (A) "avaient" = they had, is not possible, nor is (D) "ont eu." (B) "a eu" = had, in the *passé composé*, is sometimes possible when the sense is "suddenly" or a change from the prevailing situation, which the speaker wishes to emphasize. Here, however, we are simply describing the state of the group of friends, and therefore the imperfect tense is called for. (C) "avait" = had, is the only correct choice.

51. **(D)**

The adjective "tout" (A) is masculine singular, used to describe all of one thing: "Je comprends tout le livre." (B) "toute" is the feminine singular form, with the same meaning as (A). (C) "toutes" refers to all of several feminine things: "Toutes les femmes," "Toutes les tables," etc. Since we are describing "les restaurants," we need the masculine plural form, "tous" (D), which is the proper choice.

52. **(B)**

This example deals with idioms based on "avoir." Avoir (A) "honte" = to be ashamed, (C) "mal" = to have pain, and (D) "peur" = to be afraid, make no sense in this context. However, (B) [avoir] "envie" = to feel like (doing something), is perfectly plausible and the correct response.

53. **(C)**

Before a plural adjective that precedes a noun ("bons copains") it is most correct to use "de" (C). (A) "– –" (nothing) is incorrect, as are (B) "des," and (C) "les."

54. **(A)**

After the verb "aimer," no preposition is required before an infinitive. Therefore, (A) "– –" is the only correct choice in this example.

55. **(D)**

Expressions of quantity, e.g., "plus," "assez," "beaucoup," "trop," etc., require "de," even before a plural noun. Thus, (D) is the proper reply.

56. **(A)**

The example is in the present tense; thus, neither (C) "étudiaient" = (imperfect), they were studying or they used to study; nor (D) "ont étudié" = (*passé composé*), they studied, is correct. (B) "études" = (a noun) studies ("J'aime les études de Chopin;" "Il fait ses études à Nice," etc.) is obviously incorrect. Only (A) "étudient" = (they) are studying, study, do study, is correct.

57. **(B)**

In the long interrogative form, (B) "qu'est-ce que" = what? is required when describing a thing; (literally) : "What is it that you have to say to each other?" Although (A) "que," is theoretically correct, only (B) "qu'" is correct here, since it is followed by a vowel. (C) "qui" stands for a person, and (D) "quoi" = what?, is used after a preposition and not in the interrogative form given in the example.

58. **(D)**

Since "journée" = all day long, is feminine singular, the adjective form of "tout" must also be feminine singular: (D) "toute." (A) "tout" is masculine, while (B) "tous" is masculine plural and (C) "toutes" is feminine plural.

59. **(C)**

The context of the passage is in the present tense and therefore requires the present form of "vouloir" in the third person plural. (A) "voulaient" is in the imperfect tense; (B) "voudrons" = (we) will want, is first person plural, future tense; (D) "veuillent" is the subjunctive form, uncalled for in the example. (C) "veulent" = (they) want, is the correct choice.

60. **(B)**

Here the subjunctive is necessary, because there are two subjects ("Les parents" and "le téléphone") connected by "que," and the verb "vouloir" is being used to express the parents' wishes. Thus, (A) "être," (C) "sera," and (D) "est," are all incorrect. The subjunctive, (B) "soit," is the proper choice.

61. **(D)**

After "chez" and other prepositions, the disjunctive pronoun must be used. Since (A) "ils" and (C) "elles" are subject pronouns and (B) "leurs" is a plural possessive pronoun (= their), only (D) "eux" is correct.

62. **(A)**

"Promettre" takes "à" before a person and therefore requires an indirect object pronoun. We are speaking of the friends' parents; thus (A) "leur" = to them, is the correct choice. (B) "les" is the direct object pronoun; (C) "leurs" is plural possessive; and (D) "lui" is an indirect object pronoun, but it is singular.

63. **(C)**

After "promettre" and before an infinitive, you must use "de": "promettre à quelqu'un de faire quelque chose" is a good way to remember this construction. (A) "– –", (B) "à," and (D) "que," are all incorrect.

64. **(B)**

The Tour de France is the most grueling bicycle race in the world, "un concours difficile." It is not (A) "un monument célèbre de Paris" = a famous Parisian monument, or (C) "un concert international." It is certainly not (D) "un voyage tranquille" = a quiet trip, since it lasts for 23 days and covers an extremely arduous route through many areas and all sorts of terrain throughout France.

65. **(C)**

This question calls for some mathematical calculation! Since we are told that 1986 was the 73rd Tour, and since the race is held annually, it is safe to say that it began more than 70 years ago (C) [depuis] "plus de soixante-dix ans." (A) "le 19ème siècle" = the 19th century, would make it too old, as would (D) "le Moyen-Age" = the Middle Ages, while (B) "1973," would make it too recent.

66. **(D)**

The nickname "giants of the road" refers to the racers, (D) "les cyclistes du Tour," not to (A) "des montagnes énormes" = high mountains, (B) "les gens qui parlent à la télé" = the television commentators, or (C) "des grands arbres à la campagne" = big trees in the countryside.

67. **(B)**

To give an image of class and luxury to this watch, the Blancpain company primarily accentuates (B) la tradition que représente le nom Blancpain et la finition du produit (the tradition that the Blancpain name represents and the product's finish). Since there is no mention of price in this ad, the answer cannot be (A), le rapport qualité-prix (literally, "quality-price relationship"). Nor is the fact that it is sold in many large cities (le fait qu'elle est vendue dans de nombreuses grandes villes) relevant in this case, which rules out (C) as a legitimate answer. Lastly, one of Blancpain's selling points, listed in bold type at the top, is that Blancpain does not make quartz watches and never will ([. . .] il n'existe pas de montre Blancpain à quartz. Et il n'y en aura jamais), so (D) is clearly not the answer.

68. **(C)**

This ad clearly suggests that this watch is made for discerning customers in search of quality and fine craftsmanship; hence, Blancpain "s'adresse avant tout à une clientèle (C) fine" (discerning, sophisticated). This obviously rules out (A) pragmatique (pragmatic, practical), (B) rurale (rural), and (D) modeste (humble).

69. **(D)**

Nicolas is very nervous and excited about showing his friend his favorite painting. He is hardly (A) "assez ennuyeux" = quite boring, (B) "détendu" = relaxed, or (C) "fatigué" = tired. He is, however, very (D) "agité" = restless.

70. **(B)**

The expression "difficile à vivre" means someone is hard to get along with, or live with. Therefore (A) "est gravement malade" = is gravely ill, (C) "fait toujours plaisir aux autres" = always makes others happy, and (D) "ne s'énerve jamais" = never gets upset, are all inappropriate. Only (B) "s'impatiente facilement" = gets impatient very easily, is the correct choice.

71. **(A)**

The "maître hollandais" = Dutch master, to which the question refers, is Jan Vermeer, and not (B) "une peinture fameuse" = a famous painting, (C) "un cigare coûteux" = an expensive cigar, nor (D) "un professeur d'art." Only (A) "un peintre célèbre" = a famous painter, is correct.

72. **(D)**

Since Nicolas is an art student (D) "il est étudiant d'art," he spends lots of time copying great works, in order to improve his own skills. There is nothing in the passage to suggest that (A) "il veut la vendre" = he wants to sell it [his copy of "The Lacemaker"] or that (C) "il veut la montrer à ses amis" = he wants to show his work to his friends, nor does he think that (B) "il peut faire mieux" = he can do better (than the original artist).

73. **(A)**

Remember that "déçus" means disappointed. Although (D) "ils sont fatigués" = they are tired, is a tempting reason, it is not logical as a reason for their disappointment. Both (B) "le musée est vide" = the museum is empty, and (C) "le tableau n'est pas bon" = the picture is not good, are untrue. Therefore, only (A) "la peinture n'est pas visible" = the painting is not visible (because there is such a crowd, they can't get near enough to see it) is correct.

74. **(D)**

"Zut!" expresses negative feelings — either anger, disappointment, or frustration of some kind. Thus, a positive feeling, as expressed in (A) "joie" is incorrect. (B) "tristesse" = sadness, and (C) "surprise" are not generally associated with "Zut!" Only (D) "colère" = anger, is appropriate.

75. **(A)**

Although Jean de La Bruyère published a series of portraits, he was not a (B) "peintre," as these were written portraits or descriptions, indicated by both the fact that they were published, and that the public tried to guess the identities of the persons depicted, which would have been much more evident had the subjects been painted. (C) "compositeur" = composer and (D) "dramaturge" = playwright are not suggested by anything in the passage. (A) "écrivain" = writer, is the correct answer.

76. **(D)**

The sketches that La Bruyère created reflected the society in which he lived, (D) "des images de la société." They were not about (A) "une pièce de théâtre" = a play, (B) "un roman historique" = an historical novel, nor (C) "des contes de fée" = fairy tales.

77. **(B)**

La Bruyère's enemies tried to prevent his election to the Académie française, the most prestigious honor accorded to a creative artist. Thus, (B) "l'élection de l'auteur à l'Académie française" is the correct choice. There was no attempt to prevent (A) "la publication de l'œuvre" = the publication of the work or (C) "l'identification des personnages" = the identification of La Bruyère's models for the book. (D) "la vente des portraits" = the sale of the portraits, is not applicable to the passage, since there is no mention of selling these written portraits.

78. **(A)**

La Bruyère's work was popular because (A) "elle dépeignit des personnes réelles" = it portrayed real people (albeit their identity was disguised). (B) "les lecteurs reconnaissaient les personnages" = readers recognized the characters in the book, is not true, since there were attempts to sell "keys" to the identity of those described by the author. (C) "l'auteur publia des "clefs" pour identifier les gens" = the author published "keys" to identify his models, we know is not the case, since La Bruyère attempted to prevent such publication. (D) "l'auteur avait beaucoup d'amis dans la société" = the author had many friends in society, may or may not be the case, but this is not the most appropriate choice, based on the information in the text.

79. **(D)**

Giton is "not very admirable" because of his selfish disregard for anyone but himself, thus (D) "il ne respecte personne." (A) "tout le monde l'imite" = everyone imitates him, while perhaps true up to a point, is not a logical conclusion from the statement given, nor are (B) "il dort beaucoup" = he sleeps a great deal, or (C) "il n'aime pas l'exercice" = he doesn't like exercise. Only (D) is a logical and therefore appropriate choice.

80. **(B)**

The terse summation given by La Bruyère: "Il est riche" explains (B), why Giton is tolerated by those who surround him. (A) "implique que les riches sont impolis" = implies that rich people are impolite, is too general an assumption. (C) "montre les problèmes de Giton" = [the conclusion] shows Giton's problems, is not correct, since he apparently does not have any; (D) "est une déclaration basée sur les faits" = is a factual statement, is not true; it is instead the author's personal opinion.

81. **(C)**

Barbara and Frédo speak French every chance they get, whenever they are together (C) "quand ils sont ensemble." Thus, (A) "seulement au cours" = only in class, is obviously not correct. And, while it is true that they like to "pass" for French people, the passage does not tell us that they use the language (B) "pour impressionner leurs parents" = to impress their parents, or (D) "à la maison" = at home.

82. **(A)**

A "veston en cuir noir" refers to the black leather jackets which young French people seem to like so much. They are worn (A) "quand il fait frais" = when it's cool outside. (B) "quand il fait chaud" is therefore inappropriate, as are (C) "pour se baigner" = to go swimming, and (D) "quand on se couche" = when one goes to bed.

83. **(D)**

Barbara and her friend try very hard to look and act French, and in their small town, they often succeed in fooling people in the street ("les passants"). (A) "ils accompagnent des touristes" = they guide tourists, is not stated or implied in the passage; (B) "tout le monde parle français dans la ville" = everyone speaks French in the town, is obviously incorrect. (C) "ils portent des lunettes de soleil" = they wear sun-glasses, does not make them "Parisiens," since Americans wear them too. The correct choice is (D) "ils essaient d'avoir l'air français" = they try to appear French.

84. **(A)**

"Franglais" = a combination of half-French, half-English words, is being resisted by many authorities of grammar and linguistics but is very popular with young people in France. (A) "Super cool," a somewhat curious hybrid, is an example of this phenomenon. (B) "de l'ancien français" = [an example] of old French, (C) "de l'influence italienne" = of the Italian influence, and (D) "du français formel" = of formal French, are all incorrect.

85. **(C)**

The two friends go to Chicago to celebrate Barbara's birthday (C) "pour fêter l'anniversaire de Barbara." They do not go (A) "pour rencontrer des touristes" = to meet tourists, (B) "pour visiter la grande ville" = to see the big city, nor (D) "pour acheter des vêtements français" = to buy French clothes, a possibility, but not indicated in the passage.

86. **(B)**

The friends (B) "sont ravis de pouvoir parler français" = are delighted to be able to speak French in the French restaurant, is the correct reply. (A) [ils] "sont un peu perdus" = are a bit lost, is not true, nor is (C) "ont des gros problèmes avec le serveur" = they have a lot of trouble with the waiter, since they seem to be getting along fabulously as they chat with him. (D) "ne savent pas ce qu'il faut faire" = they don't know what to do, is quite untrue, since they have ordered their meal in French and are enjoying themselves greatly.

87. **(D)**

Salad is eaten in France (D) "après le plat principal" = after the main course, unlike the American custom, which is to eat it (A) "avant le repas" = before the meal. (B) "comme entrée" = as an introductory course, and (C) "avec le plat principal" = with the main dish, are also incorrect.

88. **(C)**

Frédo can pay for the birthday celebration because (C) "son père lui a donné assez d'argent" = his father gave him enough money. (A) "il prend de l'argent de Barbara" = he takes money from Barbara, is not true. While (B) "c'est l'anniversaire de son amie" = it's his friend's birthday, is a true statement, that is no reason for him to be able to pay the bill. (D) "il a une carte de crédit" = he has a credit card, may be true, but we do not know this from the text.

89. **(D)**

The answer is (D): Cet immeuble appartient à "une société privée" (This building belongs to a private company). Nothing suggests that it belongs to (A) un particulier qui loue des chambres (an individual who rents out rooms), (B) une famille nombreuse (a large family), or (C) la ville de Paris (the city of Paris).

90. **(B)**

What makes *Le Kennedy* exceptional (ce qui rend « Le Kennedy » exceptionnel) is the fact that it's adjacent to a park while being a short distance from the Eiffel Tower (le fait qu'il se situe à côté d'un parc tout en étant à deux pas de la Tour Eiffel). Hence the answer is (B). There is no mention of "un barème de prix [. . .]" (a sliding scale pay system), nor of sa proximité des transports publics (its proximity to public transportation) — even if this is not an unreasonable assumption. As for the fact that its sales office is open on Wednesday (le fait que son espace de vente est ouvert le mercredi), this hardly seems relevant or exceptional, and hence is not a valid answer choice.

SAT II:
SUBJECT TEST IN
FRENCH

PRACTICE
TEST V

FRENCH TEST V

PART A

Time: 1 Hour
         90 Questions

DIRECTIONS: This part consists of a number of incomplete statements, each followed by four suggested completions. Select the most appropriate completion and blacken the corresponding space on the answer sheet.

1.   Quand on part en voyage, il faut ...

   (A) faire la vaisselle   (C) faire les valises

   (B) faire vite   (D) faire la lessive

2.   Hier je suis allé visiter une fortresse. Pour monter à la tour il a fallu ...

   (A) prendre les chaussures

   (B) descendre dans l'ascenseur

   (C) montrer le guide

   (D) prendre l'escalier

3.   Quelquefois il y a beaucoup de monde au cinéma, et il faut ... pour acheter son ticket.

   (A) faire la queue   (C) courir dans les magasins

   (B) laver le linge   (D) voir les agents

4.   Tous les hommes courtisent Honorine plus encore pour ... que pour sa gentillesse.

   (A) sa mauvaise humeur   (C) sa laideur

   (B) sa monnaie   (D) son argent

5. En automne ... tombent par terre.

   (A) les animaux
   (C) les feuilles mortes

   (B) les assiettes
   (D) les fourmis

6. Ma jupe s'est dechirée en montant l'escalier. Maintenant je ne pourrai pas ... au bal ce soir.

   (A) l'habiter
   (C) l'apporter

   (B) m'habiller
   (D) la porter

7. Le soir s'annonce; la mer s'est retirée bien loin, et là-bas, à l'horizon, on voit le soleil ...

   (A) qui se lève
   (C) qui se couche

   (B) qui revient
   (D) qui arrive

8. L'hiver, parfois, il y a ..., et c'est extrêmement dangereux de marcher ou de rouler en voiture car ça glisse.

   (A) du vent
   (C) du brouillard

   (B) du soleil
   (D) du verglas

9. Une pluie fine venait de ... ; les toits s'égouttaient.

   (A) s'élever
   (C) s'échapper

   (B) tomber
   (D) déborder

10. Intéressée, la vieille dame, les mains sur les hanches, regardait les enfants qui ... ; ils étaient si heureux!

    (A) craignaient le pire
    (C) pleuraient

    (B) avaient peur
    (D) jouaient

11. L'été il faisait chaud, lourd et humide, et souvent vers le soir ...

    (A) il faisait de l'orage

    (B) il faisait un vent terrible et glacé

    (C) le brouillard était glacé

    (D) il neigeait

12. Il venait de … ; tout le monde …

    (A) chanter … avait peur

    (B) pleuvoir … était mouillé

    (C) neiger … avait trop chaud

    (D) pleurer … était ravi

13. Ce soir, après le festival, il n'y aura plus de bruit, tout …

    (A) se sera couché   (C) se sera levé

    (B) se sera dépêché   (D) se sera tu

14. La bonne odeur qui s'échappait de la cuisine était …

    (A) désagréable   (C) accueillante

    (B) malodorante   (D) repoussante

15. Quel merveilleux spectacle créent ces légers et gracieux … qui volent sans cesse autour de nous!

    (A) papillons   (C) mouches

    (B) guêpes   (D) corbeaux

16. Les mœurs sociales d'un pays se reflètent dans …

    (A) sa récolte   (C) sa couture

    (B) ses fermes   (D) sa culture

17. Toute la nature renaît, tout reverdit, tout revit; c'est …

    (A) le printemps   (C) l'automne

    (B) l'été   (D) l'hiver

18. C'est un homme charmant, gentil, humble, patient, généreux, et …; il a vraiment toutes les qualités.

    (A) malicieux   (C) malpropre

    (B) bienveillant   (D) ennuyeux

19. L'audace de cet adolescent était telle qu'elle ...; ce jeune homme me gênait.

    (A) me satisfaisait

    (B) m'émerveillait

    (C) me réjouissait

    (D) me chagrinait

20. Quelquefois les gens oublient d'exprimer ... après un service qu'on leur a rendu.

    (A) leur oisiveté

    (B) leur avis

    (C) leur gratitude

    (D) leur admiration

21. Nous avons entendu sonner ... au clocher du village.

    (A) cinq heures

    (B) le tonnerre

    (C) quelques mots

    (D) le matin

22. Tous les jeunes ... sur la glace.

    (A) écrivaient

    (B) patinaient

    (C) nageaient

    (D) ouvraient

23. Je me rappelle de ces jours délicieux que j'ai passés dans ce petit village avec Ursule; oui, j'en garde ...

    (A) des enfants

    (B) un mémoire

    (C) la vérité

    (D) des beaux souvenirs

24. Ce sont les abeilles qui font ...

    (A) le sucre

    (B) le beurre

    (C) le miel

    (D) le lait

25. Est-ce que vous pouvez ... à l'aéroport ce soir?

    (A) m'apporter

    (B) me porter

    (C) me déménager

    (D) m'amener

26. Les fleurs odorantes … leurs parfums.

    (A) ont exhalé

    (C) ont embaumé

    (B) ont senti

    (D) ont apprécié

27. Avec ses longues … le héron peut entrer dans l'eau de plus d'un pied sans se mouiller les plumes.

    (A) jambes

    (C) ailes

    (B) plumes

    (D) pattes

PART B

DIRECTIONS: In each of the sentences in this part of the test, one or more words are underlined. One of the four choices following each sentence can be correctly substituted for the underlined word(s) to form a grammatically correct statement or question. The new sentence may differ in meaning from the original example. Select the one choice which fits grammatically into the original sentence and blacken the corresponding space on the answer sheet.

---

28. Il faut <u>à tout prix</u> passer la frontière.

  (A) joliment

  (B) coûte que coûte

  (C) hier

  (D) la semaine dernière

29. La petite fille a <u>les joues</u> toutes rouges.

  (A) les mains

  (B) les doigts

  (C) ses lèvres

  (D) ses jupes

30. La jeune fille <u>s'enveloppa</u> de sa pèlerine.

  (A) s'envenima

  (B) envisagea

  (C) se couvrit

  (D) s'envoya

31. Il faut qu'elle <u>écrive</u> à ses parents.

  (A) écrire

  (B) écrite

  (C) obéit

  (D) obéisse

32. <u>En me promenant</u> dans les jardins du château, j'ai entendu des voix.

  (A) Quand je me promenais

  (B) En se promenant

  (C) Quand je m'étais promené

  (D) En promenant

33. Nous <u>lui</u> avons demandé de partir.

   (A) nous

   (B) tu

   (C) leur

   (D) nos

34. Qu'est-ce que <u>vous</u> lui <u>avez</u> dit?

   (A) tu, as

   (B) leur, avons

   (C) se, a

   (D) moi, ai

35. Elle a acheté <u>la robe</u> qu'elle avait vue dans la vitrine.

   (A) celui

   (B) cela

   (C) celle

   (D) celles

36. <u>Il y a</u> deux mois que j'habite ici.

   (A) Cela fait

   (B) Depuis

   (C) Ils sont

   (D) Pendant

37. Il est devenu ermite; il <u>ne quitte jamais</u> sa maison.

   (A) ne quitte plus

   (B) ne plus quitter

   (C) ne jamais quitter

   (D) ne quitte que

38. Aucun de ces objets <u>ne m'appartient</u>.

   (A) ne plaît pas

   (B) est à moi

   (C) ne sera pas pour moi

   (D) n'est à moi

39. Le nageur <u>se lança</u> du haut de son perchoir et fit un plongeon en spirale.

   (A) renonça

   (B) se jeta

   (C) s'envola

   (D) s'éloigna

40. Sa mère lui avait tellement manqué pendant ses années à l'université qu'il a décidé de ne plus <u>la quitter</u>.

   (A) manquer d'elle

   (B) se débarrasser d'elle

   (C) la revoir

   (D) se séparer d'elle

41. <u>Quoique</u> mon père m'en empêche, j'irai danser ce soir.

    (A) même si   (C) de même que

    (B) c'est pareil   (D) la même chose

42. Elle lui demanda de l'assurer qu'elle s'était <u>expliquée</u> clairement.

    (A) lavée   (C) exprimée

    (B) confondue   (D) parlée

43. Les parents épargnent leur argent pour <u>pouvoir</u> envoyer leurs enfants aux meilleures écoles.

    (A) vouloir   (C) devoir

    (B) qu'ils peuvent   (D) qu'ils puissent

44. Le boxeur <u>s'entraînait</u> pour gagner le match.

    (A) se frappait   (C) se produisait

    (B) se traînait   (D) se formait

45. <u>C'est</u> un acrobate incomparable.

    (A) Il était   (C) C'était

    (B) Ils étaient   (D) Le jeune homme

PART C

DIRECTIONS: The following paragraphs contain blank spaces which indicate omissions in the text. Below each blank are four choices. Choose the answer which best completes the sentence in the given context and blacken the corresponding space on the answer sheet. Note that in some instances choice A consists of dashes, which indicate that no insertion is required at that point.

— Est-ce que cet hôtel est bon? Oui, certainement, mais _____

46. (A) celui

    (B) celui-là

    (C) celle-ci

    (D) celle-là

est _____. J'aime _____ l'hôtel Continental

47. (A) mieux   48. (A) bien

    (B) meilleur   (B) mieux

    (C) la meilleure   (C) très

    (D) le mieux   (D) trop

que l'hôtel de Savoie.

— Avez-vous trouvé _____ qui _____

49. (A) quelqu'un   50. (A) a pu

    (B) quelque chose   (B) puisse

    (C) qui est-ce   (C) ait pu

    (D) qu'est-ce   (D) peut

lui enseigner le français? Non, je n'ai trouvé _____.

51. (A) quelqu'un

    (B) personne

    (C) pas personne

    (D) aucun

— Voulez-vous bien _____ dire que je _____

52. (A) le   53. (A) le

    (B) les   (B) l'

    (C) la   (C) leur

    (D) lui   (D) me

verrai demain? Oui, je _____ _____ dirai.

54. (A) la   55. (A) les

    (B) le   (B) lui

    (C) lui   (C) le

    (D) moi   (D) me

— J'ai perdu _____ stylo; voulez-vous bien me prêter _____?

56. (A) mon   57. (A) le tien

    (B) ma   (B) le vôtre

    (C) le mien   (C) le mien

    (D) la mienne   (D) la mienne

Oui, certainement, servez-vous _____.

58. (A) à la mienne

    (B) de la mienne

    (C) du mien

    (D) au mien

— Aimez-vous _____ pêches? Oh, mais oui, bien sûr, j'aime

59. (A) les

    (B) beaucoup des

    (C) des

    (D) beaucoup de

beaucoup _____ pêches; mais je voudrais que vous me _____

60. (A) de   61. (A) donneriez

    (B) des   (B) donniez

    (C) une   (C) donnez

    (D) les   (D) donnerez

des poires car la poire est _____ fruit _____.

62. (A) ma   63. (A) favori

    (B) mes   (B) favorite

    (C) mon   (C) préférée

    (D) sa   (D) préférable

PART D

> **DIRECTIONS:** Read the following passages carefully for comprehension. Each passage is followed by a number of questions or incomplete statements. Select the one answer or completion that is most appropriate according to the passage and blacken the corresponding space on the answer sheet.

Le soleil se lève lentement, le ciel commence à pâlir; c'est l'aube. C'est le moment où il ne fait pas encore clair, où ce n'est plus la nuit et où ce n'est pas encore le jour; c'est le début de la journée, ces quelques instants que très peu de gens peuvent voir car souvent on n'est pas encore réveillé à cette heure.

Tout est incertain, tout est confus; la forme des choses est indéfinie; l'air est immobile, rien ne bouge; pas une feuille sur les arbres ne remue; la mer, couleur d'acier, est tranquille et presque silencieuse; le vent est pour ainsi dire absent. On entend à peine le clapotis des plus petites vagues qui s'écrasent contre les bateaux de pêche qui dans une heure seront au large. Les grues sont là, rangées comme un défilé de géants squelettiques à peine visibles.

On entend sans les voir les petits chalutiers qui reviennent au port; eux aussi sont silencieux comme ils glissent doucement sur l'eau, noirs, informes. On entend quelques voix d'hommes, la voix presque indistincte des pêcheurs qui ont passé la nuit en mer. Pour eux c'est la fin du travail; ils vont se reposer.

Cependant le soleil a progressé: il a passé l'horizon et il s'élève maintenant dans le ciel nuageux. C'est une boule orange qui se reflète en stries sur la mer. On commence à distinguer les hommes et les choses; tout s'éclaire de minute en minute. C'est un jour qui recommence. C'est la vie renouvelée. Chacun se réveille et repart au travail. Tout recommence. S'il est vrai que beaucoup de gens ont disparu cette nuit, en revanche beaucoup d'enfants sont nés. C'est le renouveau.

64. L'aube est le moment de la journée

 (A) où le soleil se lève

 (B) où le soleil se couche

 (C) où généralement la mer est agitée

 (D) où on voit des géants

65. D'après ce texte, dans une ville portuaire lorsque le soleil se lève on aperçoit

 (A) des pêcheurs qui dorment

 (B) qu'il fait du vent

 (C) des bateaux revenir de la pêche et des bateaux qui s'apprêtent à y partir

 (D) qu'il y a des géants squelettes

66. L'aube, dit encore ce texte, représente ces quelques instants

 (A) où les bateaux doivent rester au port

 (B) où ce n'est plus la nuit et cependant ce n'est pas encore le jour

 (C) où les grues sont au travail

 (D) où le soleil est déjà haut et chaud

> **Offres d' emploi**
>
> **Des qualités de star?**
> Producteurs
> cherchent adultes et
> enfants pour
> publicités télévisées,
> catalogues, films et
> magazines. Jusqu'à
> €1500/ jour. Anglais
> nécessaire. Lun-sam
> **05 88 77 66 55**

67. Cette annonce propose :

    (A) 1500 euros par jour à tous les candidats anglophones se présentant du lundi au samedi

    (B) Un poste à temps plein dans une agence de publicité

    (C) Des cours de théâtre et des séances de photos pour 1500 euros

    (D) La possibilité sans garantie d'une séance d'essai

68. Les gens susceptibles d'être tentés par cette annonce :

    (A) Rêvent de travailler dans le show-business

    (B) Sont surtout à la recherche d'un travail très stable et prévisible

    (C) Souhaitent regarder des catalogues et lire des magazines

    (D) Organisent des campagnes publicitaires

L'été au crépuscule, mon frère et moi, alors enfants, étions souvent assis sur le perron en pierre de la porte d'entrée de notre grande maison. Le soleil se couchait lentement, un soleil souvent rouge qui faisait dire à ma mère, "qu'il se couchait dans l'eau et qu'il pleuvrait demain"; elle ne se trompait pas souvent.

On était en juillet, on faisait la moisson, et à cette heure tardive on entendait au loin les fermiers revenir des champs dans leurs grands chariots tirés par plusieurs chevaux qui parfois se mettaient à courir tant ils étaient pressés de regagner l'écurie. Je n'oublierai jamais le bruit énorme que faisait sur la route le roulement de ces lourds chariots et le claquement sonore qu'y faisait le pas répété des chevaux puissants.

Il avait fait très chaud dans la journée et les murs brûlaient encore de la chaleur du soleil dont ils étaient encore imprégnés. Les hannetons et les moustiques bourdonnaient autour de nous, nous faisant rentrer chez nous pour retrouver le cercle de famille.

69. Dans ce texte le narrateur nous donne quelques détails

    (A) sur son enfance   (C) en nous décrivant son frère

    (B) au sujet de sa maison   (D) sur la fin de l'été

70. Cet événement mémorable de la jeunesse du narrateur se passait

    (A) vers le soir   (C) en plein midi

    (B) au milieu de la nuit   (D) dans la matinée

71. Cela arrivait surtout pendant les vacances des deux enfants qui étaient

    (A) en hiver   (C) en septembre

    (B) en été   (D) au milieu du printemps

72. En dépit du lourd chargement qu'ils traînaient, les chevaux couraient sur la route

    (A) parce qu'ils voulaient revoir la fermière

    (B) parce qu'ils étaient fatigués

    (C) parce qu'ils étaient pressés de retrouver l'écurie

    (D) parce qu'ils avaient trop travaillé

73. Tout ce bruit énorme que les deux enfants entendaient

    (A) se produisait dans le village voisin

    (B) effrayait les enfants si bien qu'ils rentraient dans la maison

    (C) venait de la route où passaient les lourds chariots des fermiers au retour des champs

    (D) venait du vacarme des hannetons et des moustiques

74. Les murs de la maison étaient encore

    (A) brûlants après l'incendie

    (B) tout rouges

    (C) solides

    (D) imprégnés de la chaleur du soleil de la journée

75. Les deux enfants rentraient chez eux

    (A) parce qu'ils avaient sommeil

    (B) parce qu'ils avaient peur des chevaux

    (C) parce qu'ils étaient ennuyés par les insectes

    (D) parce que leurs parents les appelaient

Il était enfin dans son pays natal: la France! Depuis si longtemps il s'était promis d'y retourner, et à cette minute l'avion venait de se poser à Orly, l'aéroport d'où il était parti depuis plus de trente ans. Partout où il posait le regard rien n'était plus pareil. Même les employés en uniforme qui se pressaient autour des voitures à bagages et qu'il voyait de loin lui semblaient être bien petits (les Américains souvent sont si grands!). Peut-être son esprit était-il prisonnier de cette comparaison!

L'avion roulait encore et il allait s'arrêter. On entendit une cloche et puis une voix féminine qui invita les passagers à quitter leur siège, puis elle leur souhaita bon séjour.

Il était sorti du Boeing 747, que l'on appelle aussi en France un avion à réaction, qui avait traversé l'Océan Atlantique. Il avait tant dormi car il avait été bien dans sa carlingue sans fin. Dans cet immense jet il n'avait senti aucun mouvement. Pendant la nuit il avait même parfois eu l'impression que l'avion ne bougeait plus, et il avait eu peur. Pris de panique, son cœur avait battu très fort.

A présent il était à Paris, un Paris qui se réveillait et qui partait au travail. Il était minuit à sa montre, mais à Paris il était six heures du matin; il mit sa montre à l'heure. Il avait un peu froid et il était un peu engourdi; il ne savait pas s'il avait faim ou soif; il ne savait plus s'il devait rire ou pleurer. Mais peu à peu ce semblant d'inertie disparut et il redevint lui-même. Les bruits autour de lui étaient moins confus. La vie lui revenait, et il alla chercher ses bagages.

76. Dans cette histoire il s'agit d'un voyageur

   (A) qui a peur de voyager en avion

   (B) qui n'a pas d'esprit

   (C) qui est bien petit pour un américain

   (D) qui n'a pas vu la France depuis longtemps

77. Le voyageur est très surpris quand il arrive à Orly

   (A) parce que tout ce qu'il connaissait a changé

   (B) parce qu'il trouve que les gens sont moins petits

   (C) parce qu'il se sent prisonnier des événements

   (D) parce que l'avion ne s'arrête pas tout de suite

78. L'hôtesse de l'air a pris la parole à l'arrivée à Orly

   (A) pour recommender que l'on n'oublie rien dans l'avion

   (B) pour demander aux passagers de quitter leur siège et leur souhaiter bon séjour

   (C) parce qu'elle portait un uniforme

   (D) parce qu'elle a fait sonner la cloche

79. L'avion dans lequel la traversée avait eu lieu est aussi appelé en France

   (A) un ancien avion de guerre

   (B) un avion à réaction

   (C) un Boeing 747

   (D) un immense jet

80. Quand ce monsieur est arrivé à Paris

    (A) il a mis sa montre à l'heure car il y avait six heures de différence entre la France et les Etats-Unis.

    (B) il était encore endormi

    (C) il avait soif

    (D) il avait faim

81. Son corps et son esprit étaient un peu engourdis

    (A) parce qu'il ne savait pas s'il devait rire ou pleurer

    (B) parce qu'il avait été assis dans l'avion toute la nuit

    (C) parce qu'il y avait du bruit autour de lui

    (D) parce qu'il avait froid

En vacances chez une cousine, dans la belle campagne de France, je partais toute seule par un bel après-midi pour faire une longue promenade. Je choisis un petit sentier de terre, une belle terre presque rouge, une argile qui n'a sa pareille nulle part. Le sentier n'était pas uni mais chaussée de souliers épais, pourtant je ne craignais pas de me tordre une cheville. Dès mon entrée à travers les bois je sentis l'odeur des mûriers; les mûres étaient encore rouges mais bientôt on les cueillerait.

Si la senteur tellement agréable des mûres dominait, il y avait aussi une odeur mal définie, un mélange de parfums qu'exhalaient les arbres, le tapis de feuilles sèches qui craquaient sous mes pieds, les fleurettes très hautes sur leurs tiges, l'écorce des arbres qui tombait par endroits; une odeur humide, un musc plutôt, quelque chose qui plaît aux sens et qu'on voudrait sentir toujours. Parfois un insecte passait et bourdonnait; il passait et repassait près de moi, me faisant sans doute comprendre que j'envahissais son univers. Je poursuivais ma promenade, et je me suis promise de revenir.

Lorsque j'étais sous bois il ne faisait pas chaud, et il suffisait d'un ruisseau coulant bruyamment sur les pierres pour apporter la brise et la fraîcheur. Les oiseaux eux-mêmes me donnaient l'impression de m'accompagner, mais je ne les voyais pas souvent car ils semblaient préférer la cime des arbres. De temps en temps j'entendais le plus joli cri venu de là-haut; je levais les yeux, mais l'auteur de ce cri joyeux, un merle sans doute, avait déjà disparu.

82. La narratrice de cette histoire part en promenade

    (A) par un sentier inégal

    (B) sous la pluie

    (C) le long d'une route nationale

    (D) à travers le chemin des champignons

83. Dès son entrée dans les bois la jeune fille est agréablement surprise

    (A) à la vue d'oiseaux rares

    (B) par la bonne odeur des mûriers

    (C) par le chant des oiseaux

    (D) par les feuilles sèches

84. Les parfums sous bois sont plutôt confus, mais on sait en général d'où ils viennent; la narratrice

    (A) s'est assise pour écouter les oiseaux

    (B) a vu des insectes voler autour d'elle

    (C) a poursuivi sa promenade

    (D) nous parle du mélange des parfums

85. Ce qui est également nécessaire pour compléter la fraîcheur et le bien-être qu'on cherche dans les bois c'est

    (A) une petite rivière   (C) la chaleur

    (B) la cime des arbres   (D) le cri joyeux d'un oiseau

Cette dame âgée était ma grand-mère; son nom était Marianne, le nom de la République Française. Il est dommage que le temps ajoute les années à notre âge car en vérité beaucoup de gens s'acheminent dans la vie sans vieillir; c'était le cas de ma grand-mère. Esprit indépendant, veuve de bonne heure, elle avait su se défendre en dépit de et contre tout. Elle avait passé la Grande Guerre sans se plaindre, seule, toujours seule, à Paris. Ses filles s'étaient mariées et elles avaient pris une direction qu'elle seule avait su leur faire comprendre. Elle était contente de les voir, bien que ce soit seulement de temps en temps.

Cette femme n'avait jamais accepté l'idée que la vie est parfois compliquée; elle ne voulait pas savoir cela. Sa peau de satin, son visage sans rides, ses yeux brillants, ses beaux cheveux abondants et tressés, sans un fil d'argent, ses mains longues et fines, étaient la preuve qu'elle avait toujours ignoré le souci. Elle était belle malgré ses soixante-quinze ans, belle comme elle l'avait toujours été, belle parce que, intuitive, elle n'avait pas permis aux complexités de la vie de la détruire. Elle avait su s'en défendre, et cela est admirable.

Dame de compagnie dans de riches familles, ma grand-mère a toujours connu une vie douce, une vie sans heurts, une vie qui n'ètait qu'à elle, une vie qu'elle seule a su vivre.

86. Selon l'auteur, c'est dommage que le passage du temps nous fait vieillir car

   (A) il faut rester jeune à jamais

   (B) les riches n'aiment pas employer les vieux

   (C) il y a des gens qui ne vieillissent pas d'esprit

   (D) sa grand-mère était veuve de bonne heure

87. Cette dame âgée qui refusait de vieillir

   (A) était encore bien jolie à soixante-quinze ans

   (B) avait les cheveux blanchis

   (C) aimait la vie de vieillarde

   (D) avait bon appétit

88. Elle avait des filles à qui elle avait

   (A) enseigné que la vie est trop compliquée

   (B) enseigné que la vie est trop simple

   (C) donné une direction qu'elle seule avait su leur faire comprendre

   (D) appris que les visites fréquentes sont indispensables

GUARA

6, Place des Victoires - 75002 Paris

2 MAI 2002

LIQUIDATION TOTALE
de -30% à -75%
Avant fermeture définitive

Chaussures Homme et Femme
Roberto Cavalli, Cesare Paciotti,
Gianni Barbato, Byblos, Camper,
Stéphane Kélian.

89. Dans le contexte de cette annonce, que signifie « fermeture définitive » ?

(A) Seulement qu'il était certain que la boutique « Guara » allait être fermée le 2 mai 2002

(B) Que certaines paires de chaussures étaient en solde

(C) Que la boutique « Guara » était sur le point de fermer ses portes pour de bon

(D) Que la boutique « Guara » allait fermer ses portes avant le 2 mai pour les rouvrir par la suite

90. Et que signifie « liquidation totale » ?

(A) Que certains articles allaient se vendre à –30% et d'autres à –75%

(B) Seulement que certains articles allaient être réduits de –30% à –75%

(C) Qu'il fallait vendre les articles réduits à –30% au plus vite pour faire place à ceux réduits à –75%

(D) Qu'il fallait tout vendre au plus vite puisque la boutique « Guara » avait fait faillite

SAT II: French Subject Test
Test V

ANSWER KEY

1.	(C)	24.	(C)	47.	(B)	70.	(A)
2.	(D)	25.	(D)	48.	(B)	71.	(B)
3.	(A)	26.	(A)	49.	(A)	72.	(C)
4.	(D)	27.	(A)	50.	(B)	73.	(C)
5.	(C)	28.	(B)	51.	(B)	74.	(D)
6.	(D)	29.	(A)	52.	(D)	75.	(C)
7.	(C)	30.	(C)	53.	(A)	76.	(D)
8.	(D)	31.	(D)	54.	(B)	77.	(A)
9	(B)	32.	(A)	55.	(B)	78.	(B)
10.	(D)	33.	(C)	56.	(A)	79.	(B)
11.	(A)	34.	(A)	57.	(B)	80.	(A)
12.	(B)	35.	(C)	58.	(C)	81.	(B)
13.	(D)	36.	(A)	59.	(A)	82.	(A)
14.	(C)	37.	(A)	60.	(D)	83.	(B)
15.	(A)	38.	(D)	61.	(B)	84.	(D)
16.	(D)	39.	(B)	62.	(C)	85.	(A)
17.	(A)	40.	(D)	63.	(A)	86.	(C)
18.	(B)	41.	(A)	64.	(A)	87.	(A)
19.	(D)	42.	(C)	65.	(C)	88.	(C)
20.	(C)	43.	(D)	66.	(B)	89.	(C)
21.	(A)	44.	(D)	67.	(D)	90.	(D)
22.	(B)	45.	(C)	68.	(A)		
23.	(D)	46.	(B)	69.	(A)		

DETAILED EXPLANATIONS
OF ANSWERS
PRACTICE TEST V

1. **(C)**
   faire les valises (to pack suitcases) is the correct answer for what one does when taking a trip. (A) to do the dishes, (B) to act quickly, (D) to do the wash, are not related to travelling, and are therefore incorrect in this context.

2. **(D)**
   is the correct answer because in order to climb the tower it was necessary to take the stairs (prendre l'escalier). (A) to take one's shoes, and (C) to show the guide, are unrelated to climbing the tower. (B) to go down in the elevator is wrong because it was necessary to go up.

3. **(A)**
   is the correct answer because when there are many people waiting to buy tickets, for instance, they stand in line. (B) do the laundry, (C) run to the stores or go shopping, and (D) see the policemen, are incorrect for they do not fit in this situation.

4. **(D)**
   is the correct answer because men were courting Honorine more for her money (son argent) than for (A) her bad disposition, (B) her change (coins), (C) her ugliness; therefore, (A), (B), and (C) are incorrect.

5. **(C)**
   is the correct answer, for indeed only the dead leaves (les feuilles mortes) fall to the ground, not (A) animals, (B) plates, or (D) ants; (A), (B), and (D) are, therefore, incorrect.

6. **(D)**
   is the correct answer. Since the skirt ripped (s'est dechirée), I won't be able to wear it to the dance tonight. (A) (to) live in it, (B) (to) dress myself, and (C) (to) bring it, are not consequences of the skirt's having been ripped.

7. **(C)**

is the correct answer, for indeed it is evening, and the sun (le soleil) disappears below the horizon (il se couche). (A) rises, (B) comes back, and (D) arrives (or comes), are incorrect.

8. **(D)**

is the correct answer because it is sleet (le verglas) which causes roads and sidewalks to be slippery, which is extremely dangerous (extrêmement dangereux). No, it is not (A) the wind, (B) the sun, nor (C) the fog which cause the roads to be slippery; therefore, they are incorrect.

9. **(B)**

is the correct answer, for indeed it is the rain (la pluie) which falls (qui tombe). The rain does not (A) rise up, (C) escape, or (D) overflow; therefore, (A), (C), and (D) are incorrect.

10. **(D)**

is the correct answer, for the old lady was looking at the children (les enfants) who were playing (qui jouaient). These children were not (A) fearing the worst, (B) afraid, or (C) crying, since the end of the sentence states that they were very happy (ils étaient si heureux!).

11. **(A)**

is the correct answer because one often experiences this type of situation. In the summer it was very hot, sultry, humid, and often toward the evening there was a storm (il faisait de l'orage). (B) there was a terrible ice cold wind, (C) there was an ice cold fog, and (D) it was snowing, are incorrect, for this type of weather does not occur in the summer (l'été).

12. **(B)**

is the correct answer for indeed it had just rained (il venait de pleuvoir); everyone was wet (tout le monde était mouillé). (A) he had just sung, everyone was afraid, (C) it had just snowed, everyone was too warm, and (D) he had just cried, everyone was delighted, cannot be correct.

13. **(D)**

is the correct answer because when the festival is over there will be no more noise (quand tout se sera tu, il n'y aura plus de bruit). When "everything" (A) will be in bed, (B) will have hurried, and (C) will have gotten up, are indeed incorrect.

14. **(C)**
    is the correct answer because only a pleasant smell (<u>une bonne odeur</u>) is welcoming (<u>accueillante</u>). (A) unpleasant, (B) malodorous, and (D) repulsive, are incorrect.

15. **(A)**
    is the correct answer, for only butterflies (<u>les papillons</u>) are light and graceful; certainly not (B) wasps, (C) flies, or (D) ravens. (B), (C), and (D) are incorrect.

16. **(D)**
    is the correct answer, for the social customs or morals of a country are reflected in its culture, not in (A) its harvest, (B) its farms, or (C) its sewing.

17. **(A)**
    is the correct answer because only in the spring will nature (<u>la nature</u>) be reborn (<u>renaître</u>), be green again (<u>reverdir</u>), be alive again (<u>revivre</u>). (B) summer, (C) fall, and (D) winter are, therefore, incorrect.

18. **(B)**
    is the correct answer, for a charming man (<u>un homme charmant</u>) who, in addition, is nice (<u>gentil</u>), humble, etc., will be kind (<u>bienveillant</u>), not (A) malicious, (C) unclean, or (D) boring, and they are, of course, incorrect.

19. **(D)**
    is the correct answer, for indeed the audacity (<u>l'audace</u>) of this teenager (<u>cet adolescent</u>) was bothering (gêner) the person who expresses this statement. (A) to be satisfactory, (B) to amaze with admiration, and (C) to give joy, are incorrect.

20. **(C)**
    is the correct answer: people forget to express their thanks after someone does them a favor (<u>rendre un service</u>). (A) their idleness, (B) their opinion, and (D) their admiration, are wrong.

21. **(A)**
    is the correct answer, for indeed in many villages in France, and other countries, the bell-tower (<u>le clocher</u>) does give the time, often on the hour only. Yes, we heard (A) five o'clock ringing in the bell-tower, not (B) the

thunder, (C) a few words, nor (D) the morning, which are, therefore, incorrect.

22. **(B)**

is the correct answer because all the young people were skating on the ice (<u>patinaient sur la glace</u>); they were not (A) writing, (C) swimming, nor (D) opening on it; therefore, they are incorrect.

23. **(D)**

is the correct answer, for I have beautiful memories (<u>j'en garde des beaux souvenirs</u>) of those days. (A) (<u>garder</u>) <u>des enfants</u>, meaning to babysit, (B) memorandum, and (C) the truth, are all incorrect here.

24. **(C)**

is the correct answer, for indeed we get honey (<u>le miel</u>) from the bees (<u>les abeilles</u>); bees do not make (A) sugar, (B) butter, nor (D) milk; therefore, they are eliminated.

25. **(D)**

is the correct answer because to bring a person (somewhere) uses the verb <u>amener</u>. (A) <u>apporter</u>, used for things, (B) to wear, and (C) to move (to change domiciles), are incorrect.

26. **(A)**

is the correct answer because the sweet-smelling flowers exhaled (<u>ont exhalé</u>) their fragrances (<u>leurs parfums</u>). No, they did not (B) smell, (C) scent, nor (D) appreciate, their fragrances. Therefore, they are incorrect.

27. **(A)**

is the correct answer because the heron, with its long legs (<u>ses longues jambes</u>) can enter (<u>peut entrer</u>) into the water (<u>dans l'eau</u>) more than one foot deep (<u>de plus d'un pied</u>) without getting its feathers wet (<u>sans se mouiller les plumes</u>). (B) feathers, which are attached to (C) wings, are parts of the heron which do not get wet even when the bird's legs are more than one foot under water. (D) is incorrect because the heron's feet (<u>pattes</u>) logically get wet if its legs do.

28. **(B)**

is the correct answer because <u>à tout prix</u> and <u>coûte que coûte</u> are synonyms; they both mean "at all costs." It is also the only answer choice which is grammatically correct. (A) prettily, (C) yesterday, and (D) last week, making no sense in this sentence, are eliminated.

29. **(A)**

is the correct answer since it is feminine plural, therefore agreeing with <u>toutes rouges</u>. (B) is masculine plural, which does not agree. (C) although feminine and plural, is incorrect because the possessive pronoun (<u>ses</u>) is not used for body parts when the subject is stated and the auxiliary "avoir" is used. (D) is wrong for the reason stated in (C).

30. **(C)**

is the correct answer because <u>s'enveloppa</u> et <u>se couvrit</u> are synonyms and because (C) is the only choice which is grammatically correct. (A) to grow worse, (B) to consider, and (D) to grant oneself something, are out of context, therefore, incorrect.

31. **(D)**

is the correct answer because the expression <u>il faut que</u> requires that the subjunctive follow, and <u>obéisse</u> is the only choice in the subjunctive mood. (A) would be appropriate if the sentence structure were changed to <u>Il lui faut écrire</u>, but is incorrect here. (B) and (C) are in the indicative mood, and therefore incorrect.

32. **(A)**

is the correct answer because it is the only choice which fits grammatically into the example sentence. (B) is incorrect because the verb must reflect the first person singular, not the third person. (C) is incorrect because of its tense (pluperfect); either imperfect or *passé composé* is necessary in this construction. (D) is incorrect because <u>se promener</u> is a reflexive verb and therefore requires a reflexive pronoun, <u>me</u> in this case.

33. **(C)**

is the correct answer, for <u>leur</u> could be a substitute for <u>lui</u>; they are both indirect object pronouns, and they appear in the same position in a sentence. (A) <u>nous</u>, out of context here because <u>demander</u> is not a reflexive verb, (B) <u>tu</u>, a subject pronoun, and (D) <u>nos</u>, a possessive adjective, are incorrect because none offer the possibility of a substitution for <u>lui</u>.

34. **(A)**

is the correct answer because <u>tu</u>, like <u>vous</u>, is a subject pronoun and agrees with the verb form <u>as</u>; since (B) <u>leur</u>, (C) <u>se</u>, and (D) <u>moi</u>, are not subject pronouns, nor do they agree with their respective verb forms, they are incorrect and eliminated.

35. **(C)**

is the correct answer since it is feminine singular, which is necessary in the substitution in order to agree with vue. (A) masculine singular, and (D) feminine plural, are incorrect here. (B) cela replaces an entire preceding phrase, not just a noun.

36. **(A)**

is the correct answer since il y a and cela fait are synonyms in this context. (B) and (D) would only be grammatically correct if the que in the example were eliminated. (C) is incorrect because it is not an expression of time.

37. **(A)**

is the correct answer. (B) and (C) are both grammatical constructions which require a previous conjugated verb + "de," (i.e., Elle m'a dit de ne plus quitter la maison). (D) means he only leaves his house, which contradicts the meaning of hermit.

38. **(D)**

is the correct answer since the two expressions are synonyms, as well as grammatically interchangeable in this context. (A) and (C) are both incorrect as the expression aucun ... ne is already a negative, and therefore does not require pas. (B) is wrong because it requires ne before it to complete the negative construction begun by aucun.

39. **(B)**

is the correct answer because se lança and se jeta are synonyms. (A) renounced, or gave up, (C) flew away, and (D) went away, are incorrect.

40. **(D)**

is the correct answer because he no longer wanted to be separated from her. (A) the expression manquer de means to lack (something), but-ter, for example, and is therefore incorrect here. He no longer wanted (B) to get rid of her, and (C) to see her, are illogical here, and thus incorrect.

41. **(A)**

is the correct answer because quoique (although) and même si (even if) are considered synonyms. (B) it is the same, (C) as well as, and (D) the same thing, not fitting here, are incorrect.

42. **(C)**

is the correct answer. Although all the answers agree in gender and number, only (C) makes sense here. S'expliquer and s'exprimer (to express oneself) are similar in meaning, and one cannot (A) wash oneself , (B) confuse oneself, or (D) talk to oneself clearly (clairement).

43. **(D)**

is the correct answer because pour que is an expression of finality and requires the subjunctive. Although an infinitive may follow pour, as in the example, (A) and (B) are illogical in this context, and therefore incorrect. (C) is in the indicative mood, incorrect here.

44. **(D)**

is the correct answer because s'entraînait and se formait are synonyms in this context. (A) hit himself, (B) dragged along, and (C) occurred, are all incorrect.

45. **(C)**

is the correct answer since c'était is indentical to c'est, but in a different tense, the imperfect; (A) il était, or (B) ils étaient, could not be substitutes for c'est and c'était because il était and ils étaient cannot be followed by an indefinite article (un, une, des); they must be followed by an adjective. However, a noun of profession, nationality, or religion can function adjectively provided that it is not modified by an adjective; in this case it is definitely a noun. In this sentence the noun acrobate is modified by the adjective incomparable; therefore, it cannot be preceded by il était, or ils étaient if it were in the plural. (D) le jeune homme, since it is not followed by a verb, is also eliminated.

46. **(B)**

is the correct answer. Celui-là (that one), a demonstrative pronoun, masculine and singular, replaces the noun hôtel, also masculine and singular. (A) celui (the one) cannot be correct since it is not, in this case, explicit (definite), i.e., as precise as that one, in this particular situation; (C) and (D) are also incorrect for the simple reason that they are feminine; they could not replace a masculine noun.

47. **(B)**

is the correct answer, for meilleur (better) is the only form which can modify the noun hôtel since it is a comparative adjective; (A) mieux (better), being an adverb, (C) being the feminine superlative, and (D) being the adverbial superlative, are wrong.

48. **(B)**

is the correct answer because <u>mieux</u> (better) is the only comparative adverb capable of modifying the verb <u>aime</u> (like); (A) <u>bien</u> (well), (C) <u>très</u> (very), and (D) <u>trop</u> (too much), although adverbs themselves, cannot be correct here, for they are not comparative.

49. **(A)**

is the correct answer; "did you find someone (<u>avez-vous trouvé quelqu'un</u> ...) not (B) <u>quelque chose</u> (something), (C) <u>qui est-ce</u> (who is it) and (D) <u>qu'est-ce</u> (what is it), which are out of place here.

50. **(B)**

is the correct answer. The present subjunctive is required here because of the indefinite pronoun <u>quelqu'un</u>, which implies doubt; (A) being in the *passé composé,* (C) in the past subjunctive, and (D) in the present indicative, are all incorrect.

51. **(B)**

is the correct answer. <u>Personne</u> (no one or nobody) is indeed the only form which fits in this clause; (A) <u>quelqu'un</u> (someone) is not negative, (C) <u>pas</u> never precedes <u>personne</u>, and (D) <u>aucun</u>, although negative, cannot fit here, for as a pronoun (indefinite pronoun) it should replace a noun, which is not the case here.

52. **(D)**

is the correct answer because <u>lui</u> (to him) is the only indirect object pronoun present in this choice. (A) <u>le</u> (him, it), (B) <u>les</u> (them), and (C) <u>la</u>, (her, it), being direct object pronouns, are incorrect.

53. **(A)**

is the correct answer, for indeed <u>le</u> is the only direct object pronoun in this choice capable of functioning with regard to the meaning of the sentence: would you be so kind as to tell him (say <u>to</u> him) — <u>lui</u> — that I shall see him — <u>le</u> — tomorrow. (B) <u>l'</u> is before a consonant here, and therefore incorrect; (C) <u>leur</u>, an indirect object pronoun, and (D) <u>me</u>, making no sense, are all three incorrect.

54. **(B)**

is the correct answer, for <u>le</u> is a direct object pronoun and it precedes the indirect object pronoun (<u>je le lui dirai</u>). (A) <u>la</u>, out of context since it is feminine, (C) <u>lui</u>, being an indirect object and not in the correct slot, and (D) <u>moi</u>, a disjunctive (stressed) personal pronoun, or used with the imperative affirmative, are all three incorrect.

55. **(B)**

is the correct answer, for lui, an indirect object pronoun, always follows le before the verb. (A) les (them), (C) le (it), both direct objects, and (D) me, a direct and indirect object, cannot be correct, for they do not ever follow le.

56. **(A)**

is the correct answer because stylo, masculine and singular, must be modified by a possessive adjective in the same gender and number; (B) ma, feminine and singular, (C) le mien (mine), and (D) la mienne (mine), both possessive pronouns, cannot function here; therefore, (B), (C) and (D) are eliminated.

57. **(B)**

is the correct answer, for (A) le tien is in the "tu" form, which it not being used in this case; (C) le mien (mine) and (D) la mienne (mine) are out of context here.

58. **(C)**

is the correct answer, for servir is followed by the preposition de when it means to make use of; since stylo is masculine and singular, (B) de la mienne, feminine and singular, is incorrect; (A) à la mienne and (D) au mien, both using the preposition à, are also incorrect.

59. **(A)**

is the correct answer, for with the verb aimer a definite article (le, la, l', les) is required; indefinite or partitive articles are incorrect. (C) des, being indefinite, (B) beaucoup des, and (D) beaucoup de, being both adverbial and partitive, are all three incorrect.

60. **(D)**

is the correct answer, for, as explained in #59, the verb aimer takes only a definite article, (D) les being the only one in this choice. (A) de, (B) des, and (C) une, must be eliminated.

61. **(B)**

is the correct answer, for indeed after je voudrais que (I would like) in the main clause, the subjunctive must follow in the subordinate clause. (A) donneriez, present conditional, (C) donnez, present indicative, and (D) donnerez, future, are out of context here, and consequently incorrect.

62. **(C)**

is the correct answer, for <u>fruit</u> is a masculine and singular noun, therefore (C) <u>mon</u> (my) is the only possessive adjective capable of modifying it. (B) <u>mes</u>, being plural, (A) <u>ma</u> and (D) <u>sa</u>, being feminine and singular, do not agree with <u>fruit</u>; therefore, they are incorrect.

63. **(A)**

is the correct answer, for <u>favori</u>, masculine and singular, is the only adjective that can modify the noun <u>fruit</u>, masculine and singular. (B) <u>favorite</u> and (C) <u>préférée</u>, both feminine and singular, and (D) <u>préférable</u>, out of context here, are all three incorrect.

64. **(A)**

is the correct answer, for indeed <u>l'aube</u> (dawn) is that time of day when the sun rises (<u>le soleil se lève</u>). (B) the sun sets, (C) when the sea is generally agitated, and (D) when one sees giants, are not correct.

65. **(C)**

is the correct answer because it is true that when the sun rises in the morning there are boats coming back from fishing all night, and others which are ready to leave for the new day's fishing. (A) fishermen who sleep, (B) that it is windy, and (D) that there are giant skeletons, are incorrect.

66. **(B)**

is the correct answer. Dawn (<u>l'aube</u>) is that time of day when the night has practically disappeared and when the day has not entirely appeared yet. (A) when the boats must stay in port, (C) when the cranes are working, and (D) when the sun is already high and hot, are incorrect.

67. **(D)**

The answer is (D): This ad offers (<u>cette annonce propose</u>) the possibility without guarantee of an audition (<u>la possibilité sans garantie d'une séance d'essai</u>). There is nothing in the text to suggest that all English-speaking applicants who stop in between Monday and Saturday will earn 1500 euros, or that a full-time job in an advertising agency is being offered; hence, (A) <u>1500 euros à tous les candidats anglophones [. . .]</u> and (B) <u>un poste à temps plein dans une agence de publicité</u> are both incorrect. (C) <u>Des cours de théâtre et des séances de photos pour 1500 euros</u> (acting lessons and photo shoots for 1500 euros) is not a valid answer either.

68. **(A)**

People likely to be tempted by this ad (<u>les gens susceptibles d'être tentés par cette annonce</u>) (A) <u>rêvent de travailler dans le show-business</u> (dream of working in show business). There is little indication or reason to believe that (B) they are primarily looking for stable and predictable work (<u>sont surtout à la recherche d'un travail très stable et prévisible</u>), (C) they want to look at catalogs and read magazines (<u>souhaitent regarder des catalogues et lire des magazines</u>), or (D) organize publicity campaigns (<u>organisent des campagnes publicitaires</u>).

69. **(A)**

is the correct answer because the narrator tells us of one of his childhood memories. (B) gives details on his house, (C) gives a description of his brother, and (D) gives details on the end of summer, are eliminated, for they are incorrect.

70. **(A)**

is the correct answer, for indeed this memorable event would always occur toward the evening (<u>vers le soir</u>). (B) in the middle of the night, (C) at high noon, and (D) in the morning, are incorrect.

71. **(B)**

is the correct answer because it was July, and the farmers were busy harvesting. (A) winter time, (C) in September, and (D) in the middle of spring, are incorrect.

72. **(C)**

is the correct answer, for indeed the horses were running because they were anxious to get back to their stables. (A) because they were anxious to see the farmer's wife, (B) because they were tired, and (D) because they were overworked, are incorrect.

73. **(C)**

is the correct answer because the enormous noise which the two children were hearing was coming from the road where horses, heavy wagons, and men were returning to the farm. (A) was occuring in the neighboring village, (B) was causing such fear to the children that they would go back in the house, and (D) was coming from the din of the maybugs and the mosquitoes, are incorrect.

74. **(D)**

is the correct answer, for it is true that the walls of the house were still hot with the heat of the sun which had baked them all day. (A) burning after the fire, (B) red all over, and (C) strong, are incorrect.

75. **(C)**

is the correct answer, for it is true that the two children would go back inside the house because they were surrounded with insects (<u>des hannetons et des moustiques</u>). (A) because they were sleepy, (B) because they were afraid of the horses, and (D) because their parents were calling them, are incorrect.

76. **(D)**

is the correct answer, for indeed this is a man who has not seen France for quite some time. (A) who is afraid to travel by plane, (B) who is unintelligent, and (C) who is very small for an American, are incorrect.

77. **(A)**

is the correct answer because everything has changed since he left. (B) because he finds that people are not as small as they used to be, (C) because he feels as if he were a prisoner, and (D) because the plane does not stop immediately, are incorrect.

78. **(B)**

is the correct answer, for it is true that when they arrived at Orly (Paris) the stewardess asked the passengers to leave their seats and wished them a pleasant trip. (A) to recommend that nothing be forgotten on the plane, (C) because she was wearing a uniform, and (D) because she rang the bell, are incorrect.

79. **(B)**

is the correct answer, found in lines 1-2 of the third paragraph. The plane he had crossed the Atlantic Ocean in was a Boeing 747, but according to the author it has another name in France: <u>un avion à réaction</u>.

80. **(A)**

is the correct answer, for it is true that upon arriving at Orly (Paris) the traveller adjusted his watch to the Paris time since there was a six-hour difference between France and United States time. No, he was not (B) still asleep, (C) thirsty, or (D) hungry, when he arrived in Paris; therefore, (B), (C), and (D) are incorrect.

81. **(B)**

is the correct answer, for it is true that his body and mind were somewhat numb (<u>engourdi</u>) because he had been sitting in the plane all night. No, it was not because (A) he did not know whether to laugh or cry, (C) there was noise around him, nor (D) he was cold. Therefore, all three are incorrect.

82. **(A)**

is the correct answer, for indeed the narrator starts her walk on an uneven path (<u>le sentier n'était pas uni</u>). (B) in the rain, (C) along a high-way, and (D) through the mushroom path, are incorrect.

83. **(B)**

is the correct answer, for it is true that the narrator is pleasantly surprised by the smell, the fragrance, coming from the blackberry bushes (<u>les mûriers</u>); her pleasant surprise was not caused by (A) the sight of rare birds, (C) the songs of the birds, nor (D) the dry leaves; therefore, they are incorrect.

84. **(D)**

is the correct answer because even though the smells of the woods are mixed, in general one knows where they stem from; indeed the narrator speaks of the mixture of fragrances. No, she did not (A) sit down to listen to the birds, nor did she (B) see insects fly around her — at that time, nor (C) continue her walk — at that time. Therefore, they are incorrect.

85. **(A)**

is the correct answer because a little river (<u>une petite rivière</u> or <u>un ruisseau</u>) is necessary in the woods to complete the freshness or coolness and well-being that one seeks in the woods. Not (B) the tree tops, (C) the heat, or (D) the joyous cry of the bird; therefore, (B), (C), and (D) are incorrect.

86. **(C)**

is the correct answer, found in lines 3-4 of the first paragraph. Al-though the author's grandmother was 75 years old, she was still young at heart (<u>jeune d'esprit</u>).

87. **(A)**

is the correct answer because it is true that in spite of her being seventy-five years old, the elderly lady was still very pretty (bien jolie). No, she did not (B) have white hair, (C) like the life of an old woman, or (D) have a good appetite. Therefore, (B), (C), and (D) are incorrect.

88. **(C)**

is the correct answer because it is true that Marianne had given her daughters a direction (in life) that only she could make them understand. No, she did not (A) teach them that life is too complex, (B) teach them that life is too simple, nor (D) teach them that frequent visits are a must; therefore, (A), (B), and (D) are incorrect.

89. **(C)**

The key here was recognizing that définitive doesn't in this case mean "definitive" but rather "irrevocable, permanent." Hence fermeture définitive translates into "permanent closing," which of course means that the "Guara" shop was going out of business. The correct answer is therefore (C) [. . .] "la boutique 'Guara' était sur le point de fermer ses portes pour de bon" (the "Guara" shop was about to close its doors for good). Thus, fermeture définitive cannot mean that the shop was going to be closed on May 2 (allait être fermée le 2 mai), that certain pairs of shoes were on sale (que certaines paires de chaussures étaient en solde), or that the shop was going to close its doors prior to May 2 and then reopen afterwards (fermer ses portes avant le 2 mai pour les rouvrir par la suite). These faulty scenarios eliminate choices (A), (B), and (D), respectively.

90. **(D)**

Liquidation totale means "clearance sale," in this case because the shop was going out of business. Thus choice (D) [. . .] il fallait tout vendre au plus vite puisque la boutique "Guara" avait fait faillite (everything needed to be sold as quickly as possible seeing as the "Guara" shop was going out of business) is the correct answer. The percentages taken off from the regular prices are irrelevant in this case, which eliminates choices (A), (B), and (C) as valid answers.

SAT II:
SUBJECT TEST IN
FRENCH

PRACTICE
TEST VI

FRENCH TEST VI

PART A

Time: 1 Hour
        90 Questions

DIRECTIONS: This part consists of a number of incomplete statements, each followed by four suggested completions. Select the most appropriate completion and blacken the corresponding space on the answer sheet.

1.   A la pâtisserie, on achète ...

   (A) des pattes   (C) des gâteaux

   (B) des patates   (D) des tapis

2.   Le vieillard ne marche pas bien parce qu'il a mal ...

   (A) au cou   (C) au poignet

   (B) à l'épaule   (D) à la jambe

3.   Ce touriste va ... en première classe.

   (A) travailler   (C) séjourner

   (B) voyager   (D) voler

4.   Jean oublie qu'il faut parler ... à 4h du matin.

   (A) brusquement   (C) doucement

   (B) constamment   (D) cruellement

5.   En général, la concierge parisienne habite ...

   (A) sous le toit   (C) dans la rue

   (B) au rez-de-chaussée   (D) au troisième étage

6. Simone utilise du savon pour ...

   (A) se sauver   (C) se lever

   (B) savoir   (D) se laver

7. Mes parents ont deux fauteuils dans ... pour le confort des invités.

   (A) leur salle à manger   (C) leur chambre

   (B) leur salon   (D) leur salle de bains

8. Puisque Pierre a trop mangé ce soir, il ...

   (A) a l'envie de dîner   (C) n'a plus faim

   (B) a encore faim   (D) a besoin de pain

9. Il fait beaucoup de soleil aujourd'hui. Alors, portez ...

   (A) une cravate   (C) une chaussette

   (B) une chaussure   (D) un chapeau

10. Dans mon jardin, ... chante chaque matin.

    (A) un escargot   (C) un chat

    (B) un coq   (D) une coquille

11. La sœur de votre mère est votre ...

    (A) nièce   (C) tante

    (B) belle-sœur   (D) grand-mère

12. Va chercher le courrier. ... vient de passer.

    (A) La facture   (C) Le coureur

    (B) Le facteur   (D) Le courant

13. J'ai dix-huit ans. Je viens de commencer mes études ...

    (A) au lycée   (C) au collège

    (B) à l'université   (D) à l'école secondaire

14. Les grandes vacances ont lieu …

    (A) en été   (C) à Pâques

    (B) à Noël   (D) en automne

15. Il y avait tant de bruit au théâtre que les gens ne pouvaient pas … le dialogue.

    (A) attendre   (C) entendre

    (B) atteindre   (D) étendre

16. En relisant sa lettre, Philippe … son erreur.

    (A) se rend compte de   (C) réalise

    (B) s'agit de   (D) s'échappe de

17. Elle achète … pour suivre la mode.

    (A) les revues   (C) les modèles

    (B) les magasins   (D) les mannequins

18. Jeanne est fatiguée et elle va …

    (A) se rappeler   (C) rester

    (B) se reposer   (D) sauter

19. Simon achète de l'essence pour …

    (A) son vélo   (C) sa voiture

    (B) son violon   (D) sa voile

20. Dans la classe, mon meilleur copain est Georges. C'est …

    (A) mon bon ami   (C) mon gendarme

    (B) mon boulanger   (D) mon ennemi

21. Un bon conducteur met toujours …

    (A) sa veste   (C) sa musique

    (B) sa cravate   (D) sa ceinture de sécurité

22. En été, nous partageons l'ombre du grand arbre avec les voisins qui vivent … chez nous.

    (A) en face de

    (B) assez loin de

    (C) à côté de

    (D) dans l'hôtel près de

23. Quand le service n'est pas compris, on laisse … pour le serveur.

    (A) un pourboire

    (B) l'addition

    (C) la vaisselle

    (D) le menu

24. A la pharmacie Margot a acheté …

    (A) de la médecine

    (B) des médicaments

    (C) des médecins

    (D) des méditations

25. Si vous ne mettez pas votre écharpe, vous allez … un rhume.

    (A) rattraper

    (B) attraper

    (C) attirer

    (D) prendre

26. Pour faire cette omelette, j'ai utilisé cinq …

    (A) os

    (B) œufs

    (C) œillets

    (D) yeux

27. Quand nous arrivons devant un feu rouge, nous …

    (A) courons

    (B) roulons plus vite

    (C) nous arrêtons

    (D) téléphonons aux pompiers

PART B

DIRECTIONS: In each of the sentences in this part of the test, one or more words are underlined. One of the four choices following each sentence can be correctly substituted for the underlined word(s) to form a grammatically correct statement or question. The new sentence may differ in meaning from the original example. Select the one choice which fits grammatically into the original sentence and blacken the corresponding space on the answer sheet.

28. La <u>maison</u> qu'ils ont achetée est très belle.

    (A) parapluie   (C) magazine

    (B) arbre   (D) chaise

29. Donnez-<u>moi</u> les livres qui sont sur la table, s'il vous plaît.

    (A) toi   (C) le

    (B) lui   (D) vous

30. Ton frère joue-t-il du <u>piano</u>?

    (A) tennis   (C) violon

    (B) cartes   (D) flute

31. Quand j'avais dix ans, j'ai visité <u>Paris</u>.

    (A) ma tante Hélène   (C) des amis français

    (B) ces monuments   (D) le Président

32. La cuisine <u>française</u> est très célèbre.

    (A) Chinoise   (C) Allemagne

    (B) grec   (D) italienne

33. Un bel <u>homme</u> se trouvait devant la porte.

    (A) arbre

    (B) plante

    (C) école

    (D) amie

34. Il faut qu'elle <u>écrive</u> à ses parents.

    (A) puisse

    (B) reçoive

    (C) écoute

    (D) obéisse

35. Nous <u>essayons</u> de construire une maison.

    (A) voulons

    (B) pensons

    (C) aimons

    (D) décidons

36. Martine était ravie de dîner chez <u>nous</u>.

    (A) leur

    (B) ils

    (C) eux

    (D) ceux

37. Le petit garçon s'est mis à <u>pleurer</u> dans la rue.

    (A) nager

    (B) commencer

    (C) neiger

    (D) rire

38. Gaston <u>va</u> au cinéma avec son frère demain soir.

    (A) allait

    (B) venait

    (C) ira

    (D) pourrait

39. Dis-lui de venir ici afin que nous <u>discutions</u> ensemble.

    (A) puissions

    (B) étions

    (C) parlons

    (D) parlions

40. Cette histoire est bonne, mais l'autre est <u>plus intéressante</u>.

    (A) mieux

    (B) le meilleur

    (C) meilleure

    (D) meilleur

41. Laquelle de ces <u>maisons</u> est la vôtre?

    (A) voitures

    (C) poèmes

    (B) bateaux

    (D) garages

42. Marcel, y a-t-il de la <u>crème</u> sur la table?

    (A) argent

    (C) café

    (B) thé

    (D) soupe

43. Tes cousins vont-ils venir à la fête avec <u>tes</u> amis?

    (A) vos

    (C) leurs

    (B) leur

    (D) ses

44. Les membres du cercle étaient <u>assis</u> autour de la table.

    (A) debout

    (C) débuts

    (B) debouts

    (D) débutants

45. Le problème <u>dont</u> il parle est très sérieux.

    (A) de qui

    (C) de quoi

    (B) duquel

    (D) de laquelle

PART C

DIRECTIONS: The following paragraphs contain blank spaces which indicate omissions in the text. Below each blank are four choices. Choose the answer which best completes the sentence in the given context and blacken the corresponding space on the answer sheet. Note that in some instances choice A consists of dashes, which indicate that no insertion is required at that point.

S'il fait beau samedi prochain, nous _____ un pique-nique

46. (A) aurons

    (B) verrons

    (C) ferons

    (D) serons

à la plage. Alain va inviter Charlotte _____ venir avec nous

47. (A) — —

    (B) à

    (C) pour

    (D) de

et j'espère qu'elle _____ nous accompagner parce qu'elle est

48. (A) puisse

    (B) pourra

    (C) pouvait

    (D) pourrait

très sympathique. Alain va demander _____ son père assez _____

49. (A) — —
(B) de
(C) du
(D) à

50. (A) — —
(B) de
(C) d'
(D) de l'

argent pour acheter de bonnes choses à manger et à boire.

On va _____ une journée formidable!

51. (A) avoir
(B) passer
(C) faire
(D) dépenser

Avant _____ partir en vacances, Marie et Alice _____ prendre leurs

52. (A) — —
(B) à
(C) de
(D) que

53. (A) ont dû
(B) ont dûs
(C) ont dûes
(D) devenaient

billets. Elles _____ dans une agence de voyage où elles les ont _____

54. (A) sont venus
(B) sont partis
(C) sont allés
(D) sont allées

55. (A) vendues
(B) acheté
(C) achetées
(D) achetés

hier soir. Maintenant, il faut qu'elles _____ attention à _____

56. (A) font
   (B) fassent
   (C) feront
   (D) faisaient

57. (A) tout
   (B) toute
   (C) toutes
   (D) tous

les détails du voyage.

_____ était le nom de _____ fleur rouge _____ Hélène

58. (A) Quel
   (B) Lequel
   (C) Comment
   (D) Quoi

59. (A) cet
   (B) cette
   (C) ce
   (D) celle

60. (A) que
   (B) qui
   (C) qu'
   (D) ce qu'

_____ dans son jardin hier? Je ne la _____ pas

61. (A) trouvait
   (B) a trouvé
   (C) a trouvée
   (D) trouverait

62. (A) reconnaissais
   (B) savais
   (C) connaisse
   (D) sache

mais _____ une fleur extraordinaire.

63. (A) elle était
   (B) c'était
   (C) elle avait été
   (D) elle a été

PART D

> **DIRECTIONS:** Read the following passages carefully for comprehension. Each passage is followed by a number of questions or incomplete statements. Select the one answer or completion that is most appropriate according to the passage and blacken the corresponding space on the answer sheet.

De tous les villages de Provence que Robert visita, ce fut le célèbre Châteauneuf-du-Pape, le "Castel Gondolfo" de la Vaucluse, qui lui inspira la dévotion la plus profonde. Il l'aborda pour la première fois un beau matin de printemps et a garé sa voiture en face de "La Mule du Pape," un joli petit restaurant qui prit son appellation du charmant conte d'Alphonse Daudet.

D'un vieillard amical, Robert apprit des détails de l'histoire de cet endroit intéressant:

> Voilà plus de six siècles que Jean XXII fit construire une résidence estivale pour les papes d'Avignon. De l'édifice imposant il ne reste plus, malheureusement, que quelques pierres de la tour. En 1944, les soldats qui occupaient le village fit sauter leur stock de munitions au moment d'abandonner le castel aux Alliés.

— Mais, continua le vieillard, même si les Allemands ont détruit le château, soyons heureux qu'ils n'aient pu arracher nos vignes.

Et il fit goûter à Robert un vin splendide qui avait survécu aux guerres et aux siècles — un vin qui, pour n'être plus le vin des papes, n'en reste pas moins le pape des vins.

64. Robert arriva au village

(A) à pied

(B) à cheval

(C) par le train

(D) en auto

65. "La Mule du Pape" est

(A) un hôtel et une histoire

(B) un conte et un restaurant

(C) un bon vin

(D) le nom du château

66. Qui est-ce qui a fait bâtir le château?

(A) Jean XXII

(B) les soldats

(C) Alphonse Daudet

(D) le duc de la Vaucluse

67. Robert apprécie le village à cause de

    (A) sa tradition et son vin   (C) son soleil et ses fôrets

    (B) Alphonse Daudet   (D) ses habitants

Depuis 11 ans le **Guide Arcy-Labat** des ordinateurs est une référence. Et cette édition ne déroge pas à la règle en affirmant une volonté de procéder à un classement impitoyable des meilleurs ordinateurs.

GUIDE ARCY-LABAT DES ORDINATEURS 2002

PIERRE AUBIN

Fiches techniques, secrets de fabriquants, rapport qualité-prix, fiabilité, service après-vente, capacité de mémoire, rapidité : vous trouverez ici tout ce qu'il vous faut savoir pour éviter les mauvaises surprises. Disponible chez votre marchand de journaux.

656 pages
21,34 €

68. Selon cette annonce, quel est le principal critère pris en compte pour évaluer la qualité des ordinateurs?

    (A) Les prix que leur ont été accordés par la presse

    (B) Le rapport qualité-prix

    (C) Le nombre de chaque modèle ayant été vendu

    (D) Des sondages

69. Ce livre contient des renseignements sur tout ce qui suit sauf :

    (A) Les secrets concernant la production des ordinateurs

    (B) La qualité des différents modèles

    (C) Les lieux où l'on peut acheter les modèles qui sont cités dans ce livre

    (D) Des dossiers et des fiches techniques sur les modèles en question

A la naissance de son benjamin, Mme Renard avait presque quarante ans. Ce ne fut que vingt ans plus tard que Jacques comprit un peu mieux cette femme taciturne. Elle avait élevé ses cinq enfants dans la misère extrême et bien que le père l'aidât par son travail, ce fut elle qui eut la responsabilité complète de la famille et qui en prit toutes les décisions.

A l'occasion de son 60ème anniversaire, la famille vint fêter la mère vénérée. Après le départ des autres enfants, Jacques se mit à poser des questions à Mme Renard:

—Tu ne parles jamais de ta jeunesse, Maman, dit-il. Raconte-moi un peu comment c'était.

Très doucement, la bonne femme lui parla de ces années pénibles.

Pendant la guerre, à la suite d'un bombardement, elle devint orpheline. Après un temps, on la plaça chez un oncle aisé. Dans cette famille bourgeoise, on la traita de domestique; elle avait souvent froid et presque toujours faim. Mais ce qui lui manquait le plus c'était l'amour tendre de ses parents morts qui l'avaient chérie et même gâtée dans sa jeune enfance.

Cette situation misérable dura dix longues années, jusqu'au soir où elle rencontra Jean. Celui-ci la trouva jolie, l'épousa et l'emmena à Napoule, un petit village agricole, où les jeunes époux s'installèrent dans une ferme.

70. Un benjamin est

   (A) l'aîné de la famille

   (B) le nom d'un garçon

   (C) l'avant-dernier enfant

   (D) le plus jeune de la famille

71. Jacques comprend mieux sa mère

   (A) quand il a 60 ans

   (B) quand il a 20 ans

   (C) par moyen de son père

   (D) dès son plus jeune âge

72. Il est certain que Mme Renard

   (A) ne travailla guère

   (B) était une personne faible

   (C) menait une vie difficile

   (D) n'aimait pas sa famille

73. Puisqu'elle fut orpheline, la petite

    (A) n'avait ni mère ni père

    (B) était fille unique

    (C) avait une grande famille

    (D) avait plusieurs frères

74. Le narrateur de ce passage

    (A) semble condamner Jean

    (B) décrit une famille cruelle

    (C) est Jacques

    (D) admire Mme Renard

75. Après leur mariage, les jeunes gens

    (A) firent un long voyage de noces

    (B) habitèrent un petit village

    (C) prirent des vacances

    (D) furent très riches

Le lendemain matin, leur hôte invita Monique et Philippe à visiter le château et ses vastes jardins. Tout ce qu'il leur montra fut magnifique mais ce qui les impressionna le plus était la vue de la grande terrasse. La vallée s'étendait devant eux; chaque détail du petit village était visible. A l'horizon, des collines couvertes de fleurs fraîches encadraient cette image de beauté. Le soleil brillait doucement, les arbres se couvraient de leurs premières feuilles et une brise légère fit danser l'eau qui jaillissait gaiement de la grande fontaine.

Monique n'osa respirer devant cette scène inoubliable. Elle n'avait jamais été si heureuse mais elle savait bien que cet instant ne durerait pas et que la situation changerait bientôt. Et ainsi se passa-t-il, car tout à coup on entendit les cris d'un groupe de chasseurs qui s'approchaient du château pour emmener le baron à la chasse. Celui-ci, content de les voir, fit ses adieux à Monique et à Philippe et s'en alla, le fusil à la main, le sourire aux lèvres.

76. Le narrateur décrit une scène

    (A) effrayante

    (B) douleureuse

    (C) dangereuse

    (D) paisible

77. La chose la plus frappante fut

    (A) leur hôte

    (B) tout

    (C) la vue

    (D) la fontaine

78. La scène se passe

    (A) au printemps

    (B) en hiver

    (C) au Sahara

    (D) à minuit

79. Le bonheur de Monique se brise au moment où

    (A) elle ne peut pas respirer

    (B) le baron s'en va

    (C) des gens arrivent

    (D) elle s'impatiente

80. En partant, le baron

    (A) ne dit rien à Monique

    (B) ne veut pas s'en aller

    (C) est triste de quitter ses invités

    (D) se réjouit d'aller à la chasse

Tahiti représente "l'île des rêves" de beaucoup de gens. Découverte en 1768 par un marin anglais, le capitaine Wallis, ce fut bientôt après que des explorateurs européens y allèrent. A cause de la beauté de l'île et du caractère amical de ses habitants, les aventuriers ne tardèrent pas à les suivre.

L'île devint une colonie française en 1880, et en 1891 le peintre Paul Gauguin quitta sa famille à Paris pour y aller chercher une vie différente de celle qu'il connaissait en Europe. Il fit des toiles de couleurs vives qui traitèrent la vie quotidienne et spirituelle des Tahitiens. C'est en grande partie à cause de ces œuvres célèbres que des milliers de touristes se dirigent chaque année vers l'île, ce "paradis sur terre." Ses plages de sable blanc, ses palmiers, ses montagnes, ses eaux claires, et surtout son climat tropical, attirent les Européens qui cherchent des vacances simples et l'expérience incomparable d'une détente complète.

81. Les explorateurs européens

    (A) se sont vite établis sur l'île pour la coloniser

    (B) ont fait connaître la beauté de l'île aux aventuriers

    (C) ont découragé le tourisme

    (D) n'apprécièrent pas l'île

82. Les étrangers trouvèrent les Tahitiens

    (A) sauvages   (C) timides

    (B) paresseux   (D) hospitaliers

83. Paul Gauguin est célèbre pour

    (A) ses toiles tahitiennes   (C) ses sculptures

    (B) ses paysages parisiens   (D) ses romans

84. La "vie quotidienne" signifie la vie

    (A) folklorique   (C) simple

    (B) suffisante   (D) de tous les jours

85. Tahiti offre aux touristes

    (A) des vacances stimulantes (C) une expérience cosmopolite

    (B) la possibilité de se reposer (D) l'occasion de faire du ski

Guillaume arriva à la gare de bonne heure, tout agité de quitter sa petite ville et sa famille pour aller chercher fortune à Paris. A dix-huit ans, il n'avait voyagé que très peu dans la région, mais cette fois-ci il allait traverser presque tout le pays pour rejoindre son cousin Paul à la capitale. Celui-ci s'y était installé trois ans auparavant et avait écrit à Guillaume de venir le rejoindre. Le jeune homme travaillerait dans le petit magasin dont Paul était propriétaire et habiterait chez lui aussi.

Enfin monté dans le train et assis près de la fenêtre, Guillaume ferma les yeux et s'endormit, son rêve plein d'images de la vie fascinante qui l'attendait: les rues animées, les grands boulevards élégants, les monuments célèbres qu'il avait toujours admirés, et surtout les belles femmes parisiennes qu'il allait rencontrer.

Tout à coup il eut l'impression que le train ralentissait et il ouvrit brusquement les yeux. Une voix annonçait, "Bordeaux."

— Zut! se dit-il. Je me suis trompé de train! Celui-ci va au sud et je veux aller au nord! Que je suis bête!

Il saisit sa valise et sauta sur le quai juste au moment où le train repartait. Fâché contre lui-même, le jeune aventurier se résigna à recommencer son voyage vers une nouvelle vie.

86. Guillaume quitta sa ville natale pour

    (A) voyager   (C) être touriste

    (B) visiter Paris   (D) travailler avec Paul

87. Paul était à Paris depuis

    (A) trois ans   (C) plusieurs mois

    (B) sa naissance   (D) la guerre

88. Dans le train, Guillaume

    (A) eut un cauchemar

    (B) s'imagina la vie parisienne dans ses rêves

    (C) regarda par la fenêtre

    (D) fut très agité

ESCAPADE A PRIX DOUX

Idéalement situé sur la presqu'île de Saint-Jean-Cap-Ferrat, le **Royal Riviera** offre une des plus belles vues de la Méditerranée. Avec ses 77 chambres et suites climatisées, sa plage de sable fin et sa piscine à débordement, ce palace au décor raffiné est le cadre rêvé - entre Nice et Monaco - pour une escapade romantique. D'autant que du 22 octobre au 2 décembre 2001, un forfait deux nuits pour deux personnes, comprenant l'hébergement en chambre double, les petits déjeuners et un dîner, vous est proposé pour seulement 3 775 FF.

06230 Saint-Jean-Cap-Ferrat - Tél. : 04 93 76 31 00
Fax : 04 93 01 23 07 - www.royal-riviera.com

89. Laquelle des phrases suivantes est vraie ?

(A) Le « Royal Riviera » se situe à Monaco

(B) Les tarifs étaient réduits pour les couples du 22 octobre au 2 décembre 2001

(C) Le « Royal Riviera » est surtout connu pour son charme rustique et campagnard

(D) Le « Royal Riviera » se situe sur une île

90. On peut supposer que les gens qui séjournent au « Royal Riviera » y vont surtout pour :

(A) Un accueil luxueux et attentionné au bord de la mer

(B) Changer de piscine

(C) Regarder le sable fin et se baigner dans la piscine

(D) Prendre des vacances tout en restant à deux pas de chez eux

SAT II: French Subject Test
Test VI

ANSWER KEY

1.	(C)	24.	(B)	47.	(B)	70.	(D)
2.	(D)	25.	(B)	48.	(B)	71.	(B)
3.	(B)	26.	(B)	49.	(D)	72.	(C)
4.	(C)	27.	(C)	50.	(C)	73.	(A)
5.	(B)	28.	(D)	51.	(B)	74.	(D)
6.	(D)	29.	(B)	52.	(C)	75.	(B)
7.	(B)	30.	(C)	53.	(A)	76.	(D)
8.	(C)	31.	(B)	54.	(D)	77.	(C)
9	(D)	32.	(D)	55.	(D)	78.	(A)
10.	(B)	33.	(A)	56.	(B)	79.	(C)
11.	(C)	34.	(D)	57.	(D)	80.	(D)
12.	(B)	35.	(D)	58.	(A)	81.	(B)
13.	(B)	36.	(C)	59.	(B)	82.	(D)
14.	(A)	37.	(D)	60.	(C)	83.	(A)
15.	(C)	38.	(C)	61.	(C)	84.	(D)
16.	(A)	39.	(D)	62.	(A)	85.	(B)
17.	(A)	40.	(C)	63.	(B)	86.	(D)
18.	(B)	41.	(A)	64.	(D)	87.	(A)
19.	(C)	42.	(D)	65.	(B)	88.	(B)
20.	(A)	43.	(C)	66.	(A)	89.	(B)
21.	(D)	44.	(A)	67.	(A)	90.	(A)
22.	(C)	45.	(B)	68.	(B)		
23.	(A)	46.	(C)	69.	(C)		

DETAILED EXPLANATIONS OF ANSWERS

PRACTICE TEST VI

1. **(C)**
    (A) and (B) seem related to "pâtisserie" = a pastry shop, but have completely different meanings: "pattes" = paws, and "patates" = potatoes. (D) "tapis" is a rug or carpet, and is offered as a choice because it is easy to confuse the "t" and "p" by rearranging them.

2. **(D)**
    Although (A) "au cou," (B) "à l'épaule," and (C) "au poignet," refer to parts of the body, the most logical reason for having difficulty in walking would be because of a bad leg = "à la jambe."

3. **(B)**
    "Travailler" (A) is commonly confused with "travel" but is a *faux ami* (a "false friend") meaning "to work." (C) "séjourner" = to spend time or remain in a place, (D) "voler," is not used to mean "to fly" for people, but rather for birds or planes, i.e., the physical act of flying. Therefore, (A), (C) and (D) are all inappropriate.

4. **(C)**
    In the context of the time given in the example, 4 a.m., (C) is the most logical of these adverbs, since one should respect those who are asleep by speaking quietly = "doucement." Therefore (A) sharply = "brusquement," (B) endlessly = "constamment," or (D) cruelly = "cruellement," is inappropriate.

5. **(B)**
    Since the "concierge" is an apartment manager, she generally has an apartment on the ground floor (B) "rez-de-chaussée," where she can observe the comings and goings of tenants. (A) "sous le toit" = under the roof, and (D) "au troisième étage" = on the third floor, are therefore not logical, since they are too far from the building entrance, while (C) "dans la rue" = in the road, is immediately rejected as incorrect.

6. **(D)**

    (C) "se lever" = to get up, and (D) "se laver" = to get washed, are often confused because of similarity in spelling. (A) "se sauver" = to leave quickly, and (B) "savoir" = to know, appear similar to "savon" = soap, but have no connection with the word's meaning.

7. **(B)**

    Various rooms in the house are cited here. Logically, "deux fauteuils" = two armchairs, would be located in the (B) "salon" = living room, and not in the (A) "salle à manger" = dining room or (D) "salle de bains" = bathroom. Although armchairs might be found in the "chambre" = bedroom, it is illogical here because the armchairs are for "les invités" = guests.

8. **(C)**

    This example deals with idiomatic expressions based on "avoir" and also tests knowledge of the adverbs "encore" = still, "ne plus" = no more, and "trop" = too much. (A), (B), and (D) suggest that Pierre is still hungry, and since he has overeaten they are not correct in the context.

9. **(D)**

    Confusion is possible because of the similarity in spelling between (B) "chaussure" = shoe, (C) "chaussette" = sock, and (D) "chapeau." The fact that one is advised to wear "one" of these articles disqualifies (B) and (C) as correct, while it is irrelevant whether or not one wears a tie (A) "cravate" when it is very sunny outside.

10. **(B)**

    This question tests your knowledge of animal vocabulary. Neither (A) "escargot" = snail, (C) "chat" = cat, nor (D) "coquille" = shell, is correct since none of these sing or crow. (B) "coq" = cock, and is the proper response.

11. **(C)**

    These terms identify and describe family members and relationships. (A) "nièce" is the same as in English; (B) "belle-sœur" refers to both a sister-in-law and a step-sister; (D) "grand-mère" = the mother of your mother. The question asks you to identify the sister of your mother, your aunt = "tante."

12. **(B)**

(A) "facture" = a bill or invoice, strongly resembles the correct response, (B) "facteur" = postman. (A good hint is the "eur" ending, which often identifies "one who" ... Compare "professEUR," "lectEUR," "doctEUR," or (C) "coureur" = one who runs.) (D) "courant" = current, like (C), resembles "courrier," but does not fit logically into the context here.

13. **(B)**

An eighteen year-old would be starting his/her studies "à l'université" = at the university or college (B). All of the other choices, "au lycée" (A), "au collège" (C), and "à l'école secondaire" (D), are different ways to say "high school."

14. **(A)**

While there are school breaks at (B) "Noël" = Christmas, and at (C) "Pâques" = Easter, the really long school vacation is during the summer = "été," and not in autumn (D).

15. **(C)**

Common confusion exists regarding the meaning of these verbs: (A) "attendre" = to wait for, (B) "atteindre" = to attain, and (D) "étendre" = to extend or spread out. (C) "entendre" = to hear, is the only logical response.

16. **(A)**

(B) "s'agit de" = to be a matter of, and (D) "s'échappe de" = to escape from, are pronominal verbs but do not make sense in the context. (C) "réaliser" = to achieve or realise a goal, is frequently misused for "se rendre compte de" = to realize (intellectually).

17. **(A)**

In order to keep in fashion = "suivre la mode," she buys magazines = "revues" (A), not stores = "magasins" (B), or the actual models = "modèles" (C), or "mannequins" (D).

18. **(B)**

Although all of these verbs begin with "r", their meanings are quite different: (A) "se rappeler" = to remember; (C) "rester" is a *faux ami* and does not mean to lie down or rest. Rather it means "to remain." (D) "ranger" = to arrange or put something in place, requires a direct object and is therefore not possible here.

19. **(C)**

Despite the distraction of similar initial letters, "essence" = gas, can only be correctly associated with (C) "voiture" = car. Gasoline is not appropriate for (A) "vélo" = a bicycle, (B) "violon" = a violin, or (D) "voile" = a sail.

20. **(A)**

"Copain" is commonly used for "pal" or "close friend." Two of the other choices, (B) "boulanger" (associated with "<u>pain</u>") and (C) "gendarme" = policeman (associated with "cop"), illustrate possible confusions with French and English words that are not related to "copain." (D) "ennemi" is an antonym of "copain."

21. **(D)**

A "bon conducteur" is a good driver and has nothing to do with (C) "musique," although one might associate this *false friend* with an orchestra. (A) "sa veste" = his jacket, and (B) "sa cravate" = his tie, are not logical in this context. (D) "sa ceinture de sécurité" = his safety belt, which all safe drivers use.

22. **(C)**

The neighbors we share the shade of the tree with live (C) "à côté de" = next door to us ("chez nous"). (A) "en face de" = across from, (B) "assez loin de" = fairly far from, and (D) "dans l'hôtel près de" = in the nearby hotel, are all incorrect.

23. **(A)**

This question deals with restaurant vocabulary and an understanding of "service compris" = service included in the cost of the meal. (B) "l'addition" = the check and (C) "la vaisselle" = the dishes (upon which one eats). (D) "le menu" means the same thing in English and French. (A) "un pourboire" = a tip [literally, something with which to buy a drink] is therefore the only possible choice.

24. **(B)**

The four answers have similar initial spellings and are therefore confusing. (A) "de la médecine" = medicine [the subject one studies to become a doctor] and (C) des médecins = the people who practice that profession, i.e., doctors. (D) "des méditations" is the same as the English word and is an inappropriate action in a drug store. (B) "médicaments" = the medication one takes when one is ill. Note the difference in spelling between French "méd<u>e</u>cine" and English "med<u>i</u>cine."

25. **(B)**

If you don't put your scarf on, you will catch a cold = "attraper un rhume." This is a fixed expression, therefore, although "rattraper" (A) and "prendre" (D) can mean "to catch" in some contexts, they are incorrect here. "Attirer" = to attract (C) is also incorrect.

26. **(B)**

The first three choices begin with the same letter but are very different in meaning. (A) "os" = a bone; (C) "œillets" are carnations; (D) "yeux" is the plural of "œil" = an eye, and might remind one of (B) "œufs" = eggs, the correct answer, because of somewhat similar pronunciation.

27. **(C)**

One must know that "un feu rouge" = a red traffic light, in order to choose the correct answer. (A) "courons" = we run, and (B) "roulons plus vite" = we drive faster, are both wrong (or illegal) choices, while (D), "téléphonons aux pompiers" = we call the fire department, is obviously incorrect.

28. **(D)**

Since "achetée" agrees with a preceding direct object ("maison") in the example, the noun substituted must also be feminine singular. Neither (A) "parapluie," (B) "arbre," nor (C) "magazine" is feminine, despite the final "e" in their spelling.

29. **(B)**

(A) "toi" and (D) "vous" make no sense in the example. (C) "le" is a direct object pronoun and therefore incorrect. (B) "lui," is the only logical and grammatically correct possibility.

30. **(C)**

This example is based on the difference between "jouer à," used for playing games and sports, (A) "tennis," and (B) "cartes," and "jouer de," used for instruments. (D) is incorrect because the expression is "jouer DE LA flute," a feminine form which cannot be substituted for "jouer DU piano."

31. **(B)**

"Visiter" is used for visiting places and not people. (A) "ma tante Hélène," (C) "des amis français," and (D) "le Président," are therefore incorrect. "Rendre visite à" is used for people.

32. **(D)**

This question deals with adjectives of nationality and tests your knowledge of their form. You are replacing a feminine adjective, "française," written with a small letter. (A) "Chinoise" is incorrect because it is a noun [as shown by its capital "C."] (B) "grec" is masculine and (C) "Allemagne" = Germany (often confused with "allemand," the adjective) are also not suitable. The only correct choice is (D) "italienne."

33. **(A)**

"Bel" is a special form of "beau," used for masculine nouns with an initial vowel or an "h." (B) "plante," (C) "école," and (D) "amie" are feminine, and thus incorrect.

34. **(D)**

After "Il faut que" the subjunctive is required. There is also the preposition "à" to consider, when choosing the correct verb. (A) "puisse," (B) "reçoive," and (C) "écoute," do not take "à" after them. Therefore only (D) "obéisse," which takes "à" and is in the subjunctive form, is possible.

35. **(D)**

The structural point here is that some verbs take "de" before an infinitive, as in "essayons de + construire." Therefore, the substitute verb must also take "de" and neither (A) "voulons," (B) "pensons," nor (C) "aimons," do so. Therefore (D) "décidons" is the correct answer.

36. **(C)**

After the preposition "chez," it is necessary to use a disjunctive pronoun. (A) "leur" is either a possessive adjective or a personal pronoun, (B) "ils" is a subject pronoun, and (D) "ceux" is a demonstrative pronoun, leaving only (C) "eux" as a possible choice.

37. **(D)**

"Se mettre à" = to begin. In this context, (A) "nager" = to swim, is impossible, (B) "commencer" = to begin, is redundant and (C) "neiger" = to snow, is illogical. Therefore (D) "rire" = to laugh, is the correct answer.

38. **(C)**

Because of "demain soir," the substitute word must also express the future, as does (C) "ira." (A) "allait" and (B) "venait" are in the imperfect; (D) "pourrait" is in the conditional and is not possible here either.

39. **(D)**

After "afin que," the subjunctive is required. Although (A) "puissons" is in the subjunctive, it makes no sense in the context. (B) "étions" is in the imperfect and (C) "parlons" is in the present indicative. Therefore, the only correct choice is (D) "parlions."

40. **(C)**

This example deals with the confusion between the <u>adverb</u> "mieux" = better, and the <u>adjective</u> "meilleur(e)" = better. Such a distinction does not exist in English. Since the words to be replaced ("plus intéressante") describe a feminine noun ("histoire"), you must choose a feminine adjective to replace them. (A) "mieux" is wrong, since it is an adverb; (B) "le meilleur" is in both the masculine and the superlative forms (used for comparing more than two things); while (D) "meilleur" is the masculine form. Only (C) "meilleure" is correct.

41. **(A)**

The interrogative pronoun "Laquelle" = which, which one, is in the feminine form, and therefore is replacing a feminine noun. (A) "voitures" is the only feminine noun given; (B) "bateaux" is masculine, as are (C) "poèmes" and (D) "garages," despite the fact that they end in "e." Be careful of these *faux amis*!

42. **(D)**

The partitive form "de la" = some, any, is followed by a feminine singular noun, so the substitution chosen must also be feminine singular. (A) "argent" would require the form "de l'" and is masculine; (B) "thé" = tea, is masculine ("du thé"), as is (C) "café" = coffee ("du café"). Only (D) "soupe" is feminine singular and therefore the correct choice.

43. **(C)**

This exercise tests your knowledge of possessive adjectives. Since the first part of the sentence uses "tes" (the familiar plural form), you cannot switch to formal plural (A) "vos" at the end of the sentence. (B) "leur" = their, refers to a plural subject owning one thing (e.g., Jean et Bill ont une mère; c'est LEUR mère). (D) "ses" refers to a singular subject owning several things (e.g., Les livres de Bob sont SES livres). Since we need an adjective that reflects several people owning more than one thing, the only correct answer is (C) "leurs" = their (friends).

44. **(A)**

While the four choices have similarities in spelling, do not confuse them. (A) "debout" = standing, is an invariable adjective or adverb, used for <u>singular and plural</u> nouns. (B) "debouts" is therefore incorrect, since there is no plural form of this word. (C) "débuts" and (D) "débutants" look similar to "debout" but are nouns which are used (in English, too) to describe the beginning of a career in the arts or the social world, or beginners in general. They have nothing to do with the context of the example, which deals with members of a club around a table.

45. **(B)**

The relative pronoun "dont" = of whom, of which, replaces expressions with "de." In this example, "Il parle DE ce problème" (He's speaking about this problem) becomes "Le problème DONT il parle" (The problem ABOUT WHICH he's speaking...). In this structure, "dont" cannot be replaced by (A) "de qui" = of whom, used for <u>people</u> and not for things. (C) "de quoi" = about what, is used for very general, unspecified contexts (e.g., "Je ne sais pas DE QUOI tu parles" = I don't know what you're talking about) and is therefore incorrect, since there is a specific antecedent in the example ("Le problème"). (D) "de laquelle" is not possible either, because it is used to replace a feminine antecedent and "problème" is masculine. Thus, the only correct answer is (B) "duquel," a synonym for "dont."

46. **(C)**

The expression is "faire un pique-nique" and since the context of the example is in the future ("samedi prochain") you must choose the future of "faire" = "ferons." (A) "aurons" = we will have, is included because it is a translation of the English = "We'll have a picnic," which is incorrect in French. (B) "verrons" = we shall see, and (D) "serons" = we will be, are obviously incorrect. Be careful of the spelling of "ferons," with one "r," as compared to "verrons," with two.

47. **(B)**

In French, "on invite quelqu'un <u>à</u> faire quelque chose." Thus (A) "——," which would place no preposition between both verbs, is incorrect. (C) "pour" is obviously incorrect, while (D) "de" is tempting, since there is much confusion between which verbs take "à" and which ones take "de" before an infinitive. (D) is, however, incorrect. (B) "à" is the correct choice.

48. **(B)**

After "j'espère," there is no need for the subjunctive in French, even though it is an emotion. Thus, (A) "puisse" is incorrect. (C) "pouvait" is in the imperfect tense and, since we are discussing next Saturday, it is an improper choice. (D) "pourrait" = would be able, is in the conditional and not appropriate after "j'espère." The correct answer, (B) "pourra" = will be able to, is the only acceptable choice.

49. **(D)**

The expression is "demander à quelqu'un" = to ask someone. Thus, (D) "à" is correct. (A) "— —," is like the English form but incorrect in French; (B) "de" is tempting, but it is not "demander DE;" (C) "du" is not called for, since there is a possessive adjective ("son") and no need for a contraction.

50. **(C)**

With expressions of quantity, one uses "de" before the noun: e.g., beaucoup de, trop de, peu de, etc. (A) "— —" is therefore incorrect after "assez." (B) "de" would be correct except that you must make an elision before the initial vowel of "argent," so that (C) "d'" is more appropriate than (B). And with expressions of quantity, there is no article; (D) "de l'" is therefore incorrect.

51. **(B)**

While (A) "avoir" would be correct in English, it is not correct in French. Although there are many expressions with (C) "faire," one does not say "faire une journée formidable!" (D) "dépenser" = to spend [money], is included because of its meaning in English. The only correct answer is (B) "passer" = to pass or spend time: "on passe une bonne soirée, journée," etc.

52. **(C)**

The preposition used before an infinitive is "avant de" (C). Therefore, (B) "à" and (D) "que" are incorrect. (A) "— —" assumes incorrectly that there is no "de" between "avant" and the infinitive (as is the case with some prepositions, e.g., "sans parler," "pour voir," etc.) but not with "avant."

53. **(A)**

The past participle of "devoir" in the *passé composé* is "dû." There is no agreement with the subject, as in (B) "dûs" or (C) "dûes." (D) "devenaient" = they were becoming, [from "devenir"], makes no sense in the example and should not be confused with "devoir."

54. **(D)**

The participle must agree with the subject in verbs that take "être" in the *passé composé*. Since "Marie et Alice" is a feminine plural subject,

(D) "sont allées" is the only correct answer. (A) "sont venus," (B) "sont partis," and (C) "sont allés," are masculine.

55. (D)

With "avoir" as an auxiliary in the *passé composé*, you must make agreement with the preceding direct object. Since that object is "billets," the participle must be masculine plural, as it is in (D) "achetés." Thus (A) "vendues," (B) "acheté," and (C) "achetées" are incorrect.

56. (B)

After "il faut que," the subjunctive must be used. Only (B) "fassent" is a subjunctive form. (A) "faisaient" is the imperfect, (C) "feront" is the future, and (D) "font" is the present indicative.

57. (D)

Forms of "tout" are tested here. Since it is an adjective that must agree with the noun it modifies, ("les détails"), you must choose the masculine plural form, "tous."

58. (A)

Of these interrogative expressions, (B) "Lequel" = which one, while (C) "Comment" = how or what? [when you want something which has been said made clearer]. (D) "Quoi" = what, is used after a preposition, and should never be used in conversation to clarify what has been said; ["Comment?" has that function.] The correct choice is (A) "Quel," a masculine pronoun replacing "nom."

59. (B)

The correct form of the feminine singular demonstrative adjective is (B) "cette" ["fleur" is feminine]. (A) "cet" precedes a masculine noun with an initial vowel, while (C) "ce" modifies other masculine singular nouns. (D) "celle" is a feminine demonstrative pronoun, used to replace a noun. (See example #48.)

60. (C)

A relative pronoun is required here and since it is an object, it must be a form of "que." Because it precedes "Hélène," ["h" is a vowel in French], you must elide the final "e". Therefore, (A) "que" is not quite correct. (B) "qui" is a subject pronoun and (D) "ce qu'" cannot be used because there is an antecedent in the sentence — ("fleur"). (C) "qu'" is the most correct response.

61. (C)

There are two problems in this example: What is the proper tense of the verb (imperfect or *passé composé?*) and if you choose *p.c.*, what is the form of the participle? Helen found the flower — an action that was completed within a given time ["hier"], so the imperfect (A) "trouvait" is eliminated. (D) "trouverait" = would find, is in the conditional, and therefore incorrect here. The choice is thus between (B) "a trouvé" and (C) "a trouvée." Since the direct object precedes the verb, agreement is required with "fleur," so (C) is correct.

62. (A)

You must be aware of the difference between "connaître" = to know something [through your senses or experience] and "savoir" = to know something [intellectually, through study, etc.] "Reconnaître" = to recognize, is based on "connaître" and has similar applications. (B) "savais" and (D) "sache" are forms of "savoir" and incorrect. (C) "connaisse" is the subjunctive form of "connaître" but there is no reason to use it in this example. The only correct choice is (A) "reconnaissais."

63. (B)

This example tests your understanding of "c'est" and "il est." "C'est" is used with a noun; "il est" is followed by an adjective and is not used with "un" or "une." Thus, (A) "elle était," (D) "elle a été," and (C) "elle avait été," are all incorrect.

64. (D)

The reference to Robert's arrival in the village mentions that "il a garé sa voiture" = parked his car. Therefore, (A) "à pied," (B) "à cheval," and (C) "par le train" are all incorrect.

65. (B)

Reference is made in the passage to the restaurant, "La Mule du Pape," which took its name from the story ("conte") by Daudet. There is no mention of a hotel with this name (A), and although the passage discusses wine, the name of this wine is not mentioned, so (C) "un bon vin," is not correct. (D) "le nom du château" is incorrect since we are told that the name of the castle is "Castel Gondolfo." Thus, (B) "un conte et un restaurant," is the correct answer.

66. (A)

It states specifically in the text that "Jean XXII fit construire" le château; "construire" and "bâtir" are synonyms and therefore (A) is correct. (B) "les soldats" occupied the town and later *destroyed* the tower;

they did not build it. (C) "Alphonse Daudet" is the author of the story, "La Mule de Pape," after which the restaurant was named. (D) "le duc de la Vaucluse" is not mentioned anywhere in the text. Therefore, (B), (C) and (D) are incorrect.

67. **(A)**

Although Robert appreciates (B) "Alphonse Daudet," (C) the sun and forests of the region, and (D) its friendly inhabitants, it is really the tradition and wine (of the village) (A) that inspires his "dévotion la plus profonde."

68. **(B)**

The book primarily takes into consideration value (quality/price) when evaluating computers — *le rapport qualité-prix* — which makes choice (B) the answer. There is no mention of awards given by the press (les prix que leur ont été accordés par la presse), number of units sold for each model (le nombre de chaque modèle ayant été vendu) or polls (sondages), which eliminates (A), (C), and (D) respectively.

69. **(C)**

The book contains information on (ce livre contient des renseignements sur) all of the following except (tout ce qui suit sauf) where one can purchase the computers mentioned in the book (les lieux où l'on peut acheter les ordinateurs cités dans ce livre), answer (C). The book does address les secrets des fabriquants (computer manufacturer [trade] secrets), la qualité des différents ordinateurs (the quality of the different computers), and offer des dossiers et des fiches techniques (descriptive reports and pieces on the computers in question), which eliminates choices (A), (B), and (D), respectively.

70. **(D)**

"Le benjamin" is the youngest son in the family, while (A) "l'aîné" = the oldest son, and (C) "l'avant-dernier enfant" is the next to the youngest. (B) "le nom d'un garçon" is incorrect because the example is "un benjamin," not "Benjamin."

71. **(B)**

Although one person does celebrate a 60th birthday in the story, it is Mme Renard, not Jacques. (A) "quand il a 60 ans" is therefore incorrect. We know nothing about Jacques' relationship with his father, so (C) "par moyen de son père" is not correct. (D) "dès son plus jeune âge" does not fit with the fact that Jacques only learned about his mother's youth twenty years after his birth. The correct answer is therefore (B) "quand il a 20 ans."

72. **(C)**

We are told about the extreme poverty in which Mme Renard raised her children and about her difficult childhood. Therefore, (A) "ne travailla guère" is not true, nor is (B), which describes her as "une personne faible." There is no indication that she doesn't love her family; on the contrary, she is a "mère vénérée," so she must have given love to her children to have earned it. (D) is thus eliminated, leaving the correct answer as (C) [elle] "menait une vie difficile."

73. **(A)**

The term "orpheline" means "orphan" and therefore (A) "n'avait ni mère ni père" is the most appropriate choice. We know nothing about the rest of the girl's family, so (B) "était fille unique," (C) "avait une grande famille," and (D) "avait plusieurs frères," are only conjectural and do not refer to the loss of her parents, implied by "orpheline."

74. **(D)**

The narrator implies that Mme Renard is an admirable person by his description of the way she raised her family in dire poverty, was loved by her children, and overcame her miserable childhood, never complaining about it. (A) "semble condamner Jean," (B) "décrit une famille cruelle," and (C) "est Jacques" are incorrect.

75. **(B)**

The passage does not tell us that the newlyweds (A) "firent un long voyage de noces" or (C) "prirent des vacances," and from the context we can judge that they were never very rich (D) "furent très riches." Therefore, only (B) "habitèrent un petit village" can be correctly deduced from the text, since we know that they settled in Napoule.

76. **(D)**

The scene is neither (A) "effrayante" = frightening, (B) "douleureuse" = painful, nor (D) "dangereuse" = dangerous. Instead, it is one of calm beauty, (D) "paisible."

77. **(C)**

While Monique appreciates everything she sees, it is (C) "la vue" which impresses her most.

78. **(A)**

There are many suggestions that it is spring: the leafing trees, the soft sun, the flower-covered hills. Thus, (B) "en hiver," or (D) "à minuit" are obviously incorrect. (C) "au Sahara" is mentioned nowhere in the text, and is therefore incorrect. (A) "au printemps" is the logical answer within the context.

79. **(C)**

Monique's precious moment is shattered by the arrival of the hunters (C). (A) "elle ne peut pas respirer" is the effect of her happiness and (B) "le baron s'en va" does not break her mood, since it is already upset by the noise of the arriving men. (D) "elle s'impatiente" is not indicated in the text.

80. **(D)**

The baron says goodbye to Monique so (A) [il] "ne dit rien à Monique" is incorrect. He is happy to go off hunting and gives no indication of being sad to leave, so (B) [il] "ne veut pas partir" and (C) [il] "est triste de quitter ses invités" are not true. His joy at going hunting is obvious, since he leaves with "le sourire aux lèvres." Thus, (D) [il] "se réjouit d'aller à la chasse" is the most appropriate answer.

81. **(B)**

The island became a colony more than a century after its discovery. Therefore (A) is incorrect. Both (C) [les explorateurs] "ont découragé le tourisme," and (D) "n'apprécièrent pas l'île," are false statements. Adventurers soon followed the explorers, so (B) is correct.

82. **(D)**

Visitors to the island did not find the natives (A) "sauvages," (B) "paresseux" = lazy, or (C) "timides." Rather, they were very friendly and welcomed foreigners. Thus (D), describing them as "hospitaliers," is correct.

83. **(A)**

Gauguin painted many scenes of Tahiti and it is for these works that he is famous. Neither (B) "ses paysages parisiens," nor (C) "ses sculptures," brought him fame. Also, although he wrote a few books, he is not celebrated for his "romans" = novels, (D). The correct answer, therefore, is (A) "ses toiles tahitiennes" = his paintings of Tahiti.

84. **(D)**

The word "quotidien" means "daily," so that while Gauguin painted native life (A) "la vie folklorique," and (C) "la vie simple" in depicting Tahitian life, the question requires a definition of "quotidien." (B) "la vie suffisante" is included because "quotidien" might seem to be related to "quota" but is not. (D) [la vie] "de tous les jours," is the correct choice.

85. **(B)**
Tahiti offers neither excitement (A) "des vacances stimulantes" nor an urban adventure (C) "une expérience cosmopolite." Since it has a tropical climate, there is obviously no skiing possible on its mountains, so (D) "l'occasion de faire du ski" is also incorrect. (B) "la possibilité de se reposer" is the best choice, since the passage mentions "le détente complète" = complete relaxation.

86. **(D)**
While Guillaume will be traveling to Paris and will undoubtedly get to know the city, he has left home to seek his fortune by working with his cousin Paul. Thus, although (A) "voyager" and (B) "visiter Paris" have some elements of truth, the best answer is (D) "travailler avec Paul." (C) "être touriste" is entirely incorrect as the reason he is leaving home.

87. **(A)**
"Auparavant" refers to a period of time that precedes the time of narration = before. Therefore, Paul has been in Paris for three years when he sends for Guillaume. He has not been in the capital either since "sa naissance" (B), "plusieurs mois" (C), or "la guerre" (D).

88. **(B)**
Guillaume has a pleasant dream about his future life in the big city. It is not a "cauchemar" = nightmare (A). Also, he is not very nervous in the train, since he goes right to sleep. Therefore (D) [il] "fut tres agité" is incorrect, as is (C) [il] "regarda par la fenêtre." (B) [il] "s'imagina la vie parisienne dans ses rêves" is correct.

89. **(B)**
Les tarifs étaient réduits pour les couples du 22 octobre au 2 décembre (rates were reduced for couples between October 22 and December 2) is the only true statement (phrase vraie) here, which makes choice (B) the correct answer. (A) Le "Royal Riviera" se situe à Monaco (the "Royal Riviera" is located in Monaco) cannot be right because it is located in "Sain-Jean-Cap-Ferrat," which is entre Nice et Monaco (between Nice and Monaco). References to romance and comfort, not to mention a quick look at the picture, indicate that (C) [. . .] est surtout

connu pour son charme rustique et campagnard (is known primarily for its rustic country charm) cannot be true. Choice (D) se situe sur une île (is located on an island) is incorrect, as it is located on a presqu'île — a peninsula.

90. **(A)**

On peut supposer que les gens qui séjournent au "Royal Riviera" y vont surtout pour (it can reasonably be assumed that people who stay at the "Royal Riviera" do so primarily) (A) un accueil luxueux et attentionné au bord de la mer (for a luxurious and attentive welcome by the sea). There is no suggestion nor reason to believe that it is to change swimming pools (changer de piscine) or to look at sand and swim in the pool (regarder le sable fin et se baigner dans la piscine), which eliminates choices (B) and (C), respectively. As for choice (D), it would be illogical to assume that everyone who stays at this hotel lives a short distance from it, and there is no indication that this is the case, hence prendre des vacances tout en restant à deux pas de chez eux (because they want to take a vacation while remaining close to home) is not a valid answer.

SAT II:
SUBJECT TEST IN
FRENCH

ANSWER
SHEETS

SAT II: SUBJECT TEST IN
FRENCH
ANSWER SHEET

1. Ⓐ Ⓑ Ⓒ Ⓓ Ⓔ
2. Ⓐ Ⓑ Ⓒ Ⓓ Ⓔ
3. Ⓐ Ⓑ Ⓒ Ⓓ Ⓔ
4. Ⓐ Ⓑ Ⓒ Ⓓ Ⓔ
5. Ⓐ Ⓑ Ⓒ Ⓓ Ⓔ
6. Ⓐ Ⓑ Ⓒ Ⓓ Ⓔ
7. Ⓐ Ⓑ Ⓒ Ⓓ Ⓔ
8. Ⓐ Ⓑ Ⓒ Ⓓ Ⓔ
9. Ⓐ Ⓑ Ⓒ Ⓓ Ⓔ
10. Ⓐ Ⓑ Ⓒ Ⓓ Ⓔ
11. Ⓐ Ⓑ Ⓒ Ⓓ Ⓔ
12. Ⓐ Ⓑ Ⓒ Ⓓ Ⓔ
13. Ⓐ Ⓑ Ⓒ Ⓓ Ⓔ
14. Ⓐ Ⓑ Ⓒ Ⓓ Ⓔ
15. Ⓐ Ⓑ Ⓒ Ⓓ Ⓔ
16. Ⓐ Ⓑ Ⓒ Ⓓ Ⓔ
17. Ⓐ Ⓑ Ⓒ Ⓓ Ⓔ
18. Ⓐ Ⓑ Ⓒ Ⓓ Ⓔ
19. Ⓐ Ⓑ Ⓒ Ⓓ Ⓔ
20. Ⓐ Ⓑ Ⓒ Ⓓ Ⓔ
21. Ⓐ Ⓑ Ⓒ Ⓓ Ⓔ
22. Ⓐ Ⓑ Ⓒ Ⓓ Ⓔ
23. Ⓐ Ⓑ Ⓒ Ⓓ Ⓔ
24. Ⓐ Ⓑ Ⓒ Ⓓ Ⓔ
25. Ⓐ Ⓑ Ⓒ Ⓓ Ⓔ
26. Ⓐ Ⓑ Ⓒ Ⓓ Ⓔ
27. Ⓐ Ⓑ Ⓒ Ⓓ Ⓔ
28. Ⓐ Ⓑ Ⓒ Ⓓ Ⓔ
29. Ⓐ Ⓑ Ⓒ Ⓓ Ⓔ
30. Ⓐ Ⓑ Ⓒ Ⓓ Ⓔ
31. Ⓐ Ⓑ Ⓒ Ⓓ Ⓔ
32. Ⓐ Ⓑ Ⓒ Ⓓ Ⓔ
33. Ⓐ Ⓑ Ⓒ Ⓓ Ⓔ
34. Ⓐ Ⓑ Ⓒ Ⓓ Ⓔ
35. Ⓐ Ⓑ Ⓒ Ⓓ Ⓔ
36. Ⓐ Ⓑ Ⓒ Ⓓ Ⓔ
37. Ⓐ Ⓑ Ⓒ Ⓓ Ⓔ
38. Ⓐ Ⓑ Ⓒ Ⓓ Ⓔ
39. Ⓐ Ⓑ Ⓒ Ⓓ Ⓔ
40. Ⓐ Ⓑ Ⓒ Ⓓ Ⓔ
41. Ⓐ Ⓑ Ⓒ Ⓓ Ⓔ
42. Ⓐ Ⓑ Ⓒ Ⓓ Ⓔ
43. Ⓐ Ⓑ Ⓒ Ⓓ Ⓔ
44. Ⓐ Ⓑ Ⓒ Ⓓ Ⓔ
45. Ⓐ Ⓑ Ⓒ Ⓓ Ⓔ
46. Ⓐ Ⓑ Ⓒ Ⓓ Ⓔ
47. Ⓐ Ⓑ Ⓒ Ⓓ Ⓔ
48. Ⓐ Ⓑ Ⓒ Ⓓ Ⓔ
49. Ⓐ Ⓑ Ⓒ Ⓓ Ⓔ
50. Ⓐ Ⓑ Ⓒ Ⓓ Ⓔ
51. Ⓐ Ⓑ Ⓒ Ⓓ Ⓔ
52. Ⓐ Ⓑ Ⓒ Ⓓ Ⓔ
53. Ⓐ Ⓑ Ⓒ Ⓓ Ⓔ
54. Ⓐ Ⓑ Ⓒ Ⓓ Ⓔ
55. Ⓐ Ⓑ Ⓒ Ⓓ Ⓔ
56. Ⓐ Ⓑ Ⓒ Ⓓ Ⓔ
57. Ⓐ Ⓑ Ⓒ Ⓓ Ⓔ
58. Ⓐ Ⓑ Ⓒ Ⓓ Ⓔ
59. Ⓐ Ⓑ Ⓒ Ⓓ Ⓔ
60. Ⓐ Ⓑ Ⓒ Ⓓ Ⓔ
61. Ⓐ Ⓑ Ⓒ Ⓓ Ⓔ
62. Ⓐ Ⓑ Ⓒ Ⓓ Ⓔ
63. Ⓐ Ⓑ Ⓒ Ⓓ Ⓔ
64. Ⓐ Ⓑ Ⓒ Ⓓ Ⓔ
65. Ⓐ Ⓑ Ⓒ Ⓓ Ⓔ
66. Ⓐ Ⓑ Ⓒ Ⓓ Ⓔ
67. Ⓐ Ⓑ Ⓒ Ⓓ Ⓔ
68. Ⓐ Ⓑ Ⓒ Ⓓ Ⓔ
69. Ⓐ Ⓑ Ⓒ Ⓓ Ⓔ
70. Ⓐ Ⓑ Ⓒ Ⓓ Ⓔ
71. Ⓐ Ⓑ Ⓒ Ⓓ Ⓔ
72. Ⓐ Ⓑ Ⓒ Ⓓ Ⓔ
73. Ⓐ Ⓑ Ⓒ Ⓓ Ⓔ
74. Ⓐ Ⓑ Ⓒ Ⓓ Ⓔ
75. Ⓐ Ⓑ Ⓒ Ⓓ Ⓔ
76. Ⓐ Ⓑ Ⓒ Ⓓ Ⓔ
77. Ⓐ Ⓑ Ⓒ Ⓓ Ⓔ
78. Ⓐ Ⓑ Ⓒ Ⓓ Ⓔ
79. Ⓐ Ⓑ Ⓒ Ⓓ Ⓔ
80. Ⓐ Ⓑ Ⓒ Ⓓ Ⓔ
81. Ⓐ Ⓑ Ⓒ Ⓓ Ⓔ
82. Ⓐ Ⓑ Ⓒ Ⓓ Ⓔ
83. Ⓐ Ⓑ Ⓒ Ⓓ Ⓔ
84. Ⓐ Ⓑ Ⓒ Ⓓ Ⓔ
85. Ⓐ Ⓑ Ⓒ Ⓓ Ⓔ
86. Ⓐ Ⓑ Ⓒ Ⓓ Ⓔ
87. Ⓐ Ⓑ Ⓒ Ⓓ Ⓔ
88. Ⓐ Ⓑ Ⓒ Ⓓ Ⓔ
89. Ⓐ Ⓑ Ⓒ Ⓓ Ⓔ
90. Ⓐ Ⓑ Ⓒ Ⓓ Ⓔ

SAT II: SUBJECT TEST IN
FRENCH
ANSWER SHEET

1. Ⓐ Ⓑ Ⓒ Ⓓ Ⓔ	31. Ⓐ Ⓑ Ⓒ Ⓓ Ⓔ	61. Ⓐ Ⓑ Ⓒ Ⓓ Ⓔ
2. Ⓐ Ⓑ Ⓒ Ⓓ Ⓔ	32. Ⓐ Ⓑ Ⓒ Ⓓ Ⓔ	62. Ⓐ Ⓑ Ⓒ Ⓓ Ⓔ
3. Ⓐ Ⓑ Ⓒ Ⓓ Ⓔ	33. Ⓐ Ⓑ Ⓒ Ⓓ Ⓔ	63. Ⓐ Ⓑ Ⓒ Ⓓ Ⓔ
4. Ⓐ Ⓑ Ⓒ Ⓓ Ⓔ	34. Ⓐ Ⓑ Ⓒ Ⓓ Ⓔ	64. Ⓐ Ⓑ Ⓒ Ⓓ Ⓔ
5. Ⓐ Ⓑ Ⓒ Ⓓ Ⓔ	35. Ⓐ Ⓑ Ⓒ Ⓓ Ⓔ	65. Ⓐ Ⓑ Ⓒ Ⓓ Ⓔ
6. Ⓐ Ⓑ Ⓒ Ⓓ Ⓔ	36. Ⓐ Ⓑ Ⓒ Ⓓ Ⓔ	66. Ⓐ Ⓑ Ⓒ Ⓓ Ⓔ
7. Ⓐ Ⓑ Ⓒ Ⓓ Ⓔ	37. Ⓐ Ⓑ Ⓒ Ⓓ Ⓔ	67. Ⓐ Ⓑ Ⓒ Ⓓ Ⓔ
8. Ⓐ Ⓑ Ⓒ Ⓓ Ⓔ	38. Ⓐ Ⓑ Ⓒ Ⓓ Ⓔ	68. Ⓐ Ⓑ Ⓒ Ⓓ Ⓔ
9. Ⓐ Ⓑ Ⓒ Ⓓ Ⓔ	39. Ⓐ Ⓑ Ⓒ Ⓓ Ⓔ	69. Ⓐ Ⓑ Ⓒ Ⓓ Ⓔ
10. Ⓐ Ⓑ Ⓒ Ⓓ Ⓔ	40. Ⓐ Ⓑ Ⓒ Ⓓ Ⓔ	70. Ⓐ Ⓑ Ⓒ Ⓓ Ⓔ
11. Ⓐ Ⓑ Ⓒ Ⓓ Ⓔ	41. Ⓐ Ⓑ Ⓒ Ⓓ Ⓔ	71. Ⓐ Ⓑ Ⓒ Ⓓ Ⓔ
12. Ⓐ Ⓑ Ⓒ Ⓓ Ⓔ	42. Ⓐ Ⓑ Ⓒ Ⓓ Ⓔ	72. Ⓐ Ⓑ Ⓒ Ⓓ Ⓔ
13. Ⓐ Ⓑ Ⓒ Ⓓ Ⓔ	43. Ⓐ Ⓑ Ⓒ Ⓓ Ⓔ	73. Ⓐ Ⓑ Ⓒ Ⓓ Ⓔ
14. Ⓐ Ⓑ Ⓒ Ⓓ Ⓔ	44. Ⓐ Ⓑ Ⓒ Ⓓ Ⓔ	74. Ⓐ Ⓑ Ⓒ Ⓓ Ⓔ
15. Ⓐ Ⓑ Ⓒ Ⓓ Ⓔ	45. Ⓐ Ⓑ Ⓒ Ⓓ Ⓔ	75. Ⓐ Ⓑ Ⓒ Ⓓ Ⓔ
16. Ⓐ Ⓑ Ⓒ Ⓓ Ⓔ	46. Ⓐ Ⓑ Ⓒ Ⓓ Ⓔ	76. Ⓐ Ⓑ Ⓒ Ⓓ Ⓔ
17. Ⓐ Ⓑ Ⓒ Ⓓ Ⓔ	47. Ⓐ Ⓑ Ⓒ Ⓓ Ⓔ	77. Ⓐ Ⓑ Ⓒ Ⓓ Ⓔ
18. Ⓐ Ⓑ Ⓒ Ⓓ Ⓔ	48. Ⓐ Ⓑ Ⓒ Ⓓ Ⓔ	78. Ⓐ Ⓑ Ⓒ Ⓓ Ⓔ
19. Ⓐ Ⓑ Ⓒ Ⓓ Ⓔ	49. Ⓐ Ⓑ Ⓒ Ⓓ Ⓔ	79. Ⓐ Ⓑ Ⓒ Ⓓ Ⓔ
20. Ⓐ Ⓑ Ⓒ Ⓓ Ⓔ	50. Ⓐ Ⓑ Ⓒ Ⓓ Ⓔ	80. Ⓐ Ⓑ Ⓒ Ⓓ Ⓔ
21. Ⓐ Ⓑ Ⓒ Ⓓ Ⓔ	51. Ⓐ Ⓑ Ⓒ Ⓓ Ⓔ	81. Ⓐ Ⓑ Ⓒ Ⓓ Ⓔ
22. Ⓐ Ⓑ Ⓒ Ⓓ Ⓔ	52. Ⓐ Ⓑ Ⓒ Ⓓ Ⓔ	82. Ⓐ Ⓑ Ⓒ Ⓓ Ⓔ
23. Ⓐ Ⓑ Ⓒ Ⓓ Ⓔ	53. Ⓐ Ⓑ Ⓒ Ⓓ Ⓔ	83. Ⓐ Ⓑ Ⓒ Ⓓ Ⓔ
24. Ⓐ Ⓑ Ⓒ Ⓓ Ⓔ	54. Ⓐ Ⓑ Ⓒ Ⓓ Ⓔ	84. Ⓐ Ⓑ Ⓒ Ⓓ Ⓔ
25. Ⓐ Ⓑ Ⓒ Ⓓ Ⓔ	55. Ⓐ Ⓑ Ⓒ Ⓓ Ⓔ	85. Ⓐ Ⓑ Ⓒ Ⓓ Ⓔ
26. Ⓐ Ⓑ Ⓒ Ⓓ Ⓔ	56. Ⓐ Ⓑ Ⓒ Ⓓ Ⓔ	86. Ⓐ Ⓑ Ⓒ Ⓓ Ⓔ
27. Ⓐ Ⓑ Ⓒ Ⓓ Ⓔ	57. Ⓐ Ⓑ Ⓒ Ⓓ Ⓔ	87. Ⓐ Ⓑ Ⓒ Ⓓ Ⓔ
28. Ⓐ Ⓑ Ⓒ Ⓓ Ⓔ	58. Ⓐ Ⓑ Ⓒ Ⓓ Ⓔ	88. Ⓐ Ⓑ Ⓒ Ⓓ Ⓔ
29. Ⓐ Ⓑ Ⓒ Ⓓ Ⓔ	59. Ⓐ Ⓑ Ⓒ Ⓓ Ⓔ	89. Ⓐ Ⓑ Ⓒ Ⓓ Ⓔ
30. Ⓐ Ⓑ Ⓒ Ⓓ Ⓔ	60. Ⓐ Ⓑ Ⓒ Ⓓ Ⓔ	90. Ⓐ Ⓑ Ⓒ Ⓓ Ⓔ

SAT II: SUBJECT TEST IN
FRENCH
ANSWER SHEET

1. Ⓐ Ⓑ Ⓒ Ⓓ Ⓔ	31. Ⓐ Ⓑ Ⓒ Ⓓ Ⓔ	61. Ⓐ Ⓑ Ⓒ Ⓓ Ⓔ
2. Ⓐ Ⓑ Ⓒ Ⓓ Ⓔ	32. Ⓐ Ⓑ Ⓒ Ⓓ Ⓔ	62. Ⓐ Ⓑ Ⓒ Ⓓ Ⓔ
3. Ⓐ Ⓑ Ⓒ Ⓓ Ⓔ	33. Ⓐ Ⓑ Ⓒ Ⓓ Ⓔ	63. Ⓐ Ⓑ Ⓒ Ⓓ Ⓔ
4. Ⓐ Ⓑ Ⓒ Ⓓ Ⓔ	34. Ⓐ Ⓑ Ⓒ Ⓓ Ⓔ	64. Ⓐ Ⓑ Ⓒ Ⓓ Ⓔ
5. Ⓐ Ⓑ Ⓒ Ⓓ Ⓔ	35. Ⓐ Ⓑ Ⓒ Ⓓ Ⓔ	65. Ⓐ Ⓑ Ⓒ Ⓓ Ⓔ
6. Ⓐ Ⓑ Ⓒ Ⓓ Ⓔ	36. Ⓐ Ⓑ Ⓒ Ⓓ Ⓔ	66. Ⓐ Ⓑ Ⓒ Ⓓ Ⓔ
7. Ⓐ Ⓑ Ⓒ Ⓓ Ⓔ	37. Ⓐ Ⓑ Ⓒ Ⓓ Ⓔ	67. Ⓐ Ⓑ Ⓒ Ⓓ Ⓔ
8. Ⓐ Ⓑ Ⓒ Ⓓ Ⓔ	38. Ⓐ Ⓑ Ⓒ Ⓓ Ⓔ	68. Ⓐ Ⓑ Ⓒ Ⓓ Ⓔ
9. Ⓐ Ⓑ Ⓒ Ⓓ Ⓔ	39. Ⓐ Ⓑ Ⓒ Ⓓ Ⓔ	69. Ⓐ Ⓑ Ⓒ Ⓓ Ⓔ
10. Ⓐ Ⓑ Ⓒ Ⓓ Ⓔ	40. Ⓐ Ⓑ Ⓒ Ⓓ Ⓔ	70. Ⓐ Ⓑ Ⓒ Ⓓ Ⓔ
11. Ⓐ Ⓑ Ⓒ Ⓓ Ⓔ	41. Ⓐ Ⓑ Ⓒ Ⓓ Ⓔ	71. Ⓐ Ⓑ Ⓒ Ⓓ Ⓔ
12. Ⓐ Ⓑ Ⓒ Ⓓ Ⓔ	42. Ⓐ Ⓑ Ⓒ Ⓓ Ⓔ	72. Ⓐ Ⓑ Ⓒ Ⓓ Ⓔ
13. Ⓐ Ⓑ Ⓒ Ⓓ Ⓔ	43. Ⓐ Ⓑ Ⓒ Ⓓ Ⓔ	73. Ⓐ Ⓑ Ⓒ Ⓓ Ⓔ
14. Ⓐ Ⓑ Ⓒ Ⓓ Ⓔ	44. Ⓐ Ⓑ Ⓒ Ⓓ Ⓔ	74. Ⓐ Ⓑ Ⓒ Ⓓ Ⓔ
15. Ⓐ Ⓑ Ⓒ Ⓓ Ⓔ	45. Ⓐ Ⓑ Ⓒ Ⓓ Ⓔ	75. Ⓐ Ⓑ Ⓒ Ⓓ Ⓔ
16. Ⓐ Ⓑ Ⓒ Ⓓ Ⓔ	46. Ⓐ Ⓑ Ⓒ Ⓓ Ⓔ	76. Ⓐ Ⓑ Ⓒ Ⓓ Ⓔ
17. Ⓐ Ⓑ Ⓒ Ⓓ Ⓔ	47. Ⓐ Ⓑ Ⓒ Ⓓ Ⓔ	77. Ⓐ Ⓑ Ⓒ Ⓓ Ⓔ
18. Ⓐ Ⓑ Ⓒ Ⓓ Ⓔ	48. Ⓐ Ⓑ Ⓒ Ⓓ Ⓔ	78. Ⓐ Ⓑ Ⓒ Ⓓ Ⓔ
19. Ⓐ Ⓑ Ⓒ Ⓓ Ⓔ	49. Ⓐ Ⓑ Ⓒ Ⓓ Ⓔ	79. Ⓐ Ⓑ Ⓒ Ⓓ Ⓔ
20. Ⓐ Ⓑ Ⓒ Ⓓ Ⓔ	50. Ⓐ Ⓑ Ⓒ Ⓓ Ⓔ	80. Ⓐ Ⓑ Ⓒ Ⓓ Ⓔ
21. Ⓐ Ⓑ Ⓒ Ⓓ Ⓔ	51. Ⓐ Ⓑ Ⓒ Ⓓ Ⓔ	81. Ⓐ Ⓑ Ⓒ Ⓓ Ⓔ
22. Ⓐ Ⓑ Ⓒ Ⓓ Ⓔ	52. Ⓐ Ⓑ Ⓒ Ⓓ Ⓔ	82. Ⓐ Ⓑ Ⓒ Ⓓ Ⓔ
23. Ⓐ Ⓑ Ⓒ Ⓓ Ⓔ	53. Ⓐ Ⓑ Ⓒ Ⓓ Ⓔ	83. Ⓐ Ⓑ Ⓒ Ⓓ Ⓔ
24. Ⓐ Ⓑ Ⓒ Ⓓ Ⓔ	54. Ⓐ Ⓑ Ⓒ Ⓓ Ⓔ	84. Ⓐ Ⓑ Ⓒ Ⓓ Ⓔ
25. Ⓐ Ⓑ Ⓒ Ⓓ Ⓔ	55. Ⓐ Ⓑ Ⓒ Ⓓ Ⓔ	85. Ⓐ Ⓑ Ⓒ Ⓓ Ⓔ
26. Ⓐ Ⓑ Ⓒ Ⓓ Ⓔ	56. Ⓐ Ⓑ Ⓒ Ⓓ Ⓔ	86. Ⓐ Ⓑ Ⓒ Ⓓ Ⓔ
27. Ⓐ Ⓑ Ⓒ Ⓓ Ⓔ	57. Ⓐ Ⓑ Ⓒ Ⓓ Ⓔ	87. Ⓐ Ⓑ Ⓒ Ⓓ Ⓔ
28. Ⓐ Ⓑ Ⓒ Ⓓ Ⓔ	58. Ⓐ Ⓑ Ⓒ Ⓓ Ⓔ	88. Ⓐ Ⓑ Ⓒ Ⓓ Ⓔ
29. Ⓐ Ⓑ Ⓒ Ⓓ Ⓔ	59. Ⓐ Ⓑ Ⓒ Ⓓ Ⓔ	89. Ⓐ Ⓑ Ⓒ Ⓓ Ⓔ
30. Ⓐ Ⓑ Ⓒ Ⓓ Ⓔ	60. Ⓐ Ⓑ Ⓒ Ⓓ Ⓔ	90. Ⓐ Ⓑ Ⓒ Ⓓ Ⓔ

SAT II: SUBJECT TEST IN
FRENCH
ANSWER SHEET

1. Ⓐ Ⓑ Ⓒ Ⓓ Ⓔ	31. Ⓐ Ⓑ Ⓒ Ⓓ Ⓔ	61. Ⓐ Ⓑ Ⓒ Ⓓ Ⓔ
2. Ⓐ Ⓑ Ⓒ Ⓓ Ⓔ	32. Ⓐ Ⓑ Ⓒ Ⓓ Ⓔ	62. Ⓐ Ⓑ Ⓒ Ⓓ Ⓔ
3. Ⓐ Ⓑ Ⓒ Ⓓ Ⓔ	33. Ⓐ Ⓑ Ⓒ Ⓓ Ⓔ	63. Ⓐ Ⓑ Ⓒ Ⓓ Ⓔ
4. Ⓐ Ⓑ Ⓒ Ⓓ Ⓔ	34. Ⓐ Ⓑ Ⓒ Ⓓ Ⓔ	64. Ⓐ Ⓑ Ⓒ Ⓓ Ⓔ
5. Ⓐ Ⓑ Ⓒ Ⓓ Ⓔ	35. Ⓐ Ⓑ Ⓒ Ⓓ Ⓔ	65. Ⓐ Ⓑ Ⓒ Ⓓ Ⓔ
6. Ⓐ Ⓑ Ⓒ Ⓓ Ⓔ	36. Ⓐ Ⓑ Ⓒ Ⓓ Ⓔ	66. Ⓐ Ⓑ Ⓒ Ⓓ Ⓔ
7. Ⓐ Ⓑ Ⓒ Ⓓ Ⓔ	37. Ⓐ Ⓑ Ⓒ Ⓓ Ⓔ	67. Ⓐ Ⓑ Ⓒ Ⓓ Ⓔ
8. Ⓐ Ⓑ Ⓒ Ⓓ Ⓔ	38. Ⓐ Ⓑ Ⓒ Ⓓ Ⓔ	68. Ⓐ Ⓑ Ⓒ Ⓓ Ⓔ
9. Ⓐ Ⓑ Ⓒ Ⓓ Ⓔ	39. Ⓐ Ⓑ Ⓒ Ⓓ Ⓔ	69. Ⓐ Ⓑ Ⓒ Ⓓ Ⓔ
10. Ⓐ Ⓑ Ⓒ Ⓓ Ⓔ	40. Ⓐ Ⓑ Ⓒ Ⓓ Ⓔ	70. Ⓐ Ⓑ Ⓒ Ⓓ Ⓔ
11. Ⓐ Ⓑ Ⓒ Ⓓ Ⓔ	41. Ⓐ Ⓑ Ⓒ Ⓓ Ⓔ	71. Ⓐ Ⓑ Ⓒ Ⓓ Ⓔ
12. Ⓐ Ⓑ Ⓒ Ⓓ Ⓔ	42. Ⓐ Ⓑ Ⓒ Ⓓ Ⓔ	72. Ⓐ Ⓑ Ⓒ Ⓓ Ⓔ
13. Ⓐ Ⓑ Ⓒ Ⓓ Ⓔ	43. Ⓐ Ⓑ Ⓒ Ⓓ Ⓔ	73. Ⓐ Ⓑ Ⓒ Ⓓ Ⓔ
14. Ⓐ Ⓑ Ⓒ Ⓓ Ⓔ	44. Ⓐ Ⓑ Ⓒ Ⓓ Ⓔ	74. Ⓐ Ⓑ Ⓒ Ⓓ Ⓔ
15. Ⓐ Ⓑ Ⓒ Ⓓ Ⓔ	45. Ⓐ Ⓑ Ⓒ Ⓓ Ⓔ	75. Ⓐ Ⓑ Ⓒ Ⓓ Ⓔ
16. Ⓐ Ⓑ Ⓒ Ⓓ Ⓔ	46. Ⓐ Ⓑ Ⓒ Ⓓ Ⓔ	76. Ⓐ Ⓑ Ⓒ Ⓓ Ⓔ
17. Ⓐ Ⓑ Ⓒ Ⓓ Ⓔ	47. Ⓐ Ⓑ Ⓒ Ⓓ Ⓔ	77. Ⓐ Ⓑ Ⓒ Ⓓ Ⓔ
18. Ⓐ Ⓑ Ⓒ Ⓓ Ⓔ	48. Ⓐ Ⓑ Ⓒ Ⓓ Ⓔ	78. Ⓐ Ⓑ Ⓒ Ⓓ Ⓔ
19. Ⓐ Ⓑ Ⓒ Ⓓ Ⓔ	49. Ⓐ Ⓑ Ⓒ Ⓓ Ⓔ	79. Ⓐ Ⓑ Ⓒ Ⓓ Ⓔ
20. Ⓐ Ⓑ Ⓒ Ⓓ Ⓔ	50. Ⓐ Ⓑ Ⓒ Ⓓ Ⓔ	80. Ⓐ Ⓑ Ⓒ Ⓓ Ⓔ
21. Ⓐ Ⓑ Ⓒ Ⓓ Ⓔ	51. Ⓐ Ⓑ Ⓒ Ⓓ Ⓔ	81. Ⓐ Ⓑ Ⓒ Ⓓ Ⓔ
22. Ⓐ Ⓑ Ⓒ Ⓓ Ⓔ	52. Ⓐ Ⓑ Ⓒ Ⓓ Ⓔ	82. Ⓐ Ⓑ Ⓒ Ⓓ Ⓔ
23. Ⓐ Ⓑ Ⓒ Ⓓ Ⓔ	53. Ⓐ Ⓑ Ⓒ Ⓓ Ⓔ	83. Ⓐ Ⓑ Ⓒ Ⓓ Ⓔ
24. Ⓐ Ⓑ Ⓒ Ⓓ Ⓔ	54. Ⓐ Ⓑ Ⓒ Ⓓ Ⓔ	84. Ⓐ Ⓑ Ⓒ Ⓓ Ⓔ
25. Ⓐ Ⓑ Ⓒ Ⓓ Ⓔ	55. Ⓐ Ⓑ Ⓒ Ⓓ Ⓔ	85. Ⓐ Ⓑ Ⓒ Ⓓ Ⓔ
26. Ⓐ Ⓑ Ⓒ Ⓓ Ⓔ	56. Ⓐ Ⓑ Ⓒ Ⓓ Ⓔ	86. Ⓐ Ⓑ Ⓒ Ⓓ Ⓔ
27. Ⓐ Ⓑ Ⓒ Ⓓ Ⓔ	57. Ⓐ Ⓑ Ⓒ Ⓓ Ⓔ	87. Ⓐ Ⓑ Ⓒ Ⓓ Ⓔ
28. Ⓐ Ⓑ Ⓒ Ⓓ Ⓔ	58. Ⓐ Ⓑ Ⓒ Ⓓ Ⓔ	88. Ⓐ Ⓑ Ⓒ Ⓓ Ⓔ
29. Ⓐ Ⓑ Ⓒ Ⓓ Ⓔ	59. Ⓐ Ⓑ Ⓒ Ⓓ Ⓔ	89. Ⓐ Ⓑ Ⓒ Ⓓ Ⓔ
30. Ⓐ Ⓑ Ⓒ Ⓓ Ⓔ	60. Ⓐ Ⓑ Ⓒ Ⓓ Ⓔ	90. Ⓐ Ⓑ Ⓒ Ⓓ Ⓔ

SAT II: SUBJECT TEST IN
FRENCH
ANSWER SHEET

1. Ⓐ Ⓑ Ⓒ Ⓓ Ⓔ	31. Ⓐ Ⓑ Ⓒ Ⓓ Ⓔ	61. Ⓐ Ⓑ Ⓒ Ⓓ Ⓔ
2. Ⓐ Ⓑ Ⓒ Ⓓ Ⓔ	32. Ⓐ Ⓑ Ⓒ Ⓓ Ⓔ	62. Ⓐ Ⓑ Ⓒ Ⓓ Ⓔ
3. Ⓐ Ⓑ Ⓒ Ⓓ Ⓔ	33. Ⓐ Ⓑ Ⓒ Ⓓ Ⓔ	63. Ⓐ Ⓑ Ⓒ Ⓓ Ⓔ
4. Ⓐ Ⓑ Ⓒ Ⓓ Ⓔ	34. Ⓐ Ⓑ Ⓒ Ⓓ Ⓔ	64. Ⓐ Ⓑ Ⓒ Ⓓ Ⓔ
5. Ⓐ Ⓑ Ⓒ Ⓓ Ⓔ	35. Ⓐ Ⓑ Ⓒ Ⓓ Ⓔ	65. Ⓐ Ⓑ Ⓒ Ⓓ Ⓔ
6. Ⓐ Ⓑ Ⓒ Ⓓ Ⓔ	36. Ⓐ Ⓑ Ⓒ Ⓓ Ⓔ	66. Ⓐ Ⓑ Ⓒ Ⓓ Ⓔ
7. Ⓐ Ⓑ Ⓒ Ⓓ Ⓔ	37. Ⓐ Ⓑ Ⓒ Ⓓ Ⓔ	67. Ⓐ Ⓑ Ⓒ Ⓓ Ⓔ
8. Ⓐ Ⓑ Ⓒ Ⓓ Ⓔ	38. Ⓐ Ⓑ Ⓒ Ⓓ Ⓔ	68. Ⓐ Ⓑ Ⓒ Ⓓ Ⓔ
9. Ⓐ Ⓑ Ⓒ Ⓓ Ⓔ	39. Ⓐ Ⓑ Ⓒ Ⓓ Ⓔ	69. Ⓐ Ⓑ Ⓒ Ⓓ Ⓔ
10. Ⓐ Ⓑ Ⓒ Ⓓ Ⓔ	40. Ⓐ Ⓑ Ⓒ Ⓓ Ⓔ	70. Ⓐ Ⓑ Ⓒ Ⓓ Ⓔ
11. Ⓐ Ⓑ Ⓒ Ⓓ Ⓔ	41. Ⓐ Ⓑ Ⓒ Ⓓ Ⓔ	71. Ⓐ Ⓑ Ⓒ Ⓓ Ⓔ
12. Ⓐ Ⓑ Ⓒ Ⓓ Ⓔ	42. Ⓐ Ⓑ Ⓒ Ⓓ Ⓔ	72. Ⓐ Ⓑ Ⓒ Ⓓ Ⓔ
13. Ⓐ Ⓑ Ⓒ Ⓓ Ⓔ	43. Ⓐ Ⓑ Ⓒ Ⓓ Ⓔ	73. Ⓐ Ⓑ Ⓒ Ⓓ Ⓔ
14. Ⓐ Ⓑ Ⓒ Ⓓ Ⓔ	44. Ⓐ Ⓑ Ⓒ Ⓓ Ⓔ	74. Ⓐ Ⓑ Ⓒ Ⓓ Ⓔ
15. Ⓐ Ⓑ Ⓒ Ⓓ Ⓔ	45. Ⓐ Ⓑ Ⓒ Ⓓ Ⓔ	75. Ⓐ Ⓑ Ⓒ Ⓓ Ⓔ
16. Ⓐ Ⓑ Ⓒ Ⓓ Ⓔ	46. Ⓐ Ⓑ Ⓒ Ⓓ Ⓔ	76. Ⓐ Ⓑ Ⓒ Ⓓ Ⓔ
17. Ⓐ Ⓑ Ⓒ Ⓓ Ⓔ	47. Ⓐ Ⓑ Ⓒ Ⓓ Ⓔ	77. Ⓐ Ⓑ Ⓒ Ⓓ Ⓔ
18. Ⓐ Ⓑ Ⓒ Ⓓ Ⓔ	48. Ⓐ Ⓑ Ⓒ Ⓓ Ⓔ	78. Ⓐ Ⓑ Ⓒ Ⓓ Ⓔ
19. Ⓐ Ⓑ Ⓒ Ⓓ Ⓔ	49. Ⓐ Ⓑ Ⓒ Ⓓ Ⓔ	79. Ⓐ Ⓑ Ⓒ Ⓓ Ⓔ
20. Ⓐ Ⓑ Ⓒ Ⓓ Ⓔ	50. Ⓐ Ⓑ Ⓒ Ⓓ Ⓔ	80. Ⓐ Ⓑ Ⓒ Ⓓ Ⓔ
21. Ⓐ Ⓑ Ⓒ Ⓓ Ⓔ	51. Ⓐ Ⓑ Ⓒ Ⓓ Ⓔ	81. Ⓐ Ⓑ Ⓒ Ⓓ Ⓔ
22. Ⓐ Ⓑ Ⓒ Ⓓ Ⓔ	52. Ⓐ Ⓑ Ⓒ Ⓓ Ⓔ	82. Ⓐ Ⓑ Ⓒ Ⓓ Ⓔ
23. Ⓐ Ⓑ Ⓒ Ⓓ Ⓔ	53. Ⓐ Ⓑ Ⓒ Ⓓ Ⓔ	83. Ⓐ Ⓑ Ⓒ Ⓓ Ⓔ
24. Ⓐ Ⓑ Ⓒ Ⓓ Ⓔ	54. Ⓐ Ⓑ Ⓒ Ⓓ Ⓔ	84. Ⓐ Ⓑ Ⓒ Ⓓ Ⓔ
25. Ⓐ Ⓑ Ⓒ Ⓓ Ⓔ	55. Ⓐ Ⓑ Ⓒ Ⓓ Ⓔ	85. Ⓐ Ⓑ Ⓒ Ⓓ Ⓔ
26. Ⓐ Ⓑ Ⓒ Ⓓ Ⓔ	56. Ⓐ Ⓑ Ⓒ Ⓓ Ⓔ	86. Ⓐ Ⓑ Ⓒ Ⓓ Ⓔ
27. Ⓐ Ⓑ Ⓒ Ⓓ Ⓔ	57. Ⓐ Ⓑ Ⓒ Ⓓ Ⓔ	87. Ⓐ Ⓑ Ⓒ Ⓓ Ⓔ
28. Ⓐ Ⓑ Ⓒ Ⓓ Ⓔ	58. Ⓐ Ⓑ Ⓒ Ⓓ Ⓔ	88. Ⓐ Ⓑ Ⓒ Ⓓ Ⓔ
29. Ⓐ Ⓑ Ⓒ Ⓓ Ⓔ	59. Ⓐ Ⓑ Ⓒ Ⓓ Ⓔ	89. Ⓐ Ⓑ Ⓒ Ⓓ Ⓔ
30. Ⓐ Ⓑ Ⓒ Ⓓ Ⓔ	60. Ⓐ Ⓑ Ⓒ Ⓓ Ⓔ	90. Ⓐ Ⓑ Ⓒ Ⓓ Ⓔ

SAT II: SUBJECT TEST IN
FRENCH
ANSWER SHEET

1. Ⓐ Ⓑ Ⓒ Ⓓ Ⓔ
2. Ⓐ Ⓑ Ⓒ Ⓓ Ⓔ
3. Ⓐ Ⓑ Ⓒ Ⓓ Ⓔ
4. Ⓐ Ⓑ Ⓒ Ⓓ Ⓔ
5. Ⓐ Ⓑ Ⓒ Ⓓ Ⓔ
6. Ⓐ Ⓑ Ⓒ Ⓓ Ⓔ
7. Ⓐ Ⓑ Ⓒ Ⓓ Ⓔ
8. Ⓐ Ⓑ Ⓒ Ⓓ Ⓔ
9. Ⓐ Ⓑ Ⓒ Ⓓ Ⓔ
10. Ⓐ Ⓑ Ⓒ Ⓓ Ⓔ
11. Ⓐ Ⓑ Ⓒ Ⓓ Ⓔ
12. Ⓐ Ⓑ Ⓒ Ⓓ Ⓔ
13. Ⓐ Ⓑ Ⓒ Ⓓ Ⓔ
14. Ⓐ Ⓑ Ⓒ Ⓓ Ⓔ
15. Ⓐ Ⓑ Ⓒ Ⓓ Ⓔ
16. Ⓐ Ⓑ Ⓒ Ⓓ Ⓔ
17. Ⓐ Ⓑ Ⓒ Ⓓ Ⓔ
18. Ⓐ Ⓑ Ⓒ Ⓓ Ⓔ
19. Ⓐ Ⓑ Ⓒ Ⓓ Ⓔ
20. Ⓐ Ⓑ Ⓒ Ⓓ Ⓔ
21. Ⓐ Ⓑ Ⓒ Ⓓ Ⓔ
22. Ⓐ Ⓑ Ⓒ Ⓓ Ⓔ
23. Ⓐ Ⓑ Ⓒ Ⓓ Ⓔ
24. Ⓐ Ⓑ Ⓒ Ⓓ Ⓔ
25. Ⓐ Ⓑ Ⓒ Ⓓ Ⓔ
26. Ⓐ Ⓑ Ⓒ Ⓓ Ⓔ
27. Ⓐ Ⓑ Ⓒ Ⓓ Ⓔ
28. Ⓐ Ⓑ Ⓒ Ⓓ Ⓔ
29. Ⓐ Ⓑ Ⓒ Ⓓ Ⓔ
30. Ⓐ Ⓑ Ⓒ Ⓓ Ⓔ

31. Ⓐ Ⓑ Ⓒ Ⓓ Ⓔ
32. Ⓐ Ⓑ Ⓒ Ⓓ Ⓔ
33. Ⓐ Ⓑ Ⓒ Ⓓ Ⓔ
34. Ⓐ Ⓑ Ⓒ Ⓓ Ⓔ
35. Ⓐ Ⓑ Ⓒ Ⓓ Ⓔ
36. Ⓐ Ⓑ Ⓒ Ⓓ Ⓔ
37. Ⓐ Ⓑ Ⓒ Ⓓ Ⓔ
38. Ⓐ Ⓑ Ⓒ Ⓓ Ⓔ
39. Ⓐ Ⓑ Ⓒ Ⓓ Ⓔ
40. Ⓐ Ⓑ Ⓒ Ⓓ Ⓔ
41. Ⓐ Ⓑ Ⓒ Ⓓ Ⓔ
42. Ⓐ Ⓑ Ⓒ Ⓓ Ⓔ
43. Ⓐ Ⓑ Ⓒ Ⓓ Ⓔ
44. Ⓐ Ⓑ Ⓒ Ⓓ Ⓔ
45. Ⓐ Ⓑ Ⓒ Ⓓ Ⓔ
46. Ⓐ Ⓑ Ⓒ Ⓓ Ⓔ
47. Ⓐ Ⓑ Ⓒ Ⓓ Ⓔ
48. Ⓐ Ⓑ Ⓒ Ⓓ Ⓔ
49. Ⓐ Ⓑ Ⓒ Ⓓ Ⓔ
50. Ⓐ Ⓑ Ⓒ Ⓓ Ⓔ
51. Ⓐ Ⓑ Ⓒ Ⓓ Ⓔ
52. Ⓐ Ⓑ Ⓒ Ⓓ Ⓔ
53. Ⓐ Ⓑ Ⓒ Ⓓ Ⓔ
54. Ⓐ Ⓑ Ⓒ Ⓓ Ⓔ
55. Ⓐ Ⓑ Ⓒ Ⓓ Ⓔ
56. Ⓐ Ⓑ Ⓒ Ⓓ Ⓔ
57. Ⓐ Ⓑ Ⓒ Ⓓ Ⓔ
58. Ⓐ Ⓑ Ⓒ Ⓓ Ⓔ
59. Ⓐ Ⓑ Ⓒ Ⓓ Ⓔ
60. Ⓐ Ⓑ Ⓒ Ⓓ Ⓔ

61. Ⓐ Ⓑ Ⓒ Ⓓ Ⓔ
62. Ⓐ Ⓑ Ⓒ Ⓓ Ⓔ
63. Ⓐ Ⓑ Ⓒ Ⓓ Ⓔ
64. Ⓐ Ⓑ Ⓒ Ⓓ Ⓔ
65. Ⓐ Ⓑ Ⓒ Ⓓ Ⓔ
66. Ⓐ Ⓑ Ⓒ Ⓓ Ⓔ
67. Ⓐ Ⓑ Ⓒ Ⓓ Ⓔ
68. Ⓐ Ⓑ Ⓒ Ⓓ Ⓔ
69. Ⓐ Ⓑ Ⓒ Ⓓ Ⓔ
70. Ⓐ Ⓑ Ⓒ Ⓓ Ⓔ
71. Ⓐ Ⓑ Ⓒ Ⓓ Ⓔ
72. Ⓐ Ⓑ Ⓒ Ⓓ Ⓔ
73. Ⓐ Ⓑ Ⓒ Ⓓ Ⓔ
74. Ⓐ Ⓑ Ⓒ Ⓓ Ⓔ
75. Ⓐ Ⓑ Ⓒ Ⓓ Ⓔ
76. Ⓐ Ⓑ Ⓒ Ⓓ Ⓔ
77. Ⓐ Ⓑ Ⓒ Ⓓ Ⓔ
78. Ⓐ Ⓑ Ⓒ Ⓓ Ⓔ
79. Ⓐ Ⓑ Ⓒ Ⓓ Ⓔ
80. Ⓐ Ⓑ Ⓒ Ⓓ Ⓔ
81. Ⓐ Ⓑ Ⓒ Ⓓ Ⓔ
82. Ⓐ Ⓑ Ⓒ Ⓓ Ⓔ
83. Ⓐ Ⓑ Ⓒ Ⓓ Ⓔ
84. Ⓐ Ⓑ Ⓒ Ⓓ Ⓔ
85. Ⓐ Ⓑ Ⓒ Ⓓ Ⓔ
86. Ⓐ Ⓑ Ⓒ Ⓓ Ⓔ
87. Ⓐ Ⓑ Ⓒ Ⓓ Ⓔ
88. Ⓐ Ⓑ Ⓒ Ⓓ Ⓔ
89. Ⓐ Ⓑ Ⓒ Ⓓ Ⓔ
90. Ⓐ Ⓑ Ⓒ Ⓓ Ⓔ

SAT II:
SUBJECT TEST IN
FRENCH

GLOSSARY

GLOSSARY

A

aïeul; aïeux (m., f.) – ancestor; ancestors
aile (f.) – wing
à la carte – from the menu (singly chosen items)
Allemagne (f.) – Germany
allemand(e) (adj.) – German
américain(e) (adj.) – American
Américain(e) (m., f.) – American person
animé(e) (adj.) – lively; busy
au pair (m.) – a nanny, literally a person who works for room and board

B

berger (m.) – shepherd
beurre (m.) – butter
bœuf (m.) – beef; ox; steer
boire – to drink
boisson (f.) – a drink
bonheur (m.) – happiness
bonté (f.) – kindness
bout (m.) – end; bottom
breton(ne) (adj.) – Breton (from Brittany)
bureau (m.) – desk; office

C

cadet (m.) – younger of two children; youngest
caisse (f.) – cash register (where you pay a bill)
campagne (f.) – countryside
chaîne (f.) – TV channel
chef-d'œuvre (m.) – masterpiece
chèque (m.) – check (bank)
chez – at the house of
chiffon (m.) – rag
choisir – to choose
chronique (f.) – chronicle; newspaper column
clé; clef (f.) – key
coiffeuse (f.) – hairdresser; dressing table
commencer – to begin
compter – to count
concours (m.) – contest
connaître – to know; be acquainted with
conseiller – to advise
cou (m.) – neck
coup d'état (m.) – sudden overthrow of a government
coup de grâce (m.) – death blow
craindre – to fear
croire – to believe

D

debout (adv., adj.; invariable) – standing
déception (f.) – disappointment
déçu (adj.) – disappointed
de luxe – luxurious
demain (m.) – tomorrow
demander – to ask

détente (f.) – easing of political tensions
dette (f.) – debt
deuil (m.) – mourning
devoir– 1. to have to do something; 2. *(noun; m.)* duty
dire – to say; tell

E

eau (f.) – water
écrire – to write
empêcher – to prevent; impede
emporter – to carry off; take something along
enfant (m., f.) – child
enseigner – to teach
entendre – to hear; understand
envoyer – to send
essayer – to try
éteindre – to extinguish; shut off
étendre – to stretch

F

faire – to make; do
fait accompli (m.) – accomplished fact; a "done deed"
faveur (f.) – favor
fête (f.) – party; festival; feast
fontaine (f.) – fountain
force de frappe (f.) – striking force (army)
français(e) (adj.) – French (language or thing)
Français(e) (m., f.) – Frenchman; Frenchwoman

G

garçon (m.) – boy; waiter
gare (f.) – railway station
gêne (f.) – embarrassment; discomfort; trouble
gilet (m.) – vest; cardigan
gourmet (m.) – a discriminating eater
grand prix (m.) – first prize
guêpe (f.) – wasp
guérir – to cure; heal
guerre (f.) – war

H

habiter – to live (in a place); reside
haïr – to hate
haut; haute – high; loud
hier (m.) – yesterday

I

imiter – to imitate
inégal(e) – unequal
irréel (f.) – unreal

J

jaune – yellow
jeune – young

K

klaxon (m.) – car horn

L

liaison (f.) – a relationship; linking of consonant and vowel
lisse (adj.) – smooth; sleek

M

mal (m.) – 1. evil; pain; 2. (adverb) badly
mèche (f.) – lock of hair; wick
médecin (m.) – doctor

médecine (f.) – medicine
médicament (m.) – medication
même (adj.) – 1. same; 2. self; 3. very same
menace (f.) – a threat
mener – to lead someone
merveille (f.) – marvel
mois (m.) – month
mot-clé (m.) – key word
moulin (m.) – mill

N

naissance (f.) – birth
naître – to be born
négation (f.) – negative forms; negation
neige (f.) – snow
nom (m.) – name; noun
nuage (m.) – cloud

O

œil; yeux (m.) – eye; eyes
œuf (m.) – egg
ôter – to remove; lift; take away
ou – or
où –where

ouest (m.) – west
ouïr – to hear

P

paix (f.) – peace
palais (m.) – 1. palace; 2. palate
pareil; pareille (adj.) – similar; the same
peine (f.) – sorrow; sadness; effort
plaisir (m.) – pleasure
profond (adj.) – deep; profound

Q

quai (m.) – dock; wharf

R

raconter – to recount; tell a story
rencontrer – to meet; encounter someone
rester – to stay; remain
rhume (m.) – a cold
rire – to laugh

S

sale (adj.) – dirty
salle (f.) – room
sauce (f.) – gravy; salad dressing; sauce
savoir – to know
sec (adj.) – dry
sécheresse (f.) – drought
sel (m.) – salt
soif (f.) – thirst
soir (m.) – evening
sortie (f.) – 1. exit; 2. military action (pull-out), deployment, etc.
souffrir – to suffer
soulier (m.) – shoe

T

tête (f.) – head
tirade (f.) – long speech in a play; tirade
tôt – early
travail (m.) – work
travailler – to work
trompe-l'œil (m.) – style of art that tricks the eye
trou (m.) – hole
trouver – to find

U

usine (f.) – factory
utile – useful

V

vérité (f.) – truth
vif (adj.) – lively; bright (color)
vilain (adj.) – ugly; nasty; wicked
visiter – to see (a place, not a person); to tour
voir – to see

W

wagon (m.) – railway car

MAXnotes®

REA's Literature Study Guides

MAXnotes® are student-friendly. They offer a fresh look at masterpieces of literature, presented in a lively and interesting fashion. **MAXnotes®** offer the essentials of what you should know about the work, including outlines, explanations and discussions of the plot, character lists, analyses, and historical context. **MAXnotes®** are designed to help you think independently about literary works by raising various issues and thought-provoking ideas and questions. Written by literary experts who currently teach the subject, **MAXnotes®** enhance your understanding and enjoyment of the work.

Available **MAXnotes®** include the following:

Absalom, Absalom!
The Aeneid of Virgil
Animal Farm
Antony and Cleopatra
As I Lay Dying
As You Like It
The Autobiography of
　Malcolm X
The Awakening
Beloved
Beowulf
Billy Budd
The Bluest Eye, A Novel
Brave New World
The Canterbury Tales
The Catcher in the Rye
The Color Purple
The Crucible
Death in Venice
Death of a Salesman
Dickens Dictionary
The Divine Comedy I: Inferno
Dubliners
The Edible Woman
Emma
Euripides' Medea & Electra
Frankenstein
Gone with the Wind
The Grapes of Wrath
Great Expectations
The Great Gatsby
Gulliver's Travels
Handmaid's Tale
Hamlet
Hard Times
Heart of Darkness

Henry IV, Part I
Henry V
The House on Mango Street
Huckleberry Finn
I Know Why the Caged
　Bird Sings
The Iliad
Invisible Man
Jane Eyre
Jazz
The Joy Luck Club
Jude the Obscure
Julius Caesar
King Lear
Leaves of Grass
Les Misérables
Lord of the Flies
Macbeth
The Merchant of Venice
Metamorphoses of Ovid
Metamorphosis
Middlemarch
A Midsummer Night's Dream
Moby-Dick
Moll Flanders
Mrs. Dalloway
Much Ado About Nothing
Mules and Men
My Antonia
Native Son
1984
The Odyssey
Oedipus Trilogy
Of Mice and Men
On the Road

Othello
Paradise
Paradise Lost
A Passage to India
Plato's Republic
Portrait of a Lady
A Portrait of the Artist
　as a Young Man
Pride and Prejudice
A Raisin in the Sun
Richard II
Romeo and Juliet
The Scarlet Letter
Sir Gawain and the
　Green Knight
Slaughterhouse-Five
Song of Solomon
The Sound and the Fury
The Stranger
Sula
The Sun Also Rises
A Tale of Two Cities
The Taming of the Shrew
Tar Baby
The Tempest
Tess of the D'Urbervilles
Their Eyes Were Watching God
Things Fall Apart
To Kill a Mockingbird
To the Lighthouse
Twelfth Night
Uncle Tom's Cabin
Waiting for Godot
Wuthering Heights
Guide to Literary Terms

RESEARCH & EDUCATION ASSOCIATION
61 Ethel Road W. • Piscataway, New Jersey 08854
Phone: (732) 819-8880   **website: www.rea.com**

Please send me more information about MAXnotes®.

Name _____

Address _____

City _____ State _____ Zip _____

REA's Test Preps
The Best in Test Preparation

- REA "Test Preps" are **far more** comprehensive than any other test preparation series
- Each book contains up to **eight** full-length practice tests based on the most recent exams
- **Every** type of question likely to be given on the exams is included
- Answers are accompanied by **full** and **detailed** explanations

REA publishes over 60 Test Preparation volumes in several series. They include:

Advanced Placement Exams (APs)
Biology
Calculus AB & Calculus BC
Chemistry
Computer Science
English Language & Composition
English Literature & Composition
European History
Government & Politics
Physics
Psychology
Spanish Language
Statistics
United States History

College-Level Examination Program (CLEP)
Analyzing and Interpreting Literature
College Algebra
Freshman College Composition
General Examinations
General Examinations Review
History of the United States I
Human Growth and Development
Introductory Sociology
Principles of Marketing
Spanish

SAT II: Subject Tests
Biology E/M
Chemistry
English Language Proficiency Test
French
German
Literature

SAT II: Subject Tests (cont'd)
Mathematics Level IC, IIC
Physics
Spanish
United States History
Writing

Graduate Record Exams (GREs)
Biology
Chemistry
Computer Science
General
Literature in English
Mathematics
Physics
Psychology

ACT - ACT Assessment

ASVAB - Armed Services Vocational Aptitude Battery

CBEST - California Basic Educational Skills Test

CDL - Commercial Driver License Exam

CLAST - College-Level Academic Skills Test

ELM - Entry Level Mathematics

ExCET - Exam for the Certification of Educators in Texas

FE (EIT) - Fundamentals of Engineering Exam

FE Review - Fundamentals of Engineering Review

GED - High School Equivalency Diploma Exam (U.S. & Canadian editions)

GMAT - Graduate Management Admission Test

LSAT - Law School Admission Test

MAT - Miller Analogies Test

MCAT - Medical College Admission Test

MTEL - Massachusetts Tests for Educator Licensure

MSAT - Multiple Subjects Assessment for Teachers

NJ HSPA - New Jersey High School Proficiency Assessment

PLT - Principles of Learning & Teaching Test

PPST - Pre-Professional Skills Tests

PSAT - Preliminary Scholastic Assessment Test

SAT I - Reasoning Test

SAT I - Quick Study & Review

TASP - Texas Academic Skills Program

TOEFL - Test of English as a Foreign Language

TOEIC - Test of English for International Communication

RESEARCH & EDUCATION ASSOCIATION
61 Ethel Road W. • Piscataway, New Jersey 08854
Phone: (732) 819-8880   **website: www.rea.com**

Please send me more information about your Test Prep books

Name _____

Address _____

City _____ State _____ Zip _____

REA's Test Prep Books Are The Best!

(a sample of the <u>hundreds of letters</u> REA receives each year)

" I am writing to congratulate you on preparing an exceptional study guide. In five years of teaching this course I have never encountered a more thorough, comprehensive, concise and realistic preparation for this examination. "
Teacher, Davie, FL

" I have found your publications, *The Best Test Preparation...*, to be exactly that. "
Teacher, Aptos, CA

" I used your *CLEP Introductory Sociology* book and rank it 99% — thank you! "
Student, Jerusalem, Israel

" Your *GMAT* book greatly helped me on the test. Thank you. "
Student, Oxford, OH

" Compared to the other books that my fellow students had, your book was the most useful in helping me get a great score. "
Student, North Hollywood, CA

" Your *AP English Literature and Composition* book is most impressive. "
Student, Montgomery, AL

" Just a short note to say thanks for the great support your book gave me in helping me pass the test... I'm on my way to a B.S. degree because of you! "
Student, Orlando, FL

(more on front page)